Montana Real Estate License Exam Prep

All-in-One Review and Testing to Pass Montana's Pearson Real Estate Exam

First Edition

Stephen Mettling
David Cusic
Ryan Mettling

Performance Programs Company
6810 190th Street East
Bradenton, FL, 34211
www.performanceprogramscompany.com

Material in this book is not intended to represent legal advice and should not be so construed. Readers should consult legal counsel for advice regarding points of law.

6810 190th Street East, Bradenton, FL 34211
info@performanceprogramscompany.com
www.performanceprogramscompany.com

ISBN 978-1965482698

Contents

SECTION I: NATIONAL PRINCIPLES & LAW KEY POINT REVIEW **7**
- Rights 7
- Interests & Estates 11
- Ownership 12
- Encumbrances & Liens 14
- Transferring & Recording Title 17
- Leases 20
- Land Use 21
- Legal Descriptions 25
- Contract Law 26
- Agency 29
- Listing Agreements 32
- Brokerage 34
- Sale Contracts 36
- Economics 38
- Appraisal 40
- Finance 45
- Investment 51
- Taxation 52
- Professional Practices 56
- Closings 60
- Risk Management 63
- Property Management 65

SECTION II: REAL ESTATE MATH REVIEW **68**
- Basic Math 68
- Leases 73
- Contracts for the Sale of Real Estate 73
- Appraisal & Value 73
- Finance 76
- Investment 79
- Real Estate Taxation 82
- Commissions 83
- Closing Costs, Prorations 84
- Insurance Coverage 85

SECTION III: MONTANA LAWS & PRACTICES **86**

Part I: The Montana Regulatory Environment 88
- Board of Realty Regulation 88
- The Board's Powers 88
- Grounds for Suspension or Revocation 89
- Unprofessional Conduct 90
- Discipline and Sanctions 90
- Trust Account Compliance Citations 91
- Enforcement Against Unlicensed Practice 91

Part II: Montana Real Estate Licensing 93
- Definitions Used in Board Rules 93
- Persons Requiring a Real Estate License 93
- Exemptions From Real Estate Licensure 93
- The Salesperson License 94
- The Broker License 94
- The Supervising Broker Endorsement 95
- Display of License and Pocket Card 95
- Continuing Real Estate Education 96
- Active and Inactive Status 96
- License Renewal and Reinstatement 96
- Reciprocity 97
- License Fees 97

Part III: Montana Brokerage and Disclosure Regulation 98
- Advertising and Marketing 98
- Broker and Salesperson Relationship 99
- Unprofessional Conduct 101
- Compensation 101
- Disclosure 102
- Handling Documents and Trust Funds 104
- Listings and Buyer Brokerage Agreements 105
- Ethics and Illegal Inducements 106

Part IV: Montana Agency Regulation 108
- Agency: Authorized Relationships in Montana 108
- Agency Duties and Responsibilities 109
- Agency Disclosure Recap and Timing Summary 112

Part V: Additional Montana Laws and Practices 114
- Errors and Omissions Insurance 114
- Landlord and Tenant Relationship 114
- Foreclosure and Redemption in Montana 116
- Place of Business and Officing Regulations 117
- Montana Fair Housing 117
- Land Description 118
- Common Interest Ownership and Condominiums 119
- The Statute of Frauds in Montana 120

SECTION IV: NATIONAL PRACTICE TESTS **122**
- Test 1: Rights; Interests and Estates; Ownership 122
- Test 2: Encumbrances; Liens; Title Transfer and Recording; Leases 130
- Test 3: Land Use; Legal Descriptions; Contract Law 139
- Test 4: Agency; Listing Agreements 146
- Test 5: Brokerage Business; Sale Contracts 152
- Test 6: Economics; Appraisal 159

Test 7: Finance 167
Test 8: Investments; Taxation; Professional Practices 174
Test 9: Closings; Risk Management; Property Management 182
Test 10: Real Estate Math 189

SECTION V: MONTANA-SPECIFIC PRACTICE TESTS 197
Test 11: The Montana Regulatory Environment 198
Test 12: Montana Real Estate Licensing 200
Test 13: Montana Brokerage and Disclosure Regulation 202
Test 14: Montana Agency Regulation 207
Test 15: Additional Montana Laws and Practices 211

SECTION VI: MONTANA LICENSE EXAMINATION SAMPLE TEST 214
Sample Test: Montana Practice Exam 214

SECTION VII: ANSWER KEY 228

APPENDIX: PPC TEST-TAKING TIPS 291

APPENDIX: USEFUL WEBSITES 295

Introduction

Welcome licensee candidates and future real estate professionals!

We know you have worked hard just to get here – you've completed or nearly completed your pre-license curricula, and now all you have to do is pass the state license exam. But easier said than done – and that's where we come in. We know the exam can be tough, and very nerve-wracking to prepare for. That's why we created Montana Real Estate License Exam Prep (MT-RELEP) the way we did. Since we have been managing real estate schools and developing curriculum for forty years, we know how all this works – or fails to work. Let us assure you – you made the right decision buying this publication to prepare for your Montana exam. Here's why.

First, MT-RELEP is comprehensive in that it contains both key content review and testing practice. And the text review is Montana-specific – not just simplistic national content, but terse, relevant and accurate state laws and regulations presented as a well-organized set of state 'key point reviews' ideal for pre-test memorization. But let's not dismiss the importance of the national content either. MT-RELEP's national key point reviews are a succinct compression of tested national principles and practices that comprise the national portion of state license exams from coast to coast. Our content is drawn from our own national textbook, Principles of Real Estate Practice – one of the most widely used principles textbooks in the country. Finally, our national content, as well as our question selection, is further tailored to the state testing outline promulgated by Pearson for Montana. Thus the breadth and depth of the law reviews and test questions reflect the topic emphasis of your Montana license exam.

A word about the test questions… MT-RELEP's testing practice section consists of ten national practice tests, five state practice tests, and one state exam sample test. The test questions are designed to cover the content covered by the law reviews – which reinforces your learning of the total body of information tested by your state exam. The questions are direct, to the point, and designed to test your understanding. When you have completed a given test, you can check your answers against the answer key in the Section VII. You may also note that each question's answer is accompanied by a brief explanation, or "rationale" to further reinforce your understanding.

Your particular study and testing practice strategy using MT-RELEP is up to you. But to fully exploit its comprehensive content coverage, you should try to review and memorize the key point reviews as much as possible. Then you should make every effort to take each exam, review your mistakes, and re-read the key point reviews that cover your weaker areas.

In the end, as you know, it's all up to you. Unlike other publications, we are not going to tell you that using this book will guarantee that you pass your state exam. It still takes hard work and study to pass. But we have done our best here to get you ready. Following that, the most we can do is wish you the best of success in taking and passing your state exam. So good luck!!

About the authors

For over forty five years, Stephen Mettling and David Cusic, PhD, have operated Performance Programs Company, one of the nation's most successful training organizations specializing in real estate program development. Mr. Mettling and Dr. Cusic have jointly written over 100 books, courses, and custom programs in all facets of real estate for some of the country's largest real estate schools, associations and organizations.

Mr. Mettling has also served as vice president and author for the country's largest real estate training and publishing organization. Under various capacities, he has managed the acquisition, development, and sale of national real estate textbooks and publications, as well as directed the country's largest affiliated group of real estate schools.

Dr. Cusic, an author and educator with international real estate training experience, has been engaged in vocation-oriented education since 1966. Specializing in real estate training since 1983, he has developed numerous real estate training programs for corporate and institutional clients around the country.

Ryan Mettling, partner and publisher of Performance Programs, is an accomplished online curriculum designer, author, and course developer. He is responsible for the company's strategic planning, general management, printing and production, e-pub and retail platforms, and multi-channel marketing. Mr. Mettling is a member of the Real Estate Educators Association (REEA), and graduated Valedictorian from the University of Central Florida's College of Business Administration.

Section I: National Principles & Law
Key Point Review

Rights

Land / Real Estate / Real Property

Land: surface, all ***natural things*** attached to it, subsurface, and air above the surface.

Real estate: land + **manmade** permanent attachments

Real property: real estate + bundle of rights

Constitution guarantees private ownership of real property.

Physical Characteristics of Real Estate

Immobility

- land cannot be moved from one site to another; its location is forever fixed

Indestructibility

- land is permanent and cannot be destroyed since by definition it extends below ground and into the sky
- since land is permanent, it does not depreciate
- only improvements depreciate and are insurable

Non-homogeneity

- land is non-homogeneous; no two parcels of land are exactly the same since they have a different location

Land versus Real Estate

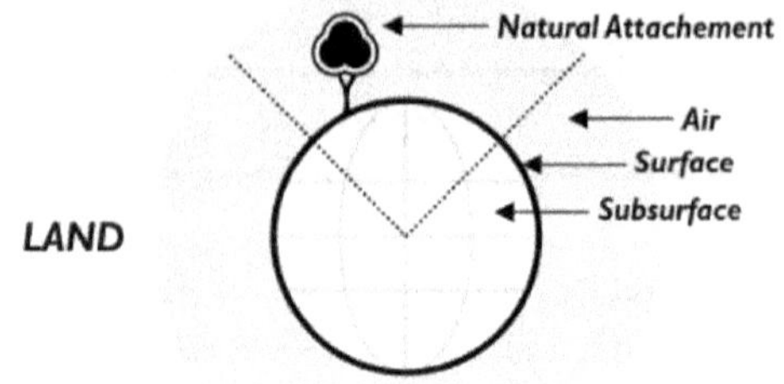

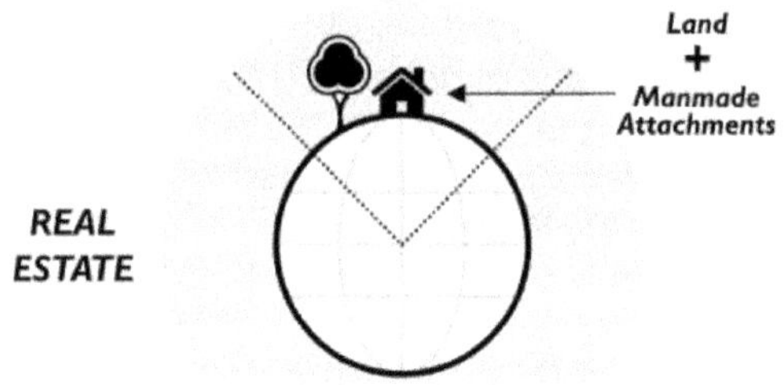

Real Estate as Property

The bundle of rights

"PUTEE":

P ossession

U se

T ransfer

E xclusion

E ncumberable

Legal Title v. Equitable title

Legal title

- full legal ownership of property and the bundle of rights as they apply to it
- contrasts with equitable title

Equitable title

- an interest that gives a lienholder or buyer the right to acquire legal title to a property if certain contractual conditions occur

Property characteristics:

- **property is** either real or personal
- property is either tangible or intangible

Real Property Rights

Airspace = air rights

Surface (of the earth) = surface rights

Subsurface = subsurface or mineral rights

Water rights:

- **Doctrine of Prior Appropriation**
  - state controls water usage
  - state grants usage permits
- **riparian rights (rivers and streams)**
  - applies to rivers and streams
  - if waterway is navigable: owners own land to water's edge
  - if waterway is not navigable: owners own land to midpoint of waterway
- **littoral rights (lakes and seas)**
  - applies to **seas and lakes**
  - abutting property owners own to **high water mark**
  - state owns underlying land

Memory Tip: **R** : **R**iver **R**iparian   **L**: **L**ake **L**ittoral

Real Property vs. Personal Property

Real property

- land
- fixtures
- attachments

Personal property

- chattels
- trade fixtures
- emblements

Differentiation criteria: item is real or personal property depending on why, how item is attached to the real estate. Depends on the owners'

- intention; adaptation; functionality; relationship of parties; contract provisions

Trade fixtures

- personal property items temporarily attached to real estate in order to conduct business

Emblements

- plants or crops that are considered personal property despite being attached to land

Conversion

- real to personal property referred to as severance
- personal to real property referred to as affixing

Factory-built housing – mobile homes and manufactured homes

- units are real or personal property: real if permanently affixed to ground; otherwise personal

Regulation Of Real Property Interests

Federal regulation

- grants rights of ownership
- controls broad land usage standards
- regulates anti-discrimination laws
  - examples: land grants; federal flood zones; fair housing laws; FHA; EPA

State regulation

- governs real estate business
- sets regional usage standards
  - examples: license laws; water rights; development regulation

Local regulation

- levies real estate taxes
- controls specific usage
  - examples: property assessing; zoning; building permits; tax levies

Judicial regulation

- applies case law and common law to disputes
- **contrasts with statutory law**

Interests & Estates

Interests and Estates in Land

Interests

Possession / Possessory

- estate in land

Non-possession / Non-possessory:

- private: encumbrance
- public: public interest

Estates In Land

- include right of possession
- leasehold = limited duration
- freehold: duration is not limited

Freehold (own)

- fee simple
  - absolute
  - defeasible
- life estates
  - conventional
  - legal

Leasehold (lease)

- estate for years
- periodic
- estate at will
- estate at sufferance

Freeholds

Fee simple

- ***not limited*** by one's lifetime
- absolute: ***highest*** form of ownership interest
- defeasible: ***reverts*** to previous owner per conditions

Life estate

- passes ***to another*** on death of named party
- remainder: ***named party*** to receive estate
- reversion: ***previous owner*** to receive estate

Conventional life estate

- ***limited*** to lifetime of life tenant/ named party
- **ordinary**: estate passes to remainderman or previous owner when life tenant dies
- **pur autre vie**: limited to lifetime of another, passes to remainderman or previous owner

Legal life estate

- created by operation of state law as opposed to a property owner's agreement
- designed to protect family survivors
- **Homestead:** rights to one's ***principal residence***
  - laws protect homestead from creditors
  - family must occupy the homestead
  - cannot be conveyed by one spouse
  - endures over life of head of household
  - interests extinguished if property destroyed

Leaseholds

Estate for years

- specific, ***stated duration***, per lease; expires at end of term; if tenant fails to vacate at lease expiration, tenancy becomes a **holdover tenancy** which is a periodic tenancy

Periodic

- lease term ***renews automatically*** upon acceptance of rent; renews indefinitely if landlord accepts rent

Estate at will

- for ***indefinite period*** subject to rent payment; cancelable with notice

Estate at sufferance

- tenancy ***against landlord's will*** and without an agreement

Ownership

Forms of Ownership

Tenancy in severalty

- ***sole*** ownership of a freehold estate; passes to heirs

Tenancy in common

- co-tenants individually own undivided interests
- ***any ownership share possible***
- no survivorship
- can convey to outside parties

Joint tenancy

- equal undivided interest jointly owned
- survivorship (may require express provision)
- requires ***four unities*** to create: time, title, interest, possession

Tenancy by the entireties

- ***husband and wife*** own equal undivided interest
- Now applies to same-sex couples in some states

Community property

- ***joint property ownership*** by spouses as opposed to separate property

Joint Tenancy & Four Unities

Unity of ownership	• owners hold single title jointly
Equal ownership	• owners always hold equal shares
Transfer	• may transfer to new owner as a tenancy in common interest with remaining joint tenants
Survivorship	• on death, interests and rights pass to other joint tenants
Creation	• requires "four unities," ***PITT***: 1. ***P***ossession: acquire same possessory rights 2. ***I***nterest: acquire equal, undivided interests 3. ***T***ime: acquire interests at same time 4. ***T***itle: acquire interests with same deed

Community Property

Separate	**Community**
• acquired ***before marriage*** • acquired by ***gift or inheritance*** • acquired with ***separate-property funds*** • ***income*** derived from ***separate property***	• all other property earned or acquired during the marriage

Estates in Trust

- ***trustor*** gives title, deed, trust agreement to trustee
- ***trustee*** renders fiduciary duties to trustor and beneficiary
- ***beneficiary*** receives ownership benefits
- **living / testamentary trust** – conveyance of real, personal property during one's lifetime
- **land trust** – grantor and beneficiary are same party; beneficiary uses, controls property but does not appear on public records

Condominiums

- ownership of a ***unit of airspace*** plus an ***undivided interes***t in the ***common elements*** as tenant in common with other owners
- may be sold, encumbered or foreclosed ***without affecting other unit owners***
- creation: by developer's declaration
- individually taxed
- managed by condo association
- owners share common area expenses

Cooperatives

- ownership of
  - ***shares in owning corporation***
  - ***proprietary lease*** in a unit
- corporation has sole, undivided ownership
- owners potentially liable for expenses of entire co-op; creditors may foreclose on entire property

Time Shares

- lease or ownership interest in property for periodic use on a scheduled basis
- **lease**: tenant leases property per the lease's schedule
- **freehold**: tenants in common own undivided interests, pay expenses per separate agreement

Encumbrances & Liens

Encumbrances

- non-possessory interests limiting legal owner's rights
- do not include possession
- two types:
  - encumbrances that affect use
  - encumbrances that affect ownership, value, transfer

Encumbrances affecting use: easements, encroachments, licenses, deed restrictions

Encumbrances affecting ownership, value, transfer: liens, deed conditions

Easements

Characteristics	• rights to use portions of another's property • affirmative easement: allows a use • negative easement: prohibits a use
Appurtenant	• ***attaches*** to the estate • ***dominant*** tenement's ***right to use*** or restrict adjacent ***servient*** tenement • ***by necessity***, to ***landlocked*** owners • party wall easement in a shared structure: to not damage or destroy
In gross	• ***does not attach*** to the estate • **personal**-- not transferrable, ends upon death of easement holder • **commercial**-- transferrable, granted to a business

By prescription

- property used without permission; can come to exist regardless of owner's consent
- obtainable through ***continuous, open, adverse use*** over a period of time which varies by state

License

- ***personal*** right to use a property
- does not attach
- non-transferrable
- revocable
- ceases upon death of owner

Encroachments

- unauthorized intrusions of one owner's real property onto another's
- may require survey to detect
- may become prescriptive easements if not remedied over prescription period

---

Deed restrictions

- conditions, covenants imposed on property by deed or subdivision plat
- goes with the property upon transfer
- established to control quality, standards of a subdivision
- apply to land use, type of structure, setbacks, minimum house size, etc.

Deed conditions

- created upon property transfer
- if violated, ownership may revert to previous owner

Deed covenants

- created by mutual agreement
- enforceable by injunction

Liens

- claims attaching to real and personal property as security for debt
- recorded on title effectively reducing equity in the amount of the lien
- does not convey ownership unless a mortgage in a title theory state
- lien attaches to the property
- property can be encumbered by multiple liens
- lien terminates upon payment, recording satisfaction

Lien types and characteristics

Voluntary / involuntary	• mortgage lien / tax lien
General / specific	• against any & all assets / against car or house
Superior / junior	• paid before juniors / paid after superiors by date of recording

Lien Priority

- order in which liens against a property are satisfied
- determined by superior v junior class and by date of recordation
- the highest priority lien is paid by foreclosure proceeds before any other lien

Superior Liens by rank (not by date of recordation; paid before junior liens)	Junior Liens (by date of recording)
• real estate tax liens • special assessment liens • federal estate tax liens • state inheritance tax liens	• federal income tax liens • judgment liens • mortgage liens • vendors' liens • mechanics' liens (by date work performed) • broker's liens (to pay commission owed)

Foreclosure

- Liquidation or transfer of collateral property by judicial, non-judicial, or strict foreclosure

Mortgage lien foreclosure	• liquidation of collateral property by ***judicial, non-judicial,*** or ***strict*** foreclosure
Judicial foreclosure	• lawsuit by creditor followed by court-ordered public sale to enforce lien; may entail ***deficiency judgments***, ***redemption rights*** • **deficiency judgment** -- judgment by court on borrower to forfeit other property to pay off any shortfalls from foreclosure • **redemption right** -- borrower's right to reclaim property before or after foreclosure sale
Non-judicial foreclosure	• ***"power of sale"*** granted to lender; no suit; ***no deficiency***
Strict foreclosure	• court orders ***legal transfer of title directly to lender*** without public sale
Deed in lieu of foreclosure	• ***"power of sale"*** granted to lender; no suit; ***no deficiency*** judgment; ***no redemption*** period after sale
Short sale	• side skirts foreclosure; lender agrees to loan concessions in the conveyance so that seller can afford to sell, since s/he owes more than property is worth • lender must approve selling terms and may take actions to recover deficiency from borrower

Lien vs. Title Theory State

- **lien theory state** -- lender of mortgaged property holds equitable title rather than legal title; **borrower holds legal title**.

- **title theory state** – **lender holds legal title** to the mortgaged property until the mortgagor satisfies the terms and obligations of the loan.

Transferring & Recording Title

Legal vs. Equitable Title

- **Legal title:** owner enjoys full bundle of rights
- **Equitable title:** party can obtain legal title subject to agreements with creditors

Notice

Notice:
- how ownership is evidenced to the public

Actual notice:
- ***knowledge acquired directly*** through demonstrable evidence, e.g., presenting or inspecting a deed, visiting a party in possession

Constructive notice:
- ***knowledge one could have obtained***, as presumed by law; imparted by recording in public records "for all to see"

Voluntary / Involuntary Title Transfer

Voluntary transfer

- deed
- will
- public grant

Involuntary transfer

- descent (without will, with heirs)
- escheat (without will nor heirs)
- foreclosure (loan default)
- eminent domain (public good)
- adverse possession (hostile, open use)

Deeds of Conveyance

Key characteristics:

- grantor grants deed to grantee
- legal title transfers upon intentional delivery and grantee's acceptance

Deed Validity

Requirements:

1. grantor
2. grantee
3. in writing
4. legal description
5. granting clause
6. consideration
7. grantor's signature
8. acknowledgement
9. delivery and acceptance

Deed Clauses

Premises	• granting
Habendum	• type of estate
Reddendum	• restrictions
Tenendum	• other property included

Deed Types

Bargain and sale	"I own but won't defend"
General warranty	"I own and will defend"
Special warranty	"I own and warrant myself only"
Quitclaim	"I may or may not own, and won't defend"
Special purpose deeds	used for different purposes, interests conveyed, or by different parties

Transfer Tax

- **Documentary stamp tax:** tax on conveyance of real property based on price of property conveyed
- Facilitates ad valorem assessment
- Payment evidenced on deed

Wills

Key characteristics

- will transfers estate to heirs upon death
- maker = owner; devisor or testator
- heir = beneficiary or devisee

Types of wills

- witnessed: in writing and two witnesses
- holographic: will in testator's handwriting
- nuncupative: oral will written by witnesses; generally not valid for property transfer

Validity of will

- legal age; mentally competent; entitled "last will & testament;" signed, witnessed, voluntary

Testate / Intestate

Order of Title Transfer

Dies testate with heirs:

- first to creditors
- then to homestead
- then **to heirs by will**

Dies intestate with heirs:	• first to creditors • then to homestead • then *to heirs by laws of descent*
Dies intestate, no heirs:	• first to creditors • then **to state by escheat**

Involuntary Title Transfer

Adverse possession

- "unwanted owner" may claim ownership to a property
- must show "claim of right" as reason
- must be notorious possession (unconcealed)
- must be hostile (possessor claims ownership)
- must be continuous for a statutory period of time

Title Records

Features

- Instruments affecting title must be recorded
- Gives public notice of ownership, condition of title
- Determines property marketability
- Protects lienholders; establishes chronology for lien priority

Key terms

- chain of title – successive property owners from original grant to present
- cloud on title – unrecorded claims
- suit to quiet title – lawsuit to settle claims
- abstract of title: written chronology of recorded owners, transfers, encumbrances

---

Forms of Title Evidence

- title insurance (best form of evidence)
- attorney's opinion of abstract (also called "opinion of title")
- title certificates
- Torrens registration
- Marketable title – must be delivered by seller; title must be free of claims, encumbrances; best assured by title insurance policy

Leases

Key characteristics

- lease is both an instrument of conveyance and contract of covenants between tenant and landlord
- lease conveys **temporary, exclusive** use of premises in exchange for rent and right of reversion

Tenant rights and obligations

- rights: use, possession, quiet enjoyment, profits
- tenant obligations: pay rent; maintain premises; follow rules

Landlord rights and obligations

- rights: receive rent; repossess upon expiration; monitor tenant compliance
- obligations: property condition, habitability, support services

Estate Types

Gross lease	• landlord pays expenses; tenant pays higher rent than net
Net lease	• tenant pays some or all expenses; rent is less than gross
Percentage lease	• landlord receives rent minimum plus percentage of retailer's sales
Residential lease	• gross lease hybrid; short term; uniform terms reflect landlord-tenant standards
Ground lease	• landlord owns and leases ground but does not own improvements
Proprietary lease	• for cooperative unit owners; indefinite term; assigned to new unit owner on sale
Leasing of rights	• leasehold transfer of rights for limited use; examples: air, mineral, water rights

Lease Termination

Causes	- default	- term expiration
	- notice	- voluntary agreement
	- property destruction	- condemnation
	- death	- abandonment under certain conditions

Uniform Residential Landlord and Tenant Act

Purposes
- balance landlord and tenant rights
- standardize leases
- have uniform eviction procedures
- protect tenants
- serve as model for state legislation

Leases
- clear lease terms
- fair market rent
- cannot waive rights

Deposits
- limits on amounts
- tenant's right to interest
- rules and deadlines for returning

Landlord Obligations
- bargain in good faith
- provide maintenance and repairs
- comply with building codes
- provide safety and access
- procedure for delivery of notices

Tenant Obligations
- maintain condition
- abide by rules and regulations
- no damage or abuse
- abide by approved uses
- no disturbance of other tenants

Land Use

Planning and Zoning Definitions

Building code: A standard of construction of an improved property established by local government officials

Certificate of occupancy: A document confirming that a newly constructed or renovated property has fully complied with all building codes and is ready for occupancy

Concurrency: A planning policy that requires developers to correct foreseen negative impacts of a development during the construction period of the project itself rather than afterward

Condemnation: 1. A decree that a parcel of private property is to be taken for public use under the power of eminent domain. 2. A government order that a property is no longer fit for use and must be demolished.

Deed restriction: A provision in a deed that limits or places rules on how the deeded property may be used or improved

Eminent domain: A power of a government entity to force the sale of private property for subsequent public use

Land use control: Regulation of how individual owners use property in a municipality or planning district. Control patterns are in accordance with a master plan

Master plan:	An amalgamated land use plan for a municipality, county, or region which incorporates community opinion, the results of intensive research, and the various land use guidelines and regulations of the state. Acts as a blueprint for subsequent zoning ordinances and rulings
Non-conforming use :	A legal or illegal land use that is not consistent with the current zoning ordinance
Police power:	A government's legal authority to create, regulate, tax, and condemn real property in the interest of the public's health, safety, and welfare
Restriction:	A limitation on the use of a property imposed by deed, zoning, state statute, or public regulation
Special exception:	A land use in conflict with current zoning that is authorized because of its perceived benefit to the public welfare
Variance:	A land use that conflicts with current zoning but is authorized for certain reasons, including undue hardship to comply and minimal negative impact to leave it alone
Zoning ordinance:	A municipal land use regulation

Land Use Planning

Goals of land use control

- preserve property values; promote highest and best use; safeguard public health, safety and welfare; control growth; incorporate community consensus
- process: develop plan; create administration; authorize controls

The master plan

- long term growth and usage strategies; often required by state law
- local plans fuse municipal goals and needs with state and regional laws

Planning objectives

- control growth rates: how much growth will occur and at what rate
- control growth patterns: type of growth desired, where it should be located
- accommodate demand for services and infrastructure

Plan development

- research trends and conditions; blend local and state objectives into master plan

Planning management

- commission makes rules, approves permits, codes, and development plans

Public Land Use Controls

Zoning

- "police power" granted by state-level enabling acts; zoning ordinance: creates zones, usage restrictions, regulations, requirements
- enables urban land managers to create separate land uses that do not conflict with one another nor create incompatible adjacencies

Types of zone

- residential, commercial, industrial, agricultural, public, PUD
- residential zoning regulates *density*, or number of dwellings in an area
- commercial zoning regulates *intensity*, or how much commercial activity is permitted in relation to size of the site

Zoning administration

- Zoning Board of Adjustment oversees rule administration and appeals

Zoning Appeals

- **Nonconforming use:** legal if use existed prior to zone creation, illegal otherwise
- **Variance:** use exception granted based on hardship
- **Special exception:** based on public interest
- **Amendment:** change of zones; rezoning

Eminent Domain

- allows a government entity to purchase a fee or easement interest in privately owned real property for the **public good** and for **public use** in exchange for "just compensation"

Planned Unit Development (PUD)

- PUD zoning designed to regulate use of whole tracts of land with a singular design
- Design purposes are to achieve optimum space efficiency and open space

Subdivision Regulation

- plat of subdivision and relevant requirements must be met and approved; must meet FHA requirements for insured financing
- location, grading, alignment, surfacing, street width, highways
- sewers and water mains
- lot and block dimensions
- building and setback lines
- public use dedications
- utility easements
- ground percolation

Building Codes

- comprehensive onsite and offsite construction and materials standards; must be met to receive certificate of occupancy

Environmental Restrictions

- flood control; solid waste disposal; air quality; water quality; marine protection; noise control; toxic substances controls; lead paint; CERCLA; Superfund

---

Private Land Use Controls

Deed Restriction

- also "covenants; conditions and restrictions", or "CC & Rs"
- limits in deed on how property can be used; cannot be discriminatory or anti-fair trade
- Eg: minimum area of residence; limits on commercial activity

Declaration restriction

- attaches to property; cannot extinguish by agreement or quit claim deed
- similar to deed restriction; purpose is to optimize, preserve value
- can enforce by injunction

Deed condition

- similar to deed restriction
- violation gives grantor right to re-possess property and sue for legal title

HOA regulation

- HOA determines rules and regs for the development via CCRs and by-laws
- Egs: fees, pet rules, rent payments; maintenance standards; occupancy limits; parking; noise; insurance requirements
- disputes settled by civil courts

Zoning Appeals

Zoning Board of Adjustment: oversees rule administration and appeals
Nonconforming use: legal if use existed prior to zone creation, illegal otherwise
Variance: use exception granted based on hardship
Special exception: based on public interest
Amendment: change of zones; rezoning

Environmental Laws

Legislation	Date	Regulated
Solid Waste Disposal Act (later part of RCRA)	1965 (1976, 1999, 2002)	landfills
Air Quality Act, Clean Air Act	1967 (1970)	air quality standards
National Environmental Policy Act (NEPA)	1969 (1970)	created EPA
Flood Control Act	amended 1969	building in flood zones; flood insurance
Resource Recovery Act	1970	solid waste disposal
Water Quality Improvement Act	1970	dumping in navigable waters; wetlands
Water Pollution Control Act amendment	1972	dumping in navigable waters; wetlands
Clean Water Act	1972 (1977)	dumping in navigable waters; wetlands
Lead-based paint ban (US Consumer Product Safety Commission rule)	1978	lead-based paint in residences
PCB ban (EPA rule)	1979	polychlorinated biphenyls
RCRA amendment	1984	underground storage tanks

Comprehensive Environmental Response, Compensation and Liability Act (CERCLA)	1980	hazardous waste disposal
Superfund Amendment and Reauthorization Act	1986	hazardous waste cleanup costs
Asbestos ban (EPA rule)	1989	asbestos in building materials
Residential Lead-based Paint Hazard Reduction Act (EPA and HUD rule)	1992 (1996)	lead-based paint disclosure and treatment
Flood Insurance Reform Act	1994	flood insurance in flood zones
Brownfields legislation	2002	industrial site cleanup

Legal Descriptions

Purpose

- to accurately locate and identify the boundaries of a parcel of real property to a degree acceptable by courts of law in the state where the property is located
- general criterion is that it alone provides sufficient data for a surveyor to locate the parcel

Metes and Bounds Method

- describes perimeter by landmarks, monuments, distances, angles
- usable within rectangular survey system
- starting at point of beginning (POB), follow perimeter, **return to POB**

Lot and Block System (Recorded Plat Method)

- used to describe properties in residential, commercial, industrial subdivisions
- tracts of land divided into lots, then grouped into blocks

Rectangular Survey System

Key points:

- simplify and standardize property descriptions
- all land in system surveyed using longitude and latitude lines
- lines created uniform grids of squares called townships

Meridians:

- north-south lines six miles apart

Parallels:

- east-west lines six miles apart

Range:

- north-south strip between meridians

Tier:	• east-west strip of area between parallels; also called township strip
Township:	• the six-mile by six-mile square at the intersection of a range and a tier
Section of a township:	• a 1 mile x 1 mile square; 1 section = 640 acres; 36 sections per township
Fractions of a section:	• going from the smallest to largest unit, indicate size and location within successively larger quarters or halves of the section: E 1/2 of the NE 1/4 of the NE 1/4 of Section 8

Contract Law

Contract Defined

- An agreement between two or more parties who have a "meeting of the minds," and have pledged to perform (or refrain from performing) some act
- A *valid* contract is *legally enforceable* by meeting certain requirements of contract law.
- If a contract does not meet requirements, it is not valid and the parties to it cannot resort to a court of law to enforce its provisions

Contract Status

Valid

- meets all requirements

Valid but unenforceable

- certain oral contracts; if performed, cannot change outcome

Void

- not valid; unenforceable

Voidable

- may be rescinded due to subsequent discoveries: if performed, cannot change outcome

Contract Validity

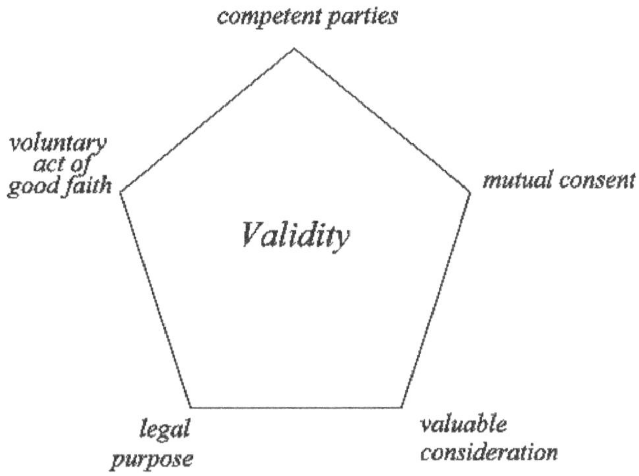

Competent parties

- legal age
- mental competency
- legitimate authority

Mutual consent

- clear and unequivocal **offer and acceptance** with an underlying **meeting of the minds**

Valuable consideration

- exchange of valuable consideration for performance by the other party; not "love and affe

Legal purpose

- promise, intent and content must be lawful; if illegal, contract is void – cannot contract to the law

Voluntary, good faith

- no duress, coercion, fraud or misrepresentation

Conveyance Contract Requirements

- must be in writing
- must contain legal description
- must be signed by one or more parties
- **exception: per Statute of Frauds,** leases for one year or less may be verbal and still be enforceable

---

Offer / Counteroffer / Acceptance

Offer

- intention to enter into contract
- must contain all intended terms
- must be in writing
- expires in "reasonable time" or date and time specified

Acceptance

- unequivocal and manifest agreement to offer
- no changes to offer whatsoever
- signed, preferably dated

Completed contract

- communication of acceptance to offeror
- if by mail, offer is communicated upon mailing

Counteroffer

- new or amended terms of a received offer
- original offer is void

Revoking an offer

- may be done at any time prior to offeree's communication of acceptance

Termination of an offer

- acceptance; rejection; revocation; expiration; counteroffer; death or insanity of either party

---

Contract Assignment

- assignable unless expressly prohibited or contract is a personal service contract (listings)

Contract Preparation

- restricted unless licensed as attorney or a party to the contract
- licensees must be aware of contract preparation restrictions in the states where they operate

---

Contract Classifications

Oral vs. written

- oral, or parol, contract may not be enforceable

Express vs. implied

- express: all terms expressly agreed to
- implied: unintentional agreement deemed to exist due to terms implied by actions

Bilateral vs. unilateral

- bilateral: both parties promise to perform
- unilateral: one party performs only if other party performs

Executed vs. executory

- executed: fully performed
- executory: performance yet to be completed

Termination

Causes

- performance
- infeasibility
- mutual agreement
- cooling-period rescission
- revocation
- abandonment
- lapse of time
- invalidity of contract
- breach of contract

Breach & Remedies

Rescission	• cancel contract; return deposits
Forfeiture	• defaulting party gives up something according to contract terms
Liquidated damages	• damages due a damaged party as stated in contract
Suit for damages	• civil suit for money damages not covered by contract
Specific performance	• suit to force party to fulfill contract promises

Agency

The Agency Relationship In Real Estate

- principal (client) hires agent (broker) to find ready, willing, and able customer (buyer, seller, tenant, landlord)
- client – agent relationship governed by fiduciary duties of trust, confidence, good faith

Universal / General / Special

Universal	• represent in all matters • can contract for principal
General	• represent in business matters • agent can contract for principal
Special	• represent in single business transaction • normally agent cannot contract for principal • characterizes the brokerage relationship

Agency Creation

- Express written **or oral** agreement (listing)
  - established for a specified transaction
  - contains an express expiration
- **Implied** agreement by actions of either party
  - can be intentional or unintentional
  - can obligate the agent to fiduciary duties and professional standards of care
  - not allowed to exist in some states

Termination

- **Voluntary**
  - fulfillment
  - expiration
  - mutual agreement
- **Involuntary**
  - incapacity
  - abandonment or destruction of property
  - renunciation
  - breach
  - bankruptcy
  - revocation of license

Duties & Obligations

Agent's Fiduciary Duties to Client

- **Skill, care and diligence:** proactive; competent; act within bounds of expertise
- **Loyalty:** place client interest above customer and self
- **Obedience:** provided actions, instructions are legal
- **Confidentiality:** extends beyond listing term indefinitely
- **Full disclosure;** property condition; customers; material facts
- **Accounting;** proper handling of monies and documents

Obligations Owed Customers

- honesty and fair dealing
- reasonable care and skill
- proper disclosure

Breach of duty: potential consequences

- loss of listing; compensation; license suspension, suit for damages

Misrepresentation and Fraud

Puffing – licensee boasting about property's benefits

Fraud

- misstatement or failure to disclose material fact
- knowledge that statement was false or fact should have been disclosed
- party relied on misstatement
- party was damaged by misstatement

Misrepresentation – misstatement or concealment of fact

- intentional misrepresentation: **purposeful misstatement** of material fact
- intentional omission: **purposeful concealment** of material fact
- negligent misrepresentation: **unintended misstatement** that agent should have known
- negligent omission: **unintended concealment** that agent should have known

Single / Dual / Sub / No Agency

Single agency

- seller or buyer agency
- tenant or landlord representation

Subagency

- outside brokers and agents who help listing agent
- listing broker's own agents
- (disallowed in some states)

Dual agency

- representing both sides
- potentially illegal or conflict of interest
- must disclose & obtain written consent
- **Types of dual agency**
    - voluntary by consent
    - involuntary by actions of parties (implied agency)
    - duties: all but full disclosure and loyalty
- **Dual agency duties**
    - disclose to both parties; obtain written consent
    - owes duties of skill, care, diligence, obedience, confidentiali accounting
    - does not owe duties of full disclosure and loyalty; exclusive representation of client's interest

Designated agency

- broker selects one subordinate to represent buyer and another to represent the seller in a given transaction under provisions of a designated agency agreement
- cannot disclose confidential information except to broker
- designated agents are not dual agents; brokers are considered disclosed consensual dual agents for that transaction

No agency

- "facilitator" or "transaction broker"
- representing neither party in the transaction
- duties to both parties: accounting; skill, care and diligence; honesty and fair dealing; disclosures affecting property value

---

Disclosure Rules

(Note: Agency disclosure rules vary by state – see State section for laws in your state.)

Objectives of disclosure

- declare
- explain
- offer choice
- obtain documented consent

Seller agent disclosures to client

- in writing
- on or before listing is executed

Seller agent disclosures to customer

- in writing
- upon first face-to-face contact, or upon substantive communication, depending on state law
- oral disclosure permitted but must have written follow-up

Buyer agent disclosures to seller

- in writing
- upon first contact with listing agent or seller
- substantive contact is assumed

Dual agent disclosures

- "informed, written consent"
- may not disclose price or financing positions or motivations unless authorized

Facilitator disclosures

- on becoming transaction broker or on substantive contact, whichever is first

---

Listing Agreements

Key characteristics

- broker's **enforceable contract** of employment
- establishes **special agency** relationship
- defines **roles** of parties
- creates **fiduciary duties** for the agent
- describes agent's **scope of authority**
- establishes compensation to be paid to the licensee

Parties

- listing broker-- fiduciary of buyer client or seller client
- subagent-- fiduciary of listing broker's client
- customer-- non-fiduciary principal in transaction

Fiduciary duties	• to client: loyalty; obedience; disclosure; skill; care; diligence; accounting; confidentiality • to customer: honesty, care and disclosure
Authority	• limited agency agreement • broker may not contract for client unless specifically authorized • clients liable only for broker's acts within scope of authority
Contract law	• unilateral contract • oral listing is valid and enforceable • exclusive listing in some states must be written to be enforceable • personal service contract-- not assignable

---

Types

Exclusive right-to-sell

- given to one broker
- usually must be written
- must expire
- broker gets commission if property transfers during period

Exclusive agency

- exclusive excepting owner
- oral or written
- must expire
- broker gets commission unless owner sells

Open listing

- non-exclusive
- oral or written
- no stated expiration
- procuring cause gets commission
- no commission if client procures customer

Net listing

- all sale proceeds above a seller's minimum price go to the broker
- discouraged, if not illegal

Multiple listing

- listing placed in MLS
- owners consent to rules and provisions of MLS

Limited services agreement

- licensee and agreement must disclose that licensee is acting as a limited service representative
- licensee provides services expressly listed in agreement as well as conventional brokerage services that will not be rendered
- agreement must be in writing
- may need to comply with minimum services requirements imposed by state regs

Buyer agency agreements

- create a fiduciary relationship with the buyer
- if exclusive, buyer agrees to only work with the buyer representative in procuring a property
- must have an expiration date along with other requirements of a valid listing

---

Compensation / Termination

Compensation

- negotiated between agent and principal
- put in writing in contract between parties
- where disputed among agents, agent with procuring cause is owed commission
- based on results: find ready willing and able customer

Causes for termination

- performance
- infeasibility
- mutual agreement
- revocation
- abandonment
- breach
- expiration
- invalidity
- incapacitation or death
- involuntary transfer
- destruction of property

Agent's performance

- may perform only authorized tasks
- must verify owner and property data
- may delegate duties to salespeople and other brokers

Revoking a listing

- clients always have power to revoke during period
- may incur liability for commission or damages

Brokerage

Who May Broker

(Varies from state to state)

Yes

1. sole proprietorship
2. for-profit corporation
3. general or limited partnership
4. joint venture

No

1. non-profit corporation
2. business trust
3. cooperative association

Broker-Agent Relationship

Legal relationship

- salesperson
  - is agent & fiduciary of broker
  - acts in broker's name
  - is subagent of client

- salesperson may not
  - have two employers
  - be paid by other parties
  - bind clients contractually

Salesperson's employment status

- employee or independent contractor
- defined by agreement

Obligations and responsibilities

- agent to broker:
  - obtain & sell listings
  - follow policies and employment provisions
  - promote ethics and broker's reputation
- broker to agent:
  - provide data, office support, compensation, training
  - uphold ethics, policies, and employment agreement

Agent compensation

- commissions per schedule after any previously negotiated splits with cooperating brokers

Commingling & Conversion

	Not allowed !!
Commingling	• mixing broker's personal or business funds with trust funds • includes failure to deposit funds in a timely manner
Conversion	• using trust funds for personal or business purposes

Advertising Requirements

- no misleading ads
- ads must contain broker's ID
- broker is responsible for content
- no blind ads (concealed identity)
- must disclose if agent owns property

Telephone Consumer Protection Act

- regulates unsolicited telemarketing calls
- solicitors must identify themselves, how they can be contacted
- must comply with any do-not-call request
- consumers can place phone numbers on Do-Not-Call list

CAN-SPAM Act

- bans sending unwanted email 'commercial messages' to wireless devices
- requires express prior authorization
- requires an 'opt out' choice to terminate the sender's messages

---

Anti-Trust Laws

Sherman, Clayton anti-trust laws	• NO restraint of trade; monopolies; • predatory pricing; exclusive dealing
no collusion:	• two or more businesses conspiring to disadvantage a competitor
no price fixing:	• two or more brokers agreeing to fix prices
no market allocation:	• colluding to restrict competition in a market segment in exchange for a competitor's reciprocal agreement
no group boycotting	• cannot "gang up" on a competitor in a given market in any way that limits the competitor's business

---

Sale Contracts

Key characteristics

- binding, bilateral contract for purchase and sale
- the enforceable "blueprint" for closing
- contract is executory, or to be fulfilled
- expires upon closing
- must be in writing
- for validity, must
  - contain valuable consideration
  - identify property
  - be signed by all

Creation / Deposit / Contingencies

Creation	• created by unqualified acceptance of an offer • gives buyer equitable title, and power to force specific performance
Deposit, or earnest money escrow	• secures contract validity and buyer's equitable interest

	• varies in amount • deposit controlled by disinterested party who must act according to escrow instructions
Contingencies	• conditions that must be met for the contract to be enforceable • must be clear • have expiration date • require diligence to satisfy
Buyer default	• seller can cancel, claim liquidated damages or sue for specific performance (i.e., buyer's deposit)
Seller default	• buyer can cancel or sue for damages or specific performance

---

Primary Clauses

- parties
- consideration
- legal description
- price and terms
- loan approval provisions
- earnest money
- escrow
- closing and possession dates
- conveyed interest
- type of deed
- title evidence
- property condition warranty/disclosures
- closing costs
- damage and destruction
- default
- broker's agency disclosure and who pays commission
- seller's representations: property condition, marketable title

---

Options

Essentials	• optionor gives option to optionee to buy at a given time and price; optionee must pay for option right • unilateral contract: seller must perform, buyer need not • if option is exercised, option becomes bilateral sale contract • options are assignable
Contract requirements	• non-refundable consideration for the option right • price and terms of the sale • option period expiration date • legal description • must be in writing • must meet contract validity requirements • option should be recorded
Common clause provisions	• how to exercise option • terms of option money forfeiture • how option money will be applied to purchase price

---

Contract for Deed

Essentials

- purchase price is paid over time in installments
- seller retains title, buyer takes possession, equitable title
- at end of period, buyer pays balance, gets legal title

Interests and rights

- seller may encumber or assign interest
- seller remains liable for underlying mortgage
- buyer may use, possess, or profit
- buyer must make periodic payments, maintain the property, and purchase at the end of the term

Default and recourse

- buyer may sue for cancellation and damages or specific performance
- seller may sue for specific performance or damages, or may need to foreclose

Economics

Supply

- the quantity of a product or service available for sale, lease, or trade at any given time

Demand

- the quantity of a product or service that is desired for purchase, lease, or trade at any given time

Supply / Demand / Price

Real Estate Supply

- property available for sale or lease; measured in dwelling units, square feet, acres

Real Estate Demand

- property buyers and tenants wishing to acquire; measured in households, square feet, acres

Interaction

- if supply increases relative to demand, price decreases
- if demand increases relative to supply, price increases

Supply-Demand Cycle

unmet demand →
construction adds supply →
market equilibrium →
construction adds more supply →
oversupply →
construction stops →
market equilibrium →
demand absorbs supply →
unmet demand →
cycle repeats

Real Estate Supply-Demand Cycle

Factors Influencing Supply and Demand

- cost, availability of financing
- availability of developable land
- construction costs
- capacity of infrastructure
- governmental regulation and police powers
- changes in the economic base
- in- and out-migrations of major employers
- labor availability
- land availability

Government Influences on the Real Estate Market

- local zoning power
- local control and permitting of new development
- local taxing power
- federal influence on interest rates
- environmental legislation and regulations

Market Indicators

- **vacancy rates**
  - increases indicate buyer / tenant market & falling prices / rents
  - decreases indicate seller / landlord market & rising prices / rents

- building **permits** – increases indicate declining vacancy; increasing prices & construction
- prices
  - increases indicate rising demand or declining supply or both
  - decreases indicate falling demand or rising supply or both

Appraisal

Concepts and Principles of Value

Supply and demand	• When demand exceeds supply, scarcity exists, values rise. • When supply exceeds demand, surplus exists, values decline. • When supply and demand are equal, the market is in balance, values stabilize.
Utility	• A property's use in the marketplace contributes to the demand for it.
Transferability	• How readily or easily title or rights to real estate can be transferred affects the property's value.
Anticipation	• The benefits a buyer expects to derive from a property over a holding period influence what the buyer is willing to pay for it.
Substitution	• A buyer will pay no more for a property than the buyer would have to pay for an equally desirable and available substitute property.
Contribution	• The contribution to value of an improvement is equal to the change in market value that the addition of the improvement causes.
Change	• Market conditions affect the benefits that can arise from the property.
Highest and best use	• A property achieves its maximum value when it is put to whichever use generates the greatest income and return. The highest and best use must be legally permissible, physically possible, financially feasible, and maximally productive.
Conformity	• A property's maximal value is attained when its form and use are consonant with surrounding properties and uses

Progression and regression
- The value of a property is influenced by the values of neighboring properties.

Assemblage
- Conjoining adjacent properties can create a combined value in excess of the values of the unassembled properties. This excess value is called **plottage value.**

Subdivision
- The division of a single property into smaller properties can result in a higher total value.

Types of Value

Market value
- an estimate of the price at which a property will sell at a particular time; this type of value is the one generally sought in appraisals and used in brokers' estimates of value

Insured value
- the face amount a casualty or hazard insurance policy will pay in case a property is rendered unusable

Reproduction value
- the value based on the cost of constructing a precise duplicate of the subject property's improvements, assuming current construction costs

Replacement value
- the value based on the cost of constructing a functional equivalent of the subject property's improvements, assuming current construction costs

Salvage value
- the nominal value of a property that has reached the end of its economic life; also an estimate of the price at which a structure will sell if it is dismantled and moved

Assessed value
- the value of a property as estimated by a taxing authority as the basis for ad valorem taxation

Depreciated value
- a value established by subtracting accumulated depreciation from the purchase price of a property

Book value
- the value of the property as carried on the accounts of the owner; the value is generally equal to the acquisition price plus capital improvements minus accumulated depreciation

Investment value
- the value of an income property as indicated by the capitalized value of the cash flow the property generates

---

Market Value Requirements

The price willing buyer and seller would agree on given:

- a cash transaction
- reasonable market exposure
- parties have market and property use information
- there is no pressure to complete the transaction
- transaction is arm's length: parties are not related
- marketable title
- no hidden influences

Measuring Living Area

Essential standards:

- Generated by American National Standards Institute and Fannie Mae
- Gross living area (GLA) = area of all rooms "above grade" measured from the exterior walls including stairwells, excluding "open areas."
- Above grade = above the surface of the ground.
- Living area below-grade must be counted as basement area
- Minimum ceiling height 7 feet.
- Two-story properties (or more) with sloped ceilings, at least 50% of the ceiling area must have a height of 7 feet or more.
- Finished space: To be counted in GLA footage, space must be finished, i.e., have a floor covering and a ceiling.
- can count entry areas but not seasonal porches
- living area must be under heat and attached
- must be attached to the main house itself; cannot count unattached outbuildings
- Attics and basements: Cannot count partially finished heated areas.
- Cannot count garage areas; may meet a local standard if fully heated, finished and improved for other household uses.
- Stairs and closets generally fully countable in GLA.

Sales Comparison Approach

1. Identify comparable sales
2. Compare comps to the subject and make adjustments to the comparables
3. Weight values indicated by adjusted comparables for the final value estimate of the subject

Adjusting Comparables

Rules for selecting comparables

- must be physically similar
- in subject's vicinity
- recently sold in arm's length sale

Rules for adjusting comparables

- never adjust the subject!
- deduct from comparable if better than subject
- add to comp if worse than subject
- Remember: ("Subtract if Superior !")

Weighting adjustments

- best indicator has fewest and smallest adjustments and smallest net adjustment from the sale price

Cost Approach

Types of cost appraised

- reproduction – cost of making a precise replica
- replacement – cost of making a functional equivalent

Steps in the approach

1. Estimate land value
2. Estimate replacement cost of improvements
3. Estimate total depreciation
4. Subtract: (cost of improvements - depreciation) = depreciated improvements cost
5. Add land back in: (land value + depreciated improvements) = value estimate of property

Key Aspects of Depreciation

Depreciation	• **loss of value** from deterioration, functional obsolescence, or economic obsolescence
Deterioration	• **wear and tear** from use and aging
Functional Obsolescence	• **outmoded** physical or design **features**: curable or incurable
Economic Obsolescence	• loss of value due to adverse **changes in surroundings**: incurable
Curability	• curable: cost to cure is less than resulting contribution to value • incurable: cost to cure exceeds contribution to value

Income Approach

- Based on the principle of anticipation: the expected future income stream of a property underlies what an investor will pay for the property
- Also based on the principle of substitution: that an investor will pay no more for a subject property with a certain income stream than the investor would have to pay for another property with a similar income stream.

Steps in the Income Approach

1. Estimate potential gross income
2. Estimate effective gross income (total potential income - vacancy)
3. Estimate net operating income (NOI) (effective income - expenses)
4. Select and apply capitalization rate (NOI ÷ cap rate)

Gross rent multipliers (GRMs)

- Simplified income-based methods to estimate value
- Method consists of applying a multiplier to the estimated gross rent of the subject
- Multiplier is derived from market data on sale prices and gross rent
- Does not necessarily produce accurate value estimates

GRM Formula

- GRM = price divided by monthly rent
- Value = GRM times monthly rent

Preparing a Comparative Market Analysis

Steps

1. Identify comparables sold, for sale properties, and expired listings
2. Compile comparison data for each comparable: price, sale date, location, age, lot size, site aspects, living area, bedrooms, etc.
3. Complete adjustments for differences; rules:
   a. Never adjust the subject
   b. Add value to the comparable if a feature is inferior to the subject
   c. Subtract value from the comp if a feature is superior to the subject
4. Derive total adjustments for each comparable
5. Reconcile all value-adjusted comps to the subject to identify a value estimate

Regulation of Appraisal Practice

FIRREA

- Financial Institutions Reform, Recovery and Enforcement Act (**FIRREA**) enacted in 1989 to regulate appraisal practices
- requires that competent individuals whose professional conduct is properly supervised perform all appraisals used in federally-related transactions
- As of January 1, 1993, federally-related appraisals must be performed only by state-certified appraisers
- **USPAP** - Uniform Standards of Professional Appraisal Practice – competency standards established by the **Appraiser Qualifications Board** of the Appraisal Foundation

USPAP

- Uniform Standards of Professional Appraisal Practice
- requires recognized appraisal methods
- must exercise a defined level of due diligence
- must properly report results
- must make proper disclosures and assumptions

Finance

Mortgage Transaction

Elements

- promissory note: promise to repay loan
- mortgage: pledge of property as collateral for loan

Mechanics

- borrower gives lender promissory note and mortgage
- lender gives borrower funds and records a lien

Hypothecation

- use of real property as collateral for a mortgage loan

Financial components

- original principal: capital amount borrowed on which interest payments are calculated
- loan balance: remaining unpaid principal at any point in the life of the loan
- interest: charge for the use of money; rate fixed or variable
- Annual Percentage Rate (APR) includes interest and all other finance charges; lender must disclose on residential properties
- point: one percent of the loan amount
- loan origination fee: charged by lender at origination to obtain required return
- term: period of time for repayment of interest and principal
- payment: the periodic payment of interest and/or principal
- down payment: borrower's cash payment applied to the purchase price
- loan-to-value ratio: the loan's share of the total value of the property
- equity: at closing, the borrower's cash invested in the property; thereafter, the difference between the market value and the loan balance

Trust Deed Transaction

Elements

- promissory note: trustor's promise to repay loan
- deed of trust: title to property as collateral for loan

Mechanics

- trust deed conveys title from the borrower/trustor to a third-party trustee
- trustee holds title on behalf of the lender/beneficiary until the debt is repaid

Promissory note

- legal instrument executed by borrower stating debt amount, loan term, method and timing of repayment, interest rate, promise to pay; may repeat other provisions from mortgage document or deed of trust; negotiable instrument assignable to a third party

Mortgage Clauses

Payment of principal and interest: prepayment and late charges

- borrower must make timely payments according to the terms of the note
- late payments or early payoffs may trigger penalties

Funds for taxes and insurance

- borrower must make monthly payments to cover taxes and hazard insurance
- borrower may also have to pay flood insurance and mortgage insurance premiums
- **escrow account:** reserve account for periodic payments of taxes and insurance.
- Real Estate Settlement Procedures Act (RESPA) limits funds the lender can require for this purpose.

PITI

- borrower's monthly payment for principal and interest is called the p&i payment (principal and interest)
- the amount which includes the escrow payment is called PITI (principal, interest, taxes, insurance).

Charges and liens

- borrower is liable for paying any charges, liens, or other expenses that may have priority over the mortgage or trust instrument.

Hazard or property insurance

- borrower must keep property insured as the lender requires.

Occupancy, preservation, maintenance and protection of the property

- borrower must take and maintain occupancy as the borrower's principal residence according to requirements
- borrower must not abuse or neglect the including use for illegal purposes, creating hazardous waste on the property, or destroying the improvements

Protection of lender's rights in the property

- lender may take actions to protect its rights in the property if the borrower jeopardizes the property's value. The costs of these actions would be charged to the borrower

Mortgage insurance

- Lender may require private mortgage insurance, or PMI which protects the lender against loss from borrower default
- applies to loans that are not backed by the Federal Housing Administration (FHA) or Veterans Administration (VA) and that have a down payment of less than 20% of the property value

Inspection

- lender may inspect the property with reasonable cause to fear damage to the collateral

Condemnation

- if the property is condemned or taken by eminent domain, lender reserves a claim on any resulting proceeds

Transfer of the property or a beneficial interest in borrower

- if borrower sells the property without the lender's approval, the lender may demand immediate repayment of the loan balance. this alienation clause, aka a due-on-sale clause, allows lender to prevent unapproved loan assumptions
- the requirement to repay the loan before the scheduled due date is called **acceleration.**

Borrower's right to reinstate

- if lender holds borrower in default, borrower has the right to reinstatement by performing certain actions, usually paying overdue payments plus expenses the lender
- clause is called a redemption clause
- gives the borrower time to satisfy obligations and prevent a forced sale

Release

- agreement to release the lien obligation when borrower has paid off the loan
- release clause, aka **defeasance** clause, may require lender to execute a **satisfaction of mortgage,** aka **release of mortgage**
- if deed of trust, lender directs trustee to execute a **release deed** or **deed of reconveyance** to the borrower as trustor.
- release deed or satisfaction should be recorded as necessary

Escalation clause

- allows lender to increase the loan's interest rate

Loan Qualification

Equal Credit Opportunity Act

- lender must evaluate applicant according to applicant's own income and credit information
- lender cannot deny credit based on
  - discounted income from part-time work
  - future plans to have family
  - locational factors
  - protected classes

Income qualification

- income ratio and debt ratio qualify borrower's income; income ratio applied to gross income determines housing expense maximum; debt ratio takes revolving debt into account
- income ratios: 25-28% conventional; 31% FHA-insured
- debt ratios: 36% conventional; 43% FHA and 41% VA

Cash qualification

- lender verifies applicant's sources of cash for down payment; extra cash enhances income qualification evaluation

Net worth

- extent to which applicant's assets exceed liabilities as a further source of reserves

Credit evaluation

- lender obtains credit reports to evaluate applicant's payment behavior

Loan commitment

- written pledge by lender to grant loan under specific terms; firm, lock-in, conditional, take-out

Loan-to-value ratio (LTV)

- relationship of loan amount to property value
- expressed as a percentage
- 80% LTV = loan is 80% of property value

Private mortgage insurance (PMI)

- must insure portions of purchase price to adjust LTVs that are too risky for conventional lenders, e.g., decreasing a 90% LTV to 80% with PMI insurance
- may be removable via increasing property value and decreasing loan balance

---

Laws Affecting Mortgage Lending

Truth-in-Lending and Regulation Z

- **Reg Z** implements **Truth-in-Lending Simplification and Reform Act** and **Consumer Credit Protection Act**
  - Lender must **disclose finance charges** and APR prior to closing;
  - Borrower has limited right of rescission, but excludes primary residence
  - Lender must follow **advertising requirements** for full disclosure of costs, loan mechanics

Equal Credit Opportunity Act (ECOA)

- prohibits discrimination in lending based on
  - race or color
  - religion
  - national origin
  - sex
  - marital status
  - age
  - dependency upon public assistance
- licensees assisting in qualifying must also comply
- denied applicants must get notice within 30 days

Real Estate Settlement Procedures Act (RESPA)

- standardizes settlement practices & ensures buyers understand settlement costs
- lender must:
  - provide CFPB booklet explaining loans, settlement costs and procedures
  - provide CFPB Loan Estimate of settlement costs within three days of application
  - provide CFPB Closing Disclosure three days before loan consummation

National Flood Insurance Act

- borrowers of "federally-related loans" must obtain flood insurance if property is in designated flood-hazard area
- flood-zone maps indicate where homeowners must obtain insurance

---

The Mortgage Market

Supply and demand for money

- relationship between supply and demand for money affects interest rates, consumer prices, availability of mortgage money; regulated by Federal Reserve

Federal Reserve control of money supply among banks

- sells T-bills to reduce money supply and increase interest rates; buys T-bills to increase supply and decrease rates
- sets the reserve requirement for member banks
- increase reserves to tighten money and raise interest rates
- decrease reserves to loosen money and lower interest rates
- sets the discount rate for member banks
- increase rate to tighten money
- decrease rate to increase money supply

Federal Home Loan Bank System (FHLBS)

- counterpart to the Fed for savings and loan associations

Federal Deposit Insurance Corporation (FDIC)

- insures deposits up to $250,000 per depositor, per insured bank, for each account ownership category

The primary mortgage market

- originates mortgage loans directly to borrowers;
- includes savings and loans, commercial banks, mutual savings banks, life insurance companies, mortgage bankers, credit unions

The secondary mortgage market

- buys existing loans to provide liquidity to primary lenders; Fannie Mae, Ginnie Mae, Freddie Mac, investment firms, life insurance companies, pension funds

Role of FNMA, GNMA, FHLMC and FAMC

- FNMA buys conventional, FHA- and VA-backed loans and pooled mortgages; guarantees payment on mortgage-backed securities
- GNMA guarantees payment on certain types of loans
- FHLMC buys and pools mortgages; sells mortgage-backed securities
- FAMC, or Farmer Mac operates in the agricultural financing markets by stimulating and expanding ag credit availability for agribusinesses

Mortgage loan originator v. lender/banker v. broker

- mortgage loan originator: solicits, negotiates mortgage loans; requires MLO license
- mortgage broker: an intermediary who brings mortgage borrowers and mortgage lenders together, but does not use its own funds to originate mortgages
- mortgage banker: person or entity who funds or services loans for others and/or who sells mortgages to the secondary market

---

Types of Mortgages

Conventional mortgages

- Originated by banks and private financial institutions
- No government-related insurance or guarantees as with FHA or VA
- Typically require 20% down payments; smaller down payments may require PMI
- Assumptions require approval

Government loan programs

- **FHA** – federally insured loan programs (see following page)
- **VA** – federally guaranteed loan programs (see following page)

Amortized fixed-rate v adjustable loans

- **Amortized:** payments include increasing increments of principal which retire loan balance over loan term
- Fixed rate: interest rate does not change – can have for amortized or interest-only loans
- Adjustable loans: interest rate fluctuates up or down with an index; payments may also vary

---

Adjustable Loan Characteristics

- **mechanics**: rate adjusts up or down with index; payments may or may not change;
- negative amortization: loan balance increases if payments are less than what is owed given the balance and rate, i.e., unpaid monthly amounts are added to the principal balance
- rate and payment caps: maximum amounts the interest rate or payments can increase in a given adjustment period or over the life of the loan; protects borrower from unaffordable increases
- index and margin: interest rate tied to any number of financial indices; margin equals a fixed point spread between the index and the interest rate
- **teaser rates:** to attract borrowers, adjustable loans may have low initial rates which increase over subsequent adjustment periods to a more permanent market level.

Custom Mortgages

- **partially amortized with a balloon:** payments will not retire principal balance over life of the loan, thus requiring a lump-sum payment, or "balloon" payment at end of term
- **interest-only loans:** loans where payments are interest only, and the principal balance is retired in full at maturity using a balloon payment
- **biweekly mortgage:** loan payments are every-two weeks, a device that reduces total interest paid, but also shortens risk period for the lender
- **package mortgage:** mortgage loans which also finance articles of personal property as part of the purchase transaction
- **home equity loans:** funds borrowed using the homeowners equity for collateral; funds can be used for any purpose
- **purchase money mortgage:** a seller-financed loan to the buyer of portions of the purchase price using the property as collateral; usually accompanied by a senior underlying first mortgage
- **reverse annuity mortgage:** a financial arrangement where the homeowner pledges equity to a lender in exchange for periodic payments of the pledged equity; in essence it is the periodic receipt of equity liquidation in exchange for an increase of debt owed on the property.

FHA Loans

Insured loans granted by approved lenders to qualified borrowers.

Loan term:
- 15, 30 years

Qualifying ratios:
- income: 31%
- debt: 43%

Minimum downpayment:
- 3.5%

Mortgage insurance:
- required at 78% LTV or above
- premium = one-time 1.75-2.25% of loan amount, plus annual premium

Points:
- None

Maximum loan amount:
- varies by Metropolitan Statistical Area

VA Loans

Guaranteed loans:
- granted by approved lenders to qualified veterans

Qualifying ratios:
- depends on lender

Minimum downpayment:
- None

Points:
- 1.25 - 3.3, depending on downpayment, type of loan, type of veteran

Investment

Investment Terminology

Appreciation: an increase in the value of a property owing to economic forces beyond the control of the investor

Asset: a tangible or intangible item of **value**

Basis; a measurement of how much is invested in the property for tax purposes; adjusted basis is the **original** cost of the asset plus capital improvements minus depreciation

Capital gain (or loss): the difference between the net **sales** proceeds of an asset and its adjusted basis

Cash flow: the remaining positive or negative amount of income an investment produces after subtracting all operating expenses and debt service from gross income

Equity: that portion of a property's value owned by the legal owner, expressed as the difference between the property's market value and all loan balances outstanding **on** the property

Leverage; the relationship between the yield rate of an investment and the interest rate of funds borrowed to finance the investment; if the yield rate is greater than the loan rate, positive leverage results; if the yield rate is less than the **loan** rate, negative leverage results

Liquidity; the degree to which an investment is readily marketable, or convertible to another form of asset; if immediately salable, an investment is liquid; the longer it takes to sell, the more illiquid the investment; real property is relatively illiquid in comparison with other types of investment

Tax shelter: an investment that produces depreciation or other non-cash losses that a taxpayer can deduct **from** other income to reduce tax liability

Investment Characteristics

Ownership benefits

- income
- appreciation
- tax shelter: depreciation and interest deductions

Ownership risks

- relatively illiquid
- management intensive
- negative leverage and price movements

Investment Entities

Direct	• investor buys directly and manages personally
Syndicate	• group of investors who combine funds to buy, develop, and/or operate a property
General partnership	• all members own and manage
Limited partnership	• general partner manages; limited partners own but do not manage
Real Estate Investment Trust	• investors buy trust certificates; trust invests in real estate assets • investors share returns per ownership percent

Taxation of Real Estate Investments

Income-producing investments are taxed on
- the annual income they make, plus
- on any gain realized when sold

Taxable income
- gross income minus allowed expenses and deductions
- net income from the investment is added to the investor's other ordinary taxable income

Cost recovery, or depreciation
- deduction of a portion of property's value from gross income each year over the depreciable life of asset
- depreciable life defined by tax laws

Depreciable basis
- the non-land, or improvement portion of an income-producing property
- cannot depreciate land value

Depreciation schedules / terms
- 27.5 years to 39 years

Capital gain and loss
- the taxable gain (profit) or loss incurred when the income property is sold
- if sales proceeds exceed the current adjusted basis there is a gain; if less, then it is a loss

Adjusted basis
- the **cost** of the investment plus **capital improvements** less **depreciation**

Interest
- deductible from income for tax purposes
- cannot deduct principal

Tax liability On Sale Of Residence

- seller of a principal residence owes tax on capital gain that results from sale unless excluded
- capital gain is the amount realized minus the adjusted basis
- gains tax exclusion: up to $250,000 for a single seller and $500,000 for a married couple can be excluded from gains tax every two years

Gain on Sale

selling price of old home	$350,000
- selling costs	35,000
= amount realized	315,000
beginning basis of old home	200,000
+ capital improvements	10,000
= adjusted basis of old home	210,000
amount realized	315,000
- adjusted basis	210,000
= gain on sale	105,000

Investment Analysis of an Income Property (See also Math Section, "Investment")

Pre-tax Cash Flow

potential rental income	$70,000
- vacancy and collection loss	4,200
= effective rental income	65,800
+ other income	2,000
= gross operating income	67,800
- operating expenses	35,000
- reserves	3,500
= net operating income (NOI)	29,300
- debt service	20,000
= pre-tax cash flow	$9,300

After-tax cash flow

pre-tax cash flow
- tax liability
= after tax cash flow

Taxable Income

NOI
+ reserves
– interest
– depreciation)
= taxable income

Tax Liability

taxable income
x tax bracket
= tax liability

Taxation

Taxing Authorities

Taxing entities

- property tax, or ad valorem taxation -- not to be confused with an income-property's annual tax on taxable income
- no federal ad valorem taxation
  - can impose a tax lien, but not annual property tax
- states may levy property taxes
  - typically delegated to **county and local jurisdictions**
  - states may also impose tax liens

Tax districts which levy property tax

- counties
- cities
- municipalities
- townships
- special tax districts
- established to collect funds for schools, fire protection, parks, community colleges, libraries, road maintenance, other public services

Property Tax Calculation

Property tax

- **ad valorem** tax levied annually on the taxable value of a property in order to help fund government and public services
- taxable value is based on assessed value

Tax base and tax rate

- **tax base**
  - the total of all assessed values in a jurisdiction excluding exemptions
- **tax rate**
  - also, the **millage** rate
  - rate applied to taxable value of each property to determine its tax levy
- **assessed value**
  - the valuation of properties for tax purposes, completed by **assessors**
- **equalization factors**
  - value-adjusting factors applied to assessed value to increase fairness, evenness of tax levies

Homestead exemption

- a tax exemption of a portion of the assessed value of a principal residence
- granted to the homeowner, provided
  - he or she is the head of the family
  - has resided at the property for the required length of time

Other exemptions

- properties immune from ad valorem tax
  - government-owned properties
- exempt from taxes
  - properties owned by non-profit-organizations

Tax rate derivation

- (1) taxing entity determines **budget requirements** to be met by ad valorem tax
- (2) divide **tax requirement** by the **tax base**

Tax rate mills

- tax rate stated as mills ($.001), or
- dollars per $100 of assessed value, or
- dollars per $1,000 of assessed value, or
- as a percentage of assessed value

Tax billing and collection

- individual tax bill
  - (rate x taxable value)
- taxable value
  - (assessed value minus exemptions and adjustments)

Special assessments

- levied against specific properties that will benefit from the planned improvement
- assessment amount based on pro rata share of benefitting properties
- creates voluntary or involuntary tax lien

Tax Lien Enforcement

Tax lien enforcement process

- tax lien enforcement & collection occurs via
  - tax certificate issuance
  - certificate buyer pays taxes due
  - application for a tax deed
  - tax sale and foreclosure initiation

Sale of tax certificates

- tax certificate buyer pays taxes due
- after a period of time may apply for a tax deed

Tax deed conveyance

- conveys title in the tax sale

Tax sale

- buyer must pay taxes due
- defaulted taxpayer may be able to redeem property
- if not redeemed, state issues tax deed to convey title to buyer

Professional Practices

Fair Housing Laws

Anti-discrimination
- federal and state laws prohibit discrimination in housing
- citizens entitled to live wherever they wish without discrimination
- **state fair housing laws** reflect national laws with certain differences
- **fair housing and local zoning**
  - fair housing does not preempt local zoning, but zoning cannot be discriminatory against protected classes

Civil Rights Act of 1866
- no discrimination in selling or leasing housing **based on race**
- **Executive Order 11063:** no **race discrimination** involving FHA- or VA-backed loans

Civil Rights Act of 1968
- Title VIII (Fair Housing Act)
- no housing discrimination based on **race, color, religion, national origin**
- certain exceptions permitted

Forms of illegal discrimination
- discriminatory misrepresentation
- advertising
- unequal services
- steering
- blockbusting
- restricting access to market
- redlining

Title VIII exemptions
- selling, leasing single family home without broker or discriminatory advertising, with conditions
- 1-4 unit rental building where owner is occupant
- leasing facilities owned by private clubs
- facilities owned by religious organizations and leased to members

Jones v. Mayer
- discrimination in selling/renting residential housing based on race is prohibited without exception or exemption

Equal Opportunity in Housing poster
- brokers must display
- affirms compliance with fair housing laws
- failure to display can be construed as discrimination
- see example on following slide

Fair Housing Amendments Act of 1988
- no discrimination based on
  - sex
  - against the handicapped
  - families with children
- **exemptions**
  - government-designated retirement housing

- retirement community (62+ years of age)
- retirement community if 80 % of dwellings have one person who is 55+
- 1-4 unit dwellings where owners have no more than three houses

Discrimination by the client

- laws apply to owners as well as agents
- agent liable if goes along with client discrimination
- agent should withdraw from relationship with discriminatory client

Violations and enforcement

- file HUD complaint
- file suit in court
- may obtain injunction, damages
- violators subject to prosecution

Fair financing laws (See also Finance Section)

- Equal Credit Opportunity Act (ECOA)
  - lenders must be fair, impartial in loan qualifying
  - may not discriminate based on race, color, religion, national origin, sex, marital status, age
  - must state reasons for credit denial
- Home Mortgage Disclosure Act
  - prohibits redlining
  - lenders must report location of loans

Americans with Disabilities Act (ADA)

- purpose is to prohibit discrimination against persons with disabilities
- applies to accessing public, employment, education, transportation facilities
- applies to private employers with 15+ employees and public employees
- Title **I: Employment**
  - must have equal opportunity, enforced by ECOA
- **Title II: State, local government**
  - cannot discriminate in state and local services
- **Title III:** Public **accommodations**
  - cannot discriminate in public accommodations, commercial facilities
- **Title IV:** Telecommunication
  - concerns accommodations in telecommunications, public service messaging
- **Title V:** miscellaneous
  - general provisions as to how ADA affects other laws, insurance, lawyers
- licensees should clearly understand provisions of Title I and III
- ADA requirements
  - landlords must modify housing to be accessible without hindrance
  - access must be equivalent to that provided for non-disabled persons
- penalties
  - violations can result in citations, license restrictions, fines, injunctions

---

Property Disclosures

Residential property condition

- Seller's Disclosure Form
  - sellers (not agents) must complete form in many states for prospective buyers
  - describes property condition at time of sale on state-approved forms
- owner's role
  - seller must affirm whether or not problems exist with property or its systems
  - if unknown, seller must so state; if a defect is known, seller must disclose

- if seller is unaware of a problem, s/he can state "no representation" which removes liability for not disclosing
- seller must sign, deliver to buyer and buyer must acknowledge receipt

- licensee's role
  - must disclose any material facts that are known or reasonably should have known
- right of rescission
  - if seller does not complete and deliver form, buyer receives a right to rescind contract and reclaim deposit
  - right to cancel continues until closing or occupancy
- property condition and material facts
  - material fact = a fact affecting the property's value or the prospect's decision to contract
  - property stigmas are not material facts (previous crime, suicide, disease, etc.)
  - no requirement to disclose non-material facts
  - material facts can include the surrounding area in addition to the immediate premises

Environmental issues

- licensees and principals are responsible for disclosing, remediating hazards
  - lead-based paint
    - if property built before 1978, must disclose possible lead hazard
    - use form "Protect Your Family from Lead in Your Home"
  - mold
    - must be disclosed if present in home
  - asbestos
    - can cause lung cancer; must be removed by experts to prevent contamination
  - air quality
    - can/should test for carbon monoxide, radon, formaldehyde, other toxic chemicals prior to sale
  - carbon monoxide
    - emitted by gas space heaters, chimneys, furnaces, stoves, etc.
    - detectors should be in every home
  - septic systems
    - can release contaminants into soil
    - should inspect periodically and prior to any conveyance
  - radon
    - detectable radioactive ground gas that can cause cancer;
  - urea formaldehyde
    - hazard in foam insulation and pressed wood products, eg, particle board
  - underground storage tanks (UST)
    - commercial hazard if leaking; should disclose presence of any UST
- Clean Air Act
  - controls air pollution, air quality on national scale
  - creates pollutant- emission standards
- Clean Water Act
  - governs, sets standards for controlling water pollution
  - applies to all waters connected to navigable waterways
- Safe Drinking Water Act
  - regulates, protects public supply of drinking water
  - sets protection standards, requires water suppliers to report discovered health risks
  - sellers must disclose property's source of drinking water, proximity to septic systems
  - should test any well system
- Brownfields Law
  - brownfields = abandoned commercial sites likely to contain toxic material
  - law provides funds, liability protections and tax exemptions for reclamation
- Environmental Protection Agency (EPA)
  - integrates federal environmental research, funding, monitoring, standard-setting, and enforcement into one agency
- licensee disclosure obligations, liabilities

        - licensees should have general awareness and know where to get expert help
        - not expected to have expert knowledge of law or physical condition
        - critical role is to
            - be aware of potential hazards
            - disclose material facts, have attorney draft disclosures
            - know where to find expert help

Warranties

- purpose and scope
    - aka, home service contracts, to cover service, repair of systems, appliances
    - typically annual contracts with costs depending on property size, location, type, degree of coverage
    - may be included in purchase price of a home
- limitations – warranties may exclude
    - pre-existing conditions, accidental breakages, poor installations, outdoor systems, certain appliances, etc.
    - homeowner must use warranty company to have services performed

Inspections

- process
    - inspections detect oversights or need for repairs
    - identify need for maintenance procedures
    - inspections uncover system, pest infestation, environmental issues
- termite inspections
    - not easily detectable by non-experts; should do annual inspections
- environmental inspections, audits
    - home inspections should include environmental issues / hazards
    - can also conduct site assessments which examine possible impairments
- environmental impact statements (EIS)
    - performed for federally, some privately funded development projects
    - addresses air, water quality, noise, health, safety, wildlife, traffic, sewer impacts of project
    - culminates in permit or permit denial
- licensee disclosure duties
    - in most states, licensees must disclose known, material facts on residential properties
    - must also disclose known results of any residential inspection
    - when not required, licensees should suggest professional inspections / audits

Homeowners' Associations

- property disclosures include homeowners' associations
    - must disclose if subject to common interest plan
    - must disclose association's membership obligation, dues, restrictions
    - association must provide required disclosure documents, forms, timing requirements
    - seller responsible for disclosures, agent must ensure seller complies

---

Codes Of Ethics

Sources of practitioner ethics

- federal, state legislation
- state license regulation
- industry self-regulation via trade associations, institutes
- predominant influence in practitioner ethics is the Code of Ethics of the National Association of Realtors®
    - covers all aspects of practice and transactions

Duties to clients

- most codes of ethics uphold commitment to fulfilling fiduciary duties, including
    - honesty in representing values, property condition
    - respecting other broker-client relationships
    - submitting all offers
    - avoiding commingling, conversion
    - maintaining transaction files
    - maintaining confidentialities
    - managing client property competently

Other Professional Practices

Duties to customers

- honesty and fair dealing
- disclosing sources of compensation
- conducting honest advertising that is not misleading

Disclosures

- comply with federal, state, and ethical disclosure requirements, including
    - disclosure in ads

Wholesaling

- the discouraged practice of simultaneously buying and selling property so that the wholesaler makes an immediate profit without actually taking possession of the property
- at closing, wholesaler assigns purchase contract to another buyer for a price that exceeds the price paid to acquire the contract
- wholesaler takes his profit as a fee
- some states require wholesaler to have a real estate license

Love letters

- the practice of buyers trying to enhance an offer's attractiveness by attaching personal letters to the seller that attempt to convince the seller that the buyer is the party the seller should sell to.
- offers can be construed as discriminatory

Professional relationships

- avoid disparagement of competitors
- do not exploit unfair advantages
- arbitrate differences, disputes rather than litigate
- respect agency relationships of others
- conform to accepted standards of co-brokerage practices

Closings

Settlement Process

- identify selling terms & costs
- determine non-prorated debits and credits
- complete prorated debits and credits
- complete closing statement
- disburse funds

Key Points On Closings

- seller must prove marketability of title (via title insurance)
- must remove all encumbrances before title transfer
- escrow officer disburses buyer's funds, loan monies once conditions are met
- conditions include survey, inspections, title insurance, reserves, PMI

RESPA

Purpose

- clarify, disclose costs; eliminate kickbacks, undisclosed fees

Applicability

- for residential property
- federally-related mortgage, including VA, FHA
- Regulated by Consumer Financial Protection Bureau (CFPB)

Information booklet

- lender must provide CFPB booklet, "Your Home Loan Toolkit"

Loan estimate

- lender must provide CFPB's H-24 Loan Estimate of settlement costs within three days of application

Closing disclosure

- lender must use CFPB's H-25 Closing Disclosure

Referral fees and kickbacks

- RESPA prohibits payment of referral fees and kickbacks
- business relationships between firms involved in the transaction must be disclosed

---

Truth-in-Lending Integrated Disclosures Rule (TRID)

Key points

- combines financial disclosure requirements of RESPA & Truth-in-Lending Act (TILA)
- replaces "Good Faith Estimate" and HUD-1 forms
- uses new "Loan Estimate" form" and "Closing Disclosure" form

Forms and procedures

- lender must provide mandatory: "Your Home Loan Toolkit" booklet at loan application
- Loan Estimate form: 3 business days after loan application
- Closing Disclosure: 3 business days before consummation
- Terms in both forms must generally be the same

Good faith

- Loan Estimate costs based on best information available
- Closing Disclosure costs equal estimate costs within certain tolerances

Types of charges

- no limitation on increase over estimate
- 10% tolerance charges
- 0 tolerance charges

Applicable transactions	• most closed-end consumer mortgages, including: construction loans, loans secured by vacant land, loans to trusts • not covered: home equity loans, reverse mortgages, loans on mobile homes, loans by small lenders (no more than 5 loans per year)
The H-25 form	• 5 pages, variable by loan type

Debits & Credits

Amount buyer must produce: excess of ***buyer's debits*** over credits

Amount seller must receive: excess of ***seller's credits*** over debits

Buyer's credits

- earnest money
- loan amount
- seller's share of prorations buyer will pay

Buyer's debits

- purchase price
- expenses (per agreement or custom)
- buyer's share of prorations prepaid by seller

Seller's credits

- purchase price
- buyer's share of prorated items prepaid by seller

Seller's debits

- expenses (per agreement or custom)
- seller's share of prorated items the buyer will pay
- loan balance and other liens to be paid off

30-Day 12-Month Proration

Formula:

Monthly Amount = (Annual amount ÷ 12)
Daily Amount = (Monthly amount ÷ 30)
Proration = (Monthly amount x no. of months) + (Daily amount x no. of days)

Example:

An annual tax bill is $1,800. Closing is on April 10. What is the seller's share of the taxes?

1. ($1,800 ÷ 12) = $150 monthly amount
2. ($150 ÷ 30) = $5.00 daily amount
3. ($150 x 3 months) = $450 Jan - Mar; ($5 x 10) = $50 Apr 1 - Apr 10; ($450 + 50) = $500 seller's share

---

365-Day Method

Formula:

Daily amount = Annual amount ÷ 365 days; or
Daily amount = Monthly amount ÷ no. of days in month
Proration = (Daily amount x no. of days)

Example:

An annual tax bill is $1,800. Closing is on April 10. What is the seller's share of the taxes?

1. ($1,800 ÷ 365) = $4.93 daily amount
2. Jan 1 thru April 10 = (31 + 28 + 31 + 10) days, or 100 days
3. ($4.93 x 100 days) = $493 seller's share

Risk Management

Four Risk Management Strategies

1) **Avoidance**
   - refrain from risky activity
     - e. g., assuring buyers a property will appreciate
2) **Reduction**
   - reduce probability of loss
   - reduce severity of loss
   - share responsibility for a decision
3) **Transference**
   - pass risk to another party
   - get E & O insurance
   - by contract; insurance
4) **Retention**
   - accept risk
   - take responsibility for consequences
   - eg, pricing strategy on a listing

Risk Management Procedures

- **education**
  - knowledge and skill reduce risk
  - understand forms and contracts
- **disclosure**
  - provide information to reduce misunderstanding & lawsuits
- **disclosure areas**
  - agency
  - property condition
  - fiduciary / statutory duties
  - personal interest in selling a property
  - documentation and record keeping
  - maintain evidence of compliance, transaction recordkeeping

---

Insurance Types–To Manage Risk

- general liability
- errors and omissions (E & O, to cover negligence in discharging service duties)
- fire and hazard
- flood
- casualty
- workers'
- personal property
- consequential loss
- surety bond

Primary Areas of Risk

Agency

- fulfill agency disclosure requirements
- discharge fiduciary duties and duties to customers
- avoid conflicts of interest
- uphold legal confidentialities

Property disclosures

- seller's property condition disclosure
- material facts disclosure
- lead paint, infestations, mold, radon

Listing and selling

- listing agreement accuracy
- comparative market analysis results
- closing cost estimates
- advertising
- authorizations and permissions
- exceeding expertise

Contracting process

- contracts for real estate must be in writing
- inaccuracy endangers contract
- avoid unauthorized practice of law
  - may fill in blanks on standard contract forms
  - do not give legal advice to public

Fair housing

- advertising may not state preference, limitation or discrimination based on race, color, religion, national origin, sex, handicap, familial status
- licensee must not be involved with discriminatory actions of a client or customer
- make sure listing and purchase contracts are in compliance

Antitrust

- cannot collude on prices; fix prices
- cannot conspire with other companies to restrict trade or unjustly impair a competitor
- cannot create monopolies
- cannot allocate markets among competitors

Rules and regulations

- prime causes of discipline
  - commission of prohibited acts
  - practicing with an expired license
  - disclosure failures
  - earnest money mishandling

Misrepresentation

- **unintentional**
  - inaccurate information conveyed unknowingly
  - occurs most often in measurements, property characterizations
- **intentional**
  - fraud
  - knowingly conveying false information

- ways to reduce risks in misrepresentation
  - measure and calculate areas accurately
  - do not over-rely on measurements by others
  - refrain from exaggeration
  - avoid stating opinions a consumer might take for expertise

Recommending providers

- risks include
  - consumer dissatisfaction
  - possible liability for undisclosed business relationship
- best practices
  - do not recommend vendors
  - provide a list of trusted vendors with a disclaimer and no recommendation

Trust fund handling

- mishandling of earnest money deposits
- commingling trust funds
- conversion of trust funds
- errors in use of trust accounts

Property Management

Management Functions

Types of manager

- individual, managing properties for multiple owners; building manager, employed to manage a single property; resident, employed to live and manage on site.
- may specialize in a property type
- manager is a fiduciary of the principal
- specific functions determined by management agreement

Reporting

- monthly, quarterly, annually
- annual operating budget, cash flow reports, profit and loss statements, budget comparison statements

Budgeting	• operating budget: rental rates, capital expenditures, reserves, salaries and wages; projects income based on past performance and current market • expenses, variable and fixed; capital expenditures: outlays for major renovations and construction; cash reserves set aside for variable expenses
Renting	• keep property rented and tenanted; • select compatible tenants and collect scheduled rents • legal issues: compliance with fair housing laws, Americans with Disabilities Act, and ECOA
Property maintenance	• balance costs of services, owner financial objectives, and tenant needs • routine, preventive, or corrective; staffed in-house or contracted out
Construction	• tenant alterations, renovations, expansion, environmental remediation • legal concerns: Americans with Disabilities Act

The Management Agreement

Components	• names; description; lease term; owner's purpose; responsibilities; authority; budget; allocation of costs; reporting; compensation; Equal Opportunity statement
Rights, duties and liabilities	• landlord: receive rent; receive premises in specified condition; enter and inspect; examine books; contract, hire vendors, set rents; pay management fee; comply with laws • manager: hire and fire; contract; perform management tasks without interference; maintain financial records, make reports, budget, collect rent, find tenants, maintain property, meet owner goals; liability for trust funds; comply with laws

Leasing Considerations

Landlord rights and responsibilities	• rights: enter premises, receive payment, retake on termination, pursue remedies • responsibilities: provide habitable conditions; maintain heating, cooling, electrical, plumbing; keep clean and in repair
Tenant rights and responsibilities	• rights: quiet enjoyment, habitable conditions, right to sue for default • responsibilities: pay rent, obey rules, give proper notice, return property in prescribed condition, use only for intended purpose

Evictions	• actual: legal procedure; notice, suit, judgment, taking • constructive: tenant vacates on account of landlord failure to maintain premises
Termination of a lease	• expiration, performance, agreement, abandonment, breach, notice, destruction of premises, condemnation, foreclosure, death of either party (tenancy at will), death of landlord (life estate)
Security deposit procedures	determined by law, rules, and agreement

Section II: Real Estate Math Review

Basic Math

Fractions

Adding and subtracting same denominator:

Formula: $a / c + b / c = (a + b) \div c$

Example: 1/2 + 1/2 = (1 + 1) / 2 = 2/2 = 1

Adding and subtracting different denominators:

Formula: $a / c + b / d = (ad + bc) / cd$

Example: 1/2 + 1/3 = (3 +2) / 6 = 5/6

Multiplying:

Formula: $(a / c) \times (b / d) = ab / cd$

Example: (2/5) x (4/6) = 8/30 = 4/15

Decimals and Percents

Converting decimals to percentages

Formula: *Decimal number x 100 = Percentage number*

Example: .022 x 100 = 2.2%

Converting percentages to decimals

Formula: *Percent number ÷ 100 = Decimal number*

Example: 2.2 ÷ 100 = .022

Multiplying percents

Formula: 1. *Percent number ÷ 100 = Decimal number*

2. *Beginning number x Decimal number = Product*

Example: 75% of 256 (75% x 256) = ?

1. 75 ÷ 100 = .75

2. 256 x .75= 192

Dividing by percents

Formula: 1. *Percent number* $\div$ *100* = *Decimal number*

2. *Beginning number* $\div$ *Decimal* = *Dividend*

Example: 240 $\div$ 75% = ?

1. 75% $\div$ 100 = .75

2. 240 $\div$ .75 = 320

Decimals, Fractions, and Percentages

Converting fractions to percents

Formula: (1) a / b or a $\div$ b = a divided by b = decimal number

(2) decimal number x 100 = percent number

Example: (1) 2 / 5 = 2 divided by 5 = 0.4

(2) .4 x 100 = 40%

Converting a percent to fraction and reducing it

Formula: (1) X% = X $\div$ 100 or X / 100

(2) $\frac{X \div a}{100 \div a}$ where a is the largest number that divides evenly into both numerator and denominator

Example: (1) 40% = 40 $\div$ 100, or 40 / 100

(2) $\frac{40 \div 20}{100 \div 20} = \frac{2}{5}$

Converting fractions to decimals and percentages

Formula: *Decimal x 100* = *Percent number*

Example: .75 x 100 = 75%

Equations

Additions and Subtractions

Formula: *if* $a = b + c$

then $b = a - c$ *(subtracting c from both sides)*

and $c = a - b$ *(subtracting b from both sides)*

Example: 10 = 6 + 4

6 = 10 - 4

4 = 10 - 6

Multiplications and Divisions

Formula: *if* $a = b \times c$

then $b = a / c$ *(dividing both sides by c)*

and $c = a / b$ *(dividing both sides by b)*

Example: 10 = 2 x 5

2 = 10 ÷ 5

5 = 10 ÷ 2

Linear and Perimeter Measurement

Linear measure of rectangles

Formula: *Side A = Area ÷ Side B*

Example: A rectangular house has one side 40' side long and area of 1,200 SF. What is the length of the other side?

Side A = (1,200' ÷ 40') = 30'

Perimeter measurement

Formula: *Perimeter = Sum of all sides of an object*

Example: A five-sided lot has the following dimensions:

Side A = 50' Side B = 60'
Side C= 70' Side D = 100'
Side E = 30'

What is the perimeter of the lot?

P = 50' + 60' + 70' + 100' + 30' = 310'

Area Measurement

Square and rectangle

Formula: *Area = Width x Depth (Horizontal) or Width x Height (Vertical)*

Width= Area ÷ Depth (Height)

Depth (Height)= Area ÷ Width

Example: A house is 40' deep and 30' wide. What is its area?

Area = 40' x 30' = 1,200 SF

Triangle

Formula: *Area = (Height* x *Base)* ÷ *2*

Note: Base is also sometimes referred to as "width"

Example: An A-frame house has a front facade measuring 30' across and 20' in height. What is the area of the facade?

Area = (30' x 20') ÷ 2 = 300 Square feet (SF)

Square foot-to-acre conversion

Formula: *Acres = Area SF ÷ 43,560 SF*

Example: How many acres is 196,020 SF?

196,020 SF ÷ 43,560 SF = 4.5 acres

Acre-to-square foot conversion

Formula: *SF = Number of acres* x *43,560 SF*

Example: How many square feet is .75 acres?

.75 acres x 43,560 SF = 32,670 SF

Linear and Area Conversion Chart

Linear measures

(cm = centimeter; m = meter; km = kilometer)

1 inch	=	1/12 foot	=	1/36 yard		
1 foot	=	12 inches	=	1/3 yard		
1 yard	=	36 inches	=	3 feet		
1 rod	=	16.5 feet	=	1/320 mile		
1 mile	=	5280 feet	=	1760 yards	=	320 rods
1 centimeter	=	1/100 m				
1 meter	=	100 cm	=	1/1000 km		
1 kilometer	=	1,000 m				

Area measures

1 square inch	=	1/144 sq. foot				
1 square foot	=	1/9 sq. yard	=	144 sq. inches		
1 square yard	=	9 sq. feet	=	1,296 sq. inches		
1 acre	=	1/640 sq. mi	=	43,560 SF	=	208.71 ft x 208.71 ft
1 square mile	=	640 acres	=	1 section	=	1/36 township
1 section	=	1 mi x 1 mi	=	640 acres	=	1/36 township
1 township	=	6 mi x 6 mi	=	36 sq. mi	=	36 sections

Metric conversions

(cm = centimeter; m = meter; km = kilometer)

1 inch	=	2.54 cm				
1 foot	=	30.48 cm	=	.3048 m		
1 yard	=	91.44 cm	=	.9144 m		
1 mile	=	1609.3 m	=	1.60 km		
1 centimeter	=	.3937 inch				
1 meter	=	39.37 inches	=	3.28 feet	=	1.094 yards
1 kilometer	=	3,281.5 feet	=	.621 mile		

Fractions of sections, acres, and linear dimensions

Fraction		# Acres
1 section	=	640 acres
1/2 section	=	320 acres
1/4 section	=	160 acres
1/8 section	=	80 acres
1/16 section	=	40 acres
1/32 section	=	20 acres
1/64 section	=	10 acres

Calculating Area from the Legal Description

Formula:

(1) *First multiply all the denominators of the fractions in the legal description together.*

(2) *Then divide 640 by the resulting product.*

Examples:

How many acres are in the Northern 1/2 of the Southwestern 1/4 of Section 6?

640 / (2 x 4) = 640 / 8 = 80 acres

How many acres are in the Western 1/2 of the Northwestern 1/4 of the Northeastern 1/4 of Section 8?

640 / (2 x 4 x 4) = 640 / 32 = 20 acres

Volume Measurement

Formula:

Volume = Width x Height x Depth *(assume objects with 90 degree angles)*

Base = Volume ÷ (Height x *Depth)*

Height = Volume ÷ (Base x Depth)

Depth = Volume ÷ (Base x Height)

Example:

What is the volume of a 40' x 30' x 20' house?

40' x 30' x 20' = 24,000 cubic feet

Leases

Percentage Lease Rent Calculation

Formula: *Monthly percentage rent = Sales x percent of sales charged*

Example: A store generates $50,000 per month. The lease calls for 1.5% percentage rent. Monthly rent amount?

($50,000 x .015) = $750 / month

Contracts for the Sale of Real Estate

Percentage of Listing Price Calculation

Formula: *Percentage of listing price = Offer ÷ Listing price*

Example: A property listed for $300,000 receives an offer for $240,000. The offer's percentage of listing price is:

$240,000 ÷ $300,000 = 80%

Earnest Money Deposit Calculation

Formula: *Deposit = Offering price x required or market-accepted percentage*

Example: A seller requires a 2% deposit on a property listed for $320,000. The required deposit (assuming a full price offer) is:

$320,000 x 2% = $6,400

Appraisal & Value

Adjusting Comparables

Rules:

1. Never adjust the subject!
2. If the comparable is superior to the subject, subtract value from the comparable.
3. If the comparable is inferior to the subject, add value to the comparable.

Example: The subject has a $10,000 pool and no porch. A comparable that sold for $250,000 has a porch ($5,000), an extra bathroom ($6,000), and no pool.

Adjustments to comp: $250,000 (+10,000 - 5,000 - 6,000) = $249,000 indicated value of subject

Gross Rent Multiplier

Formulas: *Sales price = Monthly rental income x GRM*

Monthly rental income = Sales price / Gross Rent Multiplier

Note: Gross rent multiplier is often abbreviated as GRM.

Examples:

1. What is the value of a fourplex with monthly rent of $2,800 and a GRM of 112?

   $2,800 rent x 112 GRM = $313,600

2. What is the GRM of a fourplex with monthly rent of $2,800 and a value of $313,600?

   313,600 price ÷ $2,800 rent = 112 GRM

Gross Income Multiplier

Formulas *Gross Income Multiplier = Sales price ÷ Annual income*

Sales price = Annual income x Gross Income Multiplier

Annual income = Sales price ÷ Gross Income Multiplier

Note: Gross income multiplier is often abbreviated as GIM.

Examples:

1. What is the value of a commercial property with an annual income of $33,600 and a GIM of 9.3?

   $33,600 income x 9.3 GIM = $312,480

2. What is the GIM of a commercial property with annual income of $33,600 and a value of $312,480?

   $312,480 price ÷ $33,600 = 9.3 GIM

Cost Approach Formula

Formula: *Value = Land value + (Improvements + Capital additions - Depreciation)*

Example: Land value = $150,000; home replacement cost = $450,000; new garage added @ $60,000; total depreciation = $30,000

Value = $150,000 + (450,000 + 60,000 - 30,000) = $630,000

Depreciation

Formulas: *Annual depreciation = Beginning depreciable basis ÷ Depreciation term*

Depreciable basis = (Initial property value + Any capital improvements - Land value)

Note: The depreciation term is in number of years.

Example: Property value = $500,000; land value = $110,000; depreciation term = 39 years

Step 1: ($500,000 - $110,000) = $390,000 depreciable basis

Step 2: ($390,000 ÷ 39 years) = $10,000 annual depreciation

Income Capitalization Formula

Formulas: *Value = Annual Net Operating Income ÷ Capitalization rate*

Capitalization rate = Annual Net Operating Income ÷ Value

Annual Net Operating Income = Value x Capitalization rate

Examples:

1. A property generates $490,000 net income and sells at a 7% cap rate. What is its value?

   $490,000 ÷ 7% = $7,000,000 value

2. A property has a net income of $490,000 and sells for $7,000,000. What is its cap rate?

   $490,000 ÷ 7,000,000 = .07, or 7%

3. A property's value is $7,000,000 and the cap rate is 7%. What is the property's net operating income?

   $7,000,000 x .07 = $490,000

Net Operating Income (NOI, Net Income)

Formula: *NOI = Potential rent - Vacancy loss + Other income - Operating expenses*

Note: NOI does not include debt payments!

Example: A building has 10 office suites generating annual potential rent of $10,000 each. Vacancy = 10% and annual expenses are $35,000. Vending machines yield $5,000. What is the NOI?

$100,000 rent - 10,000 vacancy + 5,000 other income - 35,000 expenses = $60,000 NOI

Finance

Points

Definition: 1 point = 1% of the loan amount or .01 x loan amount

Formulas: *Points = Fee paid ÷ Loan amount*

Fee paid = Loan amount x Points

Loan amount = Fee paid ÷ Points

Examples:

1. A borrower pays $25,000 for a $500,000 loan. How many points are paid?

   $25,000 ÷ 500,000 = .05 = 5 points

2. A borrower pays 5 points on a $500,000 loan. What is the fee paid?

   $500,000 x .05 = $25,000

3. A borrower pays $25,000 as 5 points on a loan. What is the loan amount?

   $25,000 ÷ .05 = $500,000

Rules of Thumb: 1 point charged raises lender's yield by .125%

8 points charged raises lender's yield by 1%

Example: A lender wants to yield 7% on a 6.5% loan. How many points must he or she charge?

(7% - 6.5%) = .5%

.5% ÷ .125% = 4 points

Interest Rate, Principal and Payment

Caveat!

Interest rates in mortgage financing apply to the annual interest payment and exclude principal payment. Remember to convert annual payments to monthly or vice versa as the question requires, and to exclude principal payments from your calculations!

Formulas: *Payment = Principal x Rate*

Principal = Payment ÷ Rate

Rate = Payment ÷ Principal

Examples:

1. A borrower has a $1,000,000 loan @ 6% interest. What are the annual and monthly payments?

   Annual payment = $1,000,000 x .06 = $60,000
   Monthly payment = $60,000 ÷ 12 = $5,000

2. A borrower has a $5,000 monthly payment on a 6% loan. What is the loan principal?

   Principal = ($5,000 x 12) ÷ 6% = ($60,000 ÷ .06) = $1,000,000

3. A borrower has a $5,000 monthly payment on a $1,000,000 loan. What is the loan rate?

   Rate = ($5,000 x 12) ÷ $1,000,000 = ($60,000 ÷ 1,000,000) = .06 = 6%

Total Interest, Interest Rate, and Loan Term

Formulas:

Interest-only loan: *Total interest = Loan amount x Rate x Term in years*

Amortized loan: *Total interest = (Monthly PI payment x 12 x term) - Loan amount*

Examples:

1. A borrower obtains a 10-year interest only loan of $500,000 @ 6%. How much interest will he or she pay?

   ($500,000 x .06 x 10) = $300,000

2. A borrower obtains a 10-year amortized loan of $500,000 @ 6% with monthly payments of $5,551. How much interest will he or she pay?

   ($5,551 x 12 x 10) - $500,000 = $166,120

Amortization Calculation

Formulas:

Month 1: *Principal paid = Monthly payment - (Loan amount x Rate ÷ 12)*

Month 2: *New loan amount = (Previous month principal - Principal paid)*

Principal paid = Monthly payment - (New loan amount x Rate ÷ 12)

Example: A borrower obtains a 30-year $100,000 amortized loan @ 7% with a $665.31 monthly payment. What is the principal paid in the second month?

Month 1: Principal paid = $665.31 - ($100,000 x 7% ÷ 12) = $665.31 - (583.33 interest paid) = $81.98

Month 2: New loan amount = $100,000 previous month beginning loan amount - $81.98 principal paid = $99,918.02

Principal paid = $665.31 - ($99,918.02 x 7% ÷ 12) = $665.31 - (582.86 interest paid) = $82.45

Loan Constants

Formulas:

Monthly payment = (Loan amount x Loan constant) / 1000

Loan amount = (Monthly payment ÷ Loan constant) x 1000

Loan constant = (Monthly payment ÷ Loan amount) x 1000

Examples:

1. A borrower obtains a loan for \$1,000,000 with a 6.3207 constant. What is the monthly payment?

   Monthly payment = (\$1,000,000 ÷ 1,000) x 6.3207 = \$6,320.70

2. A borrower has a monthly payment of \$6,320.70 on a loan with a monthly constant of 6.3207. What is the loan amount?

   Loan amount = (\$6,320.70 ÷ 6.3207) x 1,000 = \$1,000,000

3. A borrower obtains a loan for \$1,000,000 with a monthly payment of \$6,320.70. What is the loan constant?

   Loan constant = (\$6,320.70 ÷ \$1,000,000) x 1,000 = 6.3207

Loan - to - Value Ratio (LTV)

Formulas:

LTV ratio = Loan ÷ Price (Value)

Loan = LTV ratio x Price (Value)

Price (Value) = Loan ÷ LTV ratio

Examples:

1. A borrower can get a \$265,600 loan on a \$332,000 home. What is her LTV ratio?

   LTV Ratio = \$265,600 ÷ 332,000 = 80%

2. A borrower can get an 80% loan on a \$332,000 home. What is the loan amount?

   Loan = \$332,000 x .80 = \$265,600

3. A borrower obtained an 80% loan for \$265,600. What was the price of the home?

   Price (value) = \$265,600 ÷ .80 = \$332,000

Financial Qualification

Income ratio qualification

Formula: *Monthly Principal & Interest (PI) payment = Income ratio x Monthly gross income*

Example: A lender uses a 28% income ratio for the PI payment. A borrower grosses \$90,000 per year. What monthly PI payment can the borrower afford?

Monthly PI payment = (\$90,000 ÷ 12) x .28 = \$2,100

How much can the borrower borrow if the loan constant is 6.3207? (See also- loan constants)

Loan amount = ($2,100 ÷ 6.3207) x 1,000 = $332,241.68

Debt ratio qualification

Formulas: *Debt ratio = (Housing expense + Other debt payments) ÷ Monthly gross income*

Housing expense = (Monthly gross income x Debt ratio) - Other debt payments

Example: A lender uses a 36% debt ratio. A borrower earns $90,000 / year and has monthly non-housing debt payments of $500. What housing payment can she afford?

Housing expense = ($90,000 ÷ 12 x .36) - 500 = ($2,700 - 500) = $2,200

Investment

Appreciation Calculations

Simple appreciation

Formulas: *Total appreciation = Current value - Original price*

Total appreciation rate = Total appreciation ÷ Original price

Average annual appreciation rate = Total appreciation rate ÷ number of years

One year appreciation rate = (Annual appreciation amount) ÷ (Value at beginning of year)

Examples:

1. A home purchased for $200,000 five years ago is now worth $300,000. What are the total appreciation amount, total appreciation rate, and average appreciation rate?

   Total appreciation = ($300,000 - 200,000), or $100,000

   Total appreciation rate = ($100,000 ÷ 200,000), or 50%

   Average annual appreciation rate = 50% ÷ 5 years = 10%

2. A home costing $250,000 is worth $268,000 one year later. What is the one-year appreciation rate?

   One-year appreciation rate = ($18,000 ÷ 250,000) = 7.2%

Compounded appreciation

Formula: *Appreciated value = Beginning value x (1+ annual rate) x (1+ annual rate) ...... for the number of years in question*

Example: A $1,000,000 property is expected to appreciate 5% each year for the next 3 years. What will be its appreciated value at the end of this period?

Appreciated value = $1,000,000 x 1.05 x 1.05 x 1.05 = $1,157,625

Rate of Return, Investment Value, Income

Formulas: Where Income = net operating income (NOI); Rate = rate of return, cap rate, or percent yield; and Value = value, price or investment amount:

Rate = Income ÷ Value

Value = Income ÷ Rate

Income = Value x Rate

Examples:

1. An office building has $200,000 net income and sold for $3,200,000. What was the rate of return?

   Rate = ($200,000 NOI ÷ 3,200,000 price) = 6.25%

2. An office building has $200,000 net income and a cap rate of 6.25%. What is its value?

   Value = ($200,000 ÷ 6.25%) = $3,200,000

3. An office building sells for $3,200,000 at a cap rate of 6.25%. What is its NOI?

   Income = $3,200,000 x 6.25% = $200,000

Basis, Adjusted Basis, and Capital Gain

Formulas: *Capital gain = Amount realized - Adjusted basis, where*

Amount realized = Sale price - Selling costs

Adjusted basis = Beginning basis + Capital improvements - Total depreciation

Total depreciation = (Beginning depreciable basis ÷ Depreciation term in years) x Years depreciated

Depreciable basis = Initial property value + Capital improvements - Land value

Example: Tip: work example backwards from last formula to first formula.

An apartment building was purchased for $500,000, with the land value estimated to be $100,000. The owner added a $100,000 parking lot. The property was depreciated on a 40-year schedule (for present purposes!). Three years later the property sold for $700,000, and selling costs were $50,000. What was the capital gain?

1. depreciable basis = $500,000 purchase price + 100,000 parking lot - 100,000 land = $500,000

2. total depreciation = ($500,000 ÷ 40 years) x 3 years = $37,500

3. adjusted basis = $500,000 purchase price + 100,000 parking lot - 37,500 total depreciation = $562,500

4. amount realized = $700,000 sale price - 50,000 selling costs = $650,000

5. capital gain = $650,000 amount realized - 562,500 adjusted basis = $87,500

Depreciation

Formulas: *Annual depreciation = (Beginning depreciable basis) ÷ (Depreciation term in number of years)*

Depreciable basis = (Initial property value + Capital improvements - Land value)

Example: Property value = $500,000; land value = $110,000; depreciation term = 39 years

1. ($500,000 - 110,000) = $390,000 depreciable basis
2. ($390,000 ÷ 39 years) = $10,000 annual depreciation

Equity

Formula: *Equity = Current market value - Current loan balance(s)*

Example: A home that was purchased for $150,000 with a $100,000 loan is now worth $300,000. The current loan balance is $80,000. What is the homeowner's equity?

Equity = $300,000 value - $80,000 debt = $220,000

Net Income

Formula: *NOI = Potential rent - Vacancy loss + Other income - Operating expenses*

Note: NOI does not include debt payments!

Example: A building has 10 office suites generating annual potential rent of $10,000 each. Vacancy = 10% and annual expenses are $35,000. Vending machines yield $5,000. What is the NOI?

$100,000 rent - 10,000 vacancy + 5,000 other income - 35,000 expenses = $60,000 NOI

Cash Flow

Formula: *Cash flow = (Net Operating Income - Debt service) where debt service is PI payment*

Example: A building generates $100,000 NOI after expenses and has a debt payment of $40,000. What is its cash flow?

Cash flow = $100,000 - 40,000 = $60,000

Investment Property Income Tax Liability

Formula: *Tax liability = (NOI + Reserves - Interest expense - Depreciation) x Tax bracket*

Example: An office building has NOI of $200,000, an annual reserve expense of $20,000, interest expense of $130,000 and annual depreciation of $50,000. Assuming a 28% tax bracket, what is its income tax liability?

Tax liability = ($200,000 + 20,000 - 130,000 - 50,000) x 28% = $11,200

Return on Investment

Formula: *ROI = NOI ÷ Price*

Example: An investment property generates a cash flow of $100,000 and appraises for $1,500,000. What is the owner's return on investment?

ROI = $100,000 ÷ 1,500,000 = 6.67%

Return on Equity

Formula: *ROE = Cash flow ÷ Equity*

Example: An investment property generates a cash flow of $100,000. The owner has $500,000 equity in the property. What is the owner's return on equity?

ROE= $100,000 ÷ 500,000 = 20%

Real Estate Taxation

Converting Mill Rates

Definition: 1 mill = $.001; a mill rate of 1 mill per $1,000 = .1%; a 1% tax rate = 10 mills

Formula: *Tax = (Taxable value ÷ 1000) x Mill rate*

Example: A tax rate on a house with a $200,000 taxable value is 7 mills per thousand dollars of assessed valuation. What is the tax?

Tax = ($200,000 ÷ 1,000) x 7 mills = $1,400

Tax Base

Formula: *Tax base = Assessed valuations – Exemptions*

Example: A town has a total assessed valuation of $20,000,000 and exemptions of $4,000,000. What is the tax base?

$20,000,000 - 4,000,000 = $16,000,000

Tax Rate, Base, and Requirement

Formulas: *Tax rate = Tax requirement ÷ Tax base*

Tax base = Tax requirement ÷ Tax rate

Tax requirement = Tax base x Rate

Example: A town has a tax base of $160,000,000 and a budget of $8,000,000. What is the tax rate?

Tax rate = ($8,000,000 ÷ 160,000,000) = .05, or 5%, or 50 mills

Special Assessments

Formula: *Special assessment = Total special assessment cost x Homeowner's share*

Example: A homeowner owns 100' of an 800' seawall that must be repaired. The total assessment will be $80,000. What is the homeowner's assessment?

1. Homeowner's share = 100' ÷ 800' = .125, or 12.5%
2. Special assessment = $80,000 x 12.5% = $10,000

Commissions

Commission Splits

Formulas: *Total commission = Sale price x Commission rate*

Co-brokerage split = Total commission x Co-brokerage percent

Agent split = Co-brokerage split x Agent percent

Broker split = Co-brokerage split - Agent split

Example: A $300,000 property sells at a 7% commission with a 50-50 co-brokerage split and a 60% agent split with her broker. What are total, co-brokerage, agent's, and broker's commissions?

Total commission = \$300,000 x .07 = \$21,000

Co-brokerage splits = \$300,000 x .07 x .50 = \$10,500

Agent split = \$10,500 x .60 = \$6,300

Agent's broker's split = \$10.500 - 6,300 = \$4,200

Seller's Net

Formula: *Seller's net = Sale Price - (sale price x commission) - Other closing costs - Loan balance*

Example: A home sells for \$260,000 and has a loan balance of \$200,000 at closing. The commission is 7% and other closing costs are \$2,000. What is the seller's net?

Seller's net = (\$260,000 - (260,000 x .07) - 2,000 - 200,000) = \$39,800

Price to Net an Amount

Formula: *Sale Price = (Desired net + Closing costs + Loan payoff)) (1 - Commission rate)*

Example: A homeseller wants to net \$50,000. The commission is 7%, the loan payoff is \$150,000, and closing costs are \$4,000. What must the price be?

Sale price = (\$50,000 + 4,000 + 150,000) ÷ .93 = \$219,355

Closing Costs, Prorations

30-Day 12-Month Method

Formulas: *Monthly amount = Annual amount / 12*

Daily amount = Monthly amount / 30

Proration = (Monthly amount multiplied by the # months) + (Daily amount multiplied by the # days)

Example: An annual tax bill is \$1,800. Closing is on April 10. What is the seller's share of the taxes?

1. Monthly amount = (\$1,800 ÷ 12) = \$150; no. of months = 3
2. Daily amount = (\$150 ÷ 30) = \$5.00; no. of days = 10
3. Proration = (\$150 x 3) + (\$5 x 10) = (\$450 + 50) = \$500 seller's share

---

365-Day Method

Formula: *Daily amount = (Annual amount ÷ 365) or (Monthly amount ÷ Length of month)*

Proration = Daily amount multiplied by the # days

Example: An annual tax bill is $1,800. Closing is on April 10. What is the seller's share of the taxes?

1. Daily amount = ($1,800 ÷ 365) = $4.93
2. Jan 1 thru April 10 = (31 + 28 + 31 + 10) days, or 100 days
3. Proration = $4.93 x 100 days = $493 seller's share

Income Received in Advance (Rent)

Logic: *Credit buyer and debit seller for buyer's share*

Example: Seller receives $1,000 rent. The month is ¾ over.

1. Buyer's share is ($1,000 x 25%) = $250
2. Credit buyer / debit seller $250.

Expenses paid in Arrears (Tax)

Logic: *Credit buyer and debit seller for seller's share*

Example: Buyer will pay $1,000 taxes. The year is ¾ over.

1. Buyer's share is ($1,000 x 25%) = $250
2. Credit buyer / debit seller $750.

Insurance Coverage

Recovery with Co-Insurance Clauses

Formula: Recovery = (Damage claim) x (Percent replacement cost covered ÷ Minimum coverage requirement)

Example: An owner insures a home for $500,000. Replacement cost is $750,000. A co-insurance clause requires coverage of 80% of replacement cost to avoid penalty. Fire destroys the house. What can the owner recover from the insurer?

Claim recovery = $750,000 x (67% cost covered ÷ 80% required) = $628,125

Section III: Montana Laws & Practices

The following outline is a condensation of Montana real estate license law as codified in Title 37, Chapter 51, MCA (Real Estate Brokers and Salespersons); Title 37, Chapter 1, MCA (general licensure provisions); and Title 2, Chapter 15, Part 17, MCA (Board of Realty Regulation), together with the board's rules at ARM Title 24, Chapter 210, and related rules at ARM Title 24, Chapter 101 (Business Standards Division) and ARM Title 24, Chapter 209 (property management licensure). Other sources cited in this section include Title 37, Chapter 56, MCA (property managers); Title 70, Chapter 23, MCA (Unit Ownership Act, condominiums); Title 70, Chapter 24, MCA (Residential Landlord and Tenant Act of 1977); Title 70, Chapter 25, MCA (residential tenants' security deposits); Title 70, Chapter 26, MCA (landlord and tenant, residential and commercial); and other laws as cited.

Table of Contents

Part I: The Montana Regulatory Environment

- Board of Realty Regulation
- The Board's Powers
- Grounds for Suspension or Revocation
- Unprofessional Conduct
- Discipline and Sanctions
- Trust Account Compliance Citations
- Enforcement Against Unlicensed Practice

Part II: Montana Real Estate Licensing

- Definitions Used in Board Rules
- Persons Requiring a Real Estate License
- Exemptions From Real Estate Licensure
- The Salesperson License
- The Broker License
- The Supervising Broker Endorsement
- Display of License and Pocket Card
- Continuing Real Estate Education
- Active and Inactive Status
- License Renewal and Reinstatement
- Reciprocity
- License Fees

Part III: Montana Brokerage and Disclosure Regulation

- Advertising and Marketing
- Broker and Salesperson Relationship
- Unprofessional Conduct
- Compensation
- Disclosure
- Handling Documents and Trust Funds
- Listings and Buyer Brokerage Agreements
- Ethics and Illegal Inducements

Part IV: Montana Agency Regulation

- Agency: Authorized Relationships in Montana
- Agency Duties and Responsibilities
- Agency Disclosure Recap and Timing Summary

Part V: Additional Montana Laws and Practices

- Errors and Omissions Insurance
- Landlord and Tenant Relationship
- Foreclosure and Redemption in Montana

Place of Business and Officing Regulations
Montana Fair Housing
Land Description
Common Interest Ownership and Condominiums
The Statute of Frauds in Montana

Part One: The Montana Regulatory Environment

Board of Realty Regulation

- ❑ The Board's mission: protect the public
  - every licensing decision, rule, and disciplinary action serves public protection first
  - governing statutes: Title 37, Chapter 51, MCA; rules: ARM Title 24, Chapter 210

- ❑ Who's on the Board: five Governor-appointed members
  - the Board is created by Section 2-15-1757, MCA
  - 4 members must be active Montana real estate licensees
  - 1 member represents the public and cannot hold a real estate license
  - Senate confirmation required; all members must be Montana residents

- ❑ How the Board operates
  - allocated to the Department of Labor and Industry
  - elects its own presiding officer from within its membership
  - Board records are public; certified copies are accepted as evidence in Montana courts

- ❑ Protecting Board impartiality
  - the presiding officer and any Department employee serving the Board may not be an officer or employee of a real estate association
  - this prevents industry capture of the regulatory process

The Board's Powers

- ❑ Three core powers: licensing, rulemaking, and education
  - licensing: issues, renews, refuses, suspends, and revokes all Montana real estate licenses
  - rulemaking: adopts administrative rules that fill in the details of the licensing statute
  - education: controls the licensing exam (currently administered by Pearson) and approves all prelicense and CE courses

- ❑ Rulemaking in practice
  - Board rules cover trust accounts, internet advertising, prelicense course content, and more
  - rules have the same legal force as the statute itself
  - when the law changes in practice but the statute hasn't been updated, look to the rules

- ❑ Education authority
  - the Board can reject a course that doesn't meet its topic or quality requirements
  - CE completion records stored in Board databases verify compliance at renewal

Grounds for Suspension or Revocation

- ❑ How the process starts
  - the statutory grounds are listed in Section 37-51-321, MCA
  - the Board may investigate on its own initiative or after receiving a sworn written complaint
  - a majority vote following a hearing determines guilt

- ❑ Misrepresentation and advertising violations
  - misleading, inaccurate, or untruthful advertising in any medium
  - making false promises to influence a buyer or seller
  - a continued pattern of misrepresentation, by the licensee or through salespersons

- ❑ Financial and fiduciary violations
  - failing to account for or return money belonging to a client
  - accepting or giving undisclosed commissions, rebates, or profits
  - using the term REALTOR without authorization

- ❑ Agency and transactional violations
  - acting as both broker and undisclosed principal in the same deal
  - guaranteeing future profits from real property resale
  - advertising or showing property without the owner's written consent
  - inducing a party to break an existing contract in order to substitute a new one

- ❑ Administrative and professional violations
  - negotiating with a buyer or seller already under a written exclusive agreement with another broker
  - failing to give all parties a copy of documents they've signed
  - paying compensation to an unlicensed person

- ❑ Additional grounds
  - failing to deliver earnest money to the supervising broker promptly
  - demonstrated incompetency or unworthiness; conviction of a felony
  - violating any Board rule; failing to maintain required E&O insurance under Section 37-51-325, MCA

- ❑ Advertising other brokers' property: a specific restriction
  - a licensee may not openly advertise property belonging to others without a valid signed listing agreement on the date of the ad
  - hosting third-party ads on a licensee website is allowed, as long as no licensed services are performed for that owner

- ❑ Discipline from other states and unlicensed employees
  - discipline in another jurisdiction can be grounds for Montana action
  - a licensee is responsible for the licensed actions of every employee
    - o unlicensed staff may not perform acts requiring a license

Unprofessional Conduct

- ☐ ARM 24.210.641: conduct the Board treats as unprofessional
  - these rules add specificity beyond the statutory grounds; think of them as the Board's 'for example' list
  - violating ARM 24.210.641 is itself grounds for discipline under the main statute

- ☐ Advice, referrals, and conflicts of interest
  - never recommend a service provider (attorney, inspector, lender) without disclosing any family, financial, or business relationship with that provider
  - don't give legal advice or skip recommending that clients seek professional help when needed

- ☐ Document and transaction integrity
  - never alter a document without the client's written authority
  - verify ownership before listing; confirm the person signing has the right to list
  - never commit forgery, fraud, or conversion in any form

- ☐ Statutory compliance requirements
  - violating residential landlord-tenant law, security deposit rules, or the mobile home lot rental act is unprofessional conduct
  - same for violating radon disclosure, lead-based paint disclosure, Fair Housing laws, or the ADA

- ☐ Advertising and representation obligations
  - must comply with the internet advertising rules of ARM 24.210.430
  - must identify yourself as a licensee at first contact when seeking property information
  - must actually participate in negotiations; don't just hand off a contract and disappear unless the client has waived that in writing

- ☐ Written agreement and trust fund requirements
  - acting as a buyer agent without a written buyer broker agreement is unprofessional conduct
  - so is acting as a seller agent without a written listing agreement
  - misappropriating or failing to account for trust funds is unprofessional conduct

Discipline and Sanctions

- ☐ The Board looks at three things when choosing a sanction
  - sanctions are imposed under Section 37-1-312, MCA
  - how serious was the violation?
  - how much harm (or risk of harm) was caused to Montana consumers?
  - does the licensee have a prior disciplinary history?

- ❑ Available sanctions: revocation through restriction
  - revocation (permanent loss of license) or suspension (fixed or indefinite term)
  - probation with conditions for up to three years
  - restriction or limitation of the licensee's practice

- ❑ Additional sanctions
  - supervised practice monitored by a Board-approved supervisor
  - required remedial education or treatment
  - fines up to $1,000 per violation; denial of a new application; censure
  - the Board may stay any sanction, and may require a refund to a harmed consumer

Trust Account Compliance Citations

- ❑ Trust account citations: a faster, simpler enforcement track
  - the citation process is authorized by Section 37-51-324, MCA
  - when a broker or property manager violates trust account rules, a Department employee may issue a citation instead of full disciplinary proceedings
  - the citation is administrative; no hearing required unless the licensee disputes it

- ❑ What every citation must include
  - date and time issued; who issued it (name, title, address, signature)
  - the specific statute or rule violated; who received it (name, title, address)
  - how to pay the fine or file a dispute; the fine amount

- ❑ The 5-day response window
  - the licensee has 5 business days to pay the fine or file a written dispute
  - doing neither is itself unprofessional conduct, and triggers additional Board discipline
  - refusing to sign the citation but not disputing it is treated the same as failing to respond

- ❑ When a citation becomes a full disciplinary matter
  - the Department can escalate 'significant violations' to the Board's complaint screening panel
  - significant means
    - too many violations in one audit
    - repeat violations across audits
    - a single severe violation

Enforcement Against Unlicensed Practice

- ❑ The basic rule: you must be licensed to practice in Montana
  - acting as a broker or salesperson without a license is unlawful under Section 37-51-301, MCA
  - acting as a supervising broker without the endorsement is also unlawful

- even a single act that falls within the definition of brokerage can be a violation

- ❑ 'Within this state' has a broad reach
  - you don't have to be physically in Montana to violate Montana license law
  - marketing or dealing with Montana real estate, or soliciting Montana residents from anywhere, counts

- ❑ Enforcement tools
  - the Board uses administrative proceedings under Section 37-1-332, MCA, and can seek a court injunction to stop unlicensed activity immediately
  - an unlicensed person cannot sue in Montana courts to collect a commission; Section 37-51-401, MCA, bars the action
  - corporations and partnerships must have every officer or partner who performs licensed acts individually licensed

Part Two: Montana Real Estate Licensing

Definitions Used in Board Rules

- ❑ Key definitions that shape how the rules work
  - 'Act' includes a failure to act; inaction can be a violation
  - 'Advertising' is any information used to promote property or services; sending data to one specific prospect on request is NOT advertising
  - 'Agency' in Montana refers only to the five statutory relationships of Sections 37-51-102 and 37-51-313, MCA; common law agency concepts do not apply

- ❑ More definitions you'll use daily
  - 'Supervision' means substantially day-to-day, active overseeing, not a once-a-month check-in
  - 'Trust funds' are all money belonging to others that a licensee holds in any capacity
  - 'Residential property' includes four or fewer units used as residences, and a single condo unit sold separately

- ❑ Timing and status definitions
  - 'Cancellation' is the gap between a salesperson leaving one broker and joining another or going inactive; no practice allowed
  - 'Hour' of education equals 50 minutes of instruction
  - 'Incapacity' of a supervising broker means being wholly unable to function; voluntary absence doesn't count

Persons Requiring a Real Estate License

- ❑ Anyone practicing real estate in Montana must be licensed
  - includes brokers, salespersons, and property managers
  - supervising brokers need the license AND the supervising broker endorsement
  - advertising yourself as a real estate agent without a license is also unlawful

- ❑ Corporations and partnerships: no entity license exists
  - the entity itself can't be licensed; every person in that entity who performs licensed acts must hold an individual license
  - if the entity doesn't comply, every individual acting for it is in violation

Exemptions From Real Estate Licensure

- ❑ Who doesn't need a license: property owners
  - an owner selling or leasing property they personally own is exempt
  - an auctioneer hired by the owner for the owner's own sale is also covered

- this exemption doesn't apply to someone who regularly sells others' property and calls it their own

❑ Who doesn't need a license: legal and fiduciary roles

- attorneys performing legal duties; persons acting under a valid power of attorney
- court-appointed receivers, trustees, administrators, and executors
- trustees acting under a trust agreement, deed of trust, or will

❑ Additional exemptions

- public officials acting in their official capacity
- persons prospecting or leasing land for minerals or hydrocarbons
- managers of government-subsidized housing complexes
- persons handling rights-of-way, condemnations, or tribal or governmental permits
- generally circulated newspapers and publications, and radio and television stations, engaged in their normal business

The Salesperson License

❑ Requirements to become a Montana salesperson

- at least 18 years old with high school completion (or equivalent)
- complete 70 hours of Board-approved prelicense education
- pass the Montana licensing exam and apply with the recommendation of a supervising broker

❑ Exam and application timing

- must apply for a license within 12 months of passing; exam results expire otherwise
- the state and national portions can be taken separately; each result is valid for 12 months independently

The Broker License

❑ Becoming a broker: experience comes first

- must have worked as a licensed Montana salesperson for at least 2 years (or equivalent Board-approved experience)
- no waiver of the experience requirement, even with advanced education

❑ Broker prelicense education and exam

- 60-hour broker prelicense course covering brokerage management, trust accounting, property management, and liability
- must also demonstrate 30 activity points earned within the prior 36 months (transactions, education, supervision, instruction)
- apply within 12 months of passing the broker exam

The Supervising Broker Endorsement

- ❑ A broker license alone doesn't allow supervision
  - a separate supervising broker endorsement is required to supervise salespersons under Section 37-51-302, MCA
  - requires completing the Board-approved pre-endorsement course
  - out-of-state brokers must take the pre-endorsement course before the endorsement is issued

- ❑ Maintaining and losing the endorsement
  - 4 hours of supervising-broker-specific CE required every licensing year (those 4 hours count toward the total 12-hour CE requirement)
  - the endorsement cannot go on inactive status; fail to meet CE and it lapses
  - a lapsed endorsement can be renewed; a terminated endorsement requires starting fresh

- ❑ Temporary supervision: short-term coverage when needed
  - must be in writing, signed by both the existing and temporary broker, filed with the Board 3 or more business days in advance
  - maximum 60 days per salesperson in any 12-month period
  - the temporary supervisor is not the broker of record and cannot transfer supervision to anyone else

- ❑ Death or incapacity of the supervising broker
  - the salesperson must notify the Board within 10 days
  - temporary supervision can be arranged; the same rules apply, but no authorization from the deceased broker is needed
  - alternatively, the salesperson may transfer to a new broker or go inactive

Display of License and Pocket Card

- ❑ Where licenses must be displayed
  - a salesperson's license is held by the supervising broker; it doesn't go home with the salesperson
  - a broker with a place of business must conspicuously display the broker's own license there
  - copies of all associated salespersons' current licenses must also be displayed at the designated address

- ❑ The pocket card: a licensee's daily ID
  - issued annually by the Department; certifies the holder is a licensed Montana broker or salesperson
  - a salesperson's card names the supervising broker and the designated address
  - keep it current; if the broker changes, the card must be updated

Continuing Real Estate Education

- ☐ CE basics: 12 hours every licensing year
  - licensing year runs November 1 through October 31
  - no carry-over; hours earned beyond 12 don't count toward the following year
  - supervising brokers must include 4 hours of supervising-broker-specific topics within their 12

- ☐ What qualifies as approved CE
  - courses approved by ARELLO's Distance Education Certification program
  - courses approved by any state real estate licensing agency
  - courses endorsed by a national, state, or local REALTORS or property management association

- ☐ Attendance rules and individual course approval
  - must complete at least 90% of the first hour and 100% of each hour after that to receive credit
  - found a qualifying course that isn't yet approved? apply to the Board within 30 days of completion to get individual credit

Active and Inactive Status

- ☐ Inactive status: keeping your license without practicing
  - an inactive licensee holds the license legally but may not perform any real estate services
  - CE requirements are frozen while inactive; no hours needed, no hours earned
  - to go inactive: submit the change form, pay the fee, and surrender the license to the Board
    - a salesperson also needs a release from the supervising broker

- ☐ Coming back to active status
  - complete any CE that would have been required during the inactive period (capped at 24 hours)
  - submit the change form, pay the fee, and provide proof of E&O insurance
  - inactive licenses must still be renewed annually; ignore the renewal date and the license lapses

License Renewal and Reinstatement

- ☐ Annual renewal: October 31 deadline
  - every licensee renews by October 31, active or inactive
  - all CE must be completed before renewal; incomplete applications are returned
  - a salesperson in 'cancellation' status (between brokers) cannot renew; the license must first go inactive or transfer to a new supervising broker

- ❑ Reinstatement after discipline
  - suspension runs 1 year and revocation is permanent, unless the Board's order specifies otherwise
  - conditions for reinstatement can include retaking the licensing exam, completing a qualifying course, or both
  - the Board decides case-by-case what's needed to demonstrate the conduct has been remedied

Reciprocity

- ❑ Reciprocity: getting a Montana license if you're already licensed elsewhere
  - the Board can enter agreements that waive some prelicense education or exam requirements for licensees from other states
  - reciprocity only works both ways; the other state must grant the same privileges to Montana licensees
  - the Montana state law exam portion is often still required even under a reciprocity agreement

License Fees

- ❑ Fees: what you pay and where the money goes
  - fees are set by Board rule and can change; always verify current amounts on the Department's website before applying
  - most fees flow into the state special revenue fund reserved for Board operations; exam fees go directly to Pearson
  - no city or county may charge a separate license fee or tax as a condition of practicing real estate in Montana

Part Three: Montana Brokerage and Disclosure Regulation

Advertising and Marketing

- ❑ All advertising must be truthful, accurate, and identified
  - authority comes from Section 37-51-321, MCA, for any medium and ARM 24.210.430 for the internet
  - every ad, in any medium, must accurately describe the property or service
  - an ad may not misrepresent the property, the terms of sale, the value, brokerage policies, or the services the licensee will provide
  - franchise brokers must work their own name or trade name into franchise advertising; the franchise logo alone is not enough
  - no advertising of property belonging to another without a signed listing agreement valid on the date the ad runs

- ❑ Internet advertising: the three non-negotiables (ARM 24.210.430)
  - accurate: the ad must truthfully describe what's being offered, and a property listing must identify the city, town, or county (the full street address is not required)
  - identified: every viewable page must name the licensee and show they're a real estate professional
  - current: update or remove a listing within 7 days of a material change such as sale, expiration, or amendment
  - the rule reaches websites, blogs, video streaming, and social media; newspaper, television, radio, yard signs, and direct mail stay under the general standard

- ❑ Where identification must appear online
  - every viewable page of a website, or a link to identification from every page
  - at the beginning or end of every email, news group, discussion list, and bulletin board message
  - chat sessions and voice-over-net sessions: before licensable services are offered, or in text visible on the same page
  - multimedia advertising must display identification as part of the message; a banner ad must display it or link to a page that does
  - instant messages need no identification in each message if identification was given in another format first

- ❑ New platforms, same rules
  - social media business pages (Facebook, Instagram, TikTok, LinkedIn, YouTube) must each carry licensee identification
  - short-form video must carry identification in on-screen graphics, captions, or spoken audio
  - video tours must reflect the property's current condition; editing that hides defects is misleading advertising
  - drone footage must be accurate and the operator must hold the FAA Part 107 remote pilot certificate

- AI-generated descriptions and images remain the licensee's responsibility; virtually staged photos must be labeled as such

- Text and SMS marketing: one extra layer
  - the federal Telephone Consumer Protection Act requires consent before sending promotional texts
  - identification must appear in the message body or in a clearly visible link

- Advertising a cooperating broker's listing
  - allowed with the listing agent's cooperation and consent and the owner's consent
  - the ad must state that the property is listed with another licensee or brokerage and identify that listing agent or brokerage
  - MLS or listing-agent data may be reformatted or condensed but the content may not be changed
  - a condensed ad must state that the material was abstracted from another source and that buyers should request further information

Broker and Salesperson Relationship

- One broker at a time, no exceptions
  - a salesperson may be associated with only one supervising broker at a time
  - a salesperson may not perform real estate services for any broker other than the one designated on the license
  - the supervising broker's name and designated address appear on the salesperson's pocket card

- The broker's office and change of address (Section 37-51-308, MCA)
  - a broker must maintain a designated physical address with the broker's license prominently displayed there
  - a copy of each associated salesperson's current license must also be displayed at that address
  - notify the Department before a move or within 10 days after, designate the new address, and pay the fee

- When a salesperson leaves
  - the broker must immediately return the salesperson's license to the Board with a termination letter; a dispute is not grounds to delay
  - the broker remains supervising broker of record until the license and the release reach the Board
  - the salesperson has 10 days to name a new supervising broker or go inactive; no practice during that gap
  - listings and pending transactions belong to the broker, who must immediately notify all principals
  - a departing salesperson may request a certified statement of the transactions worked in the prior 3 years

- ❑ Supervision: what it actually means
  - reasonable supervision (ARM 24.210.605, for salespersons with 2 or more years of experience): written office policy, transaction file audits, regular contact, regular training, and review of all advertising
  - high-level supervision (ARM 24.210.606, under 2 years of experience or fewer than 10 transaction sides in a calendar year): adds office procedure training, contract preparation review, transaction monitoring, and pre-closing document review
  - a listing agreement negotiated by a salesperson is not valid until the supervising broker reviews, signs, and dates it
  - a complaint filed against a salesperson goes to the supervising broker as well, who must also respond

- ❑ Lapse of the supervising broker
  - the broker must immediately inform supervised salespersons of a lapsed license or endorsement
  - within 10 days of Board notice the salesperson must request inactive status or transfer to another broker
  - no licensed activity during the unsupervised period

- ❑ Temporary supervision: structured coverage for gaps (ARM 24.210.601)
  - must be in writing, naming the salespersons transferred and the effective beginning and ending dates
  - signed by both the existing supervising broker and the temporary supervising broker
  - filed with the Board at least 3 business days before it begins; a late filing draws a late fee against the existing broker
  - maximum 60 days per salesperson in any 12-month period; the cap follows the salesperson, not the receiving broker
  - the temporary broker is NOT the broker of record and may return supervision only to the original broker

- ❑ Death or incapacity of the supervising broker
  - the salesperson must notify the Board within 10 days and may not practice until the license is transferred
  - temporary supervision may be arranged under the same rules, without authorization from the original broker
  - alternatively the salesperson may go inactive or transfer to a new supervising broker

- ❑ Salesperson for-sale-by-owner transactions (Section 37-51-309, MCA)
  - a salesperson may handle a personal sale, exchange, lease, or rental without the supervising broker's involvement
  - before entering the transaction, disclose to the other party that it is the salesperson's personal transaction and does not involve the broker or firm
  - the broker and firm are not responsible for the transaction or for the salesperson's failure to disclose

- ❑ Paying out-of-state brokers for cooperative work
  - a Montana broker may not employ or pay an unlicensed person for acts requiring a license

- a Montana broker may pay a broker licensed in another state, provided that broker performed no services in Montana for the fee paid
- the nonresident must file written consent to Montana jurisdiction and to service on the Department; a corporation's consent must be authenticated by its seal

❑ Action for compensation (Section 37-51-401, MCA)

- no court action to recover compensation may be maintained without alleging and proving licensure at the time the cause of action arose

Unprofessional Conduct

❑ Categories most relevant to brokers

- the unauthorized practice of law: drafting complex contract provisions, advising on legal strategy, or interpreting statutes for a client
- failing to advise a principal or third party to seek outside professional services when appropriate
- recommending a service provider without disclosing any family, financial, or business relationship with that provider
- failing to verify ownership before accepting a listing; no title search is required, but making no inquiry at all can support discipline
- falsifying or altering a document without the party's written authority; forgery, fraud, misrepresentation, conversion, and theft are separate grounds
- failing to comply with internet advertising rules, fair housing law, the ADA, landlord-tenant and security deposit law, the mobile home lot rental act, radon disclosure, or the federal lead-based paint program
- failing to participate in negotiations as a seller or buyer agent, unless the principal waived that obligation in writing
- failing to account for or misappropriating trust funds

❑ Supervising broker discipline risk

- a supervising broker is exposed to discipline for the conduct of every supervised salesperson
- a pattern of complaints, or a single serious complaint, can trigger an inquiry into whether supervision was adequate
- the endorsement is a separate Board credential and can be limited or revoked even if the broker license is not

Compensation

❑ Montana statutory framework

- commissions are purely a matter of contract; Montana law has never set a rate or schedule
- paying a commission to an unlicensed person is unprofessional conduct under Section 37-51-321, MCA
- payments to a principal, reductions in the commission owed by a principal, and payments to the seller of a brokerage business are not treated as payments to an unlicensed person

- the broker earns the commission only after the transaction closes or terminates
- any division of forfeited earnest money between broker and seller must be in a written agreement between them

❑ The 2024 NAR settlement: the two key changes

- practice changes from the Sitzer-Burnett settlement took effect August 17, 2024
- offers of buyer broker compensation may no longer be communicated through an MLS, in any field or in remarks
- sellers may still offer buyer concessions on an MLS and may still negotiate buyer broker compensation off the MLS
- a written buyer broker agreement must be in place before the buyer tours a home, whether in person or by live virtual tour

❑ What the compensation clause must do

- state a specific, objectively ascertainable amount or rate; open-ended language such as 'whatever the seller is offering' is not permitted
- prohibit the licensee from receiving compensation from any source above the agreed amount or rate
- conspicuously state that broker fees and commissions are not set by law and are fully negotiable

❑ How Montana license law and the settlement fit together

- Montana already required written buyer broker agreements; the settlement adds content requirements without displacing the state rule
- ARM 24.210.641 treats acting as a buyer agent without a written buyer broker agreement, or as a seller agent without a written listing agreement, as unprofessional conduct
- the buyer agreement caps what the buyer broker may receive regardless of who pays

❑ Record-keeping for compensation

- all compensation arrangements must be documented and retained for 8 years
- the purchase contract should reflect any agreed seller concession, and the closing statement should show all compensation paid and its source

Disclosure

❑ Conflict of interest disclosure

- disclose any family relationship, financial relationship, or financial interest before engaging or recommending an attorney, title company, appraiser, escrow agent, insurance agent, or maintenance service
- a licensee may not represent a party where that representation conflicts with duties owed another, except disclosed dual agency with written consent from each principal
- a licensee may not act as a dual agent in a transaction in which the licensee is also a principal
- a licensee may not act as seller agent when the licensee is the buyer, or as buyer agent when the licensee is the seller
- acting in the dual capacity of broker and undisclosed principal, including in advertising, is unprofessional conduct

- a licensee may not submit a competing offer as a principal against the licensee's own client

- ❑ Montana has no mandatory property condition form, but disclosure duties still apply
  - the seller's duty flows from the common law of fraudulent concealment and from specific hazard statutes
  - the licensee's duty to disclose adverse material facts is independent; it belongs to the licensee, not the seller
  - adverse material facts include defects, environmental hazards, and conditions that could affect title or use
  - the licensee need not investigate beyond reasonable inquiry but may not conceal a known defect or stay silent when asked

- ❑ Hazard disclosures that do apply
  - radon (Title 75, Chapter 3, MCA): a seller who has received test results must disclose them
  - methamphetamine contamination (Title 75, Chapter 10, Part 13, MCA): required when the property is offered for sale or lease
  - lead-based paint on pre-1978 housing: federal pamphlet, disclosure of known paint or hazards, and a 10-day inspection opportunity

- ❑ Agency disclosure: required timing by role (Section 37-51-314, MCA)
  - seller agent: initial disclosure when the listing agreement is executed
  - buyer agent: initial disclosure when the buyer broker agreement is executed
  - statutory broker: initial disclosure when the broker first begins to locate property for the buyer
  - subsequent disclosure: given to the other side when negotiations commence

- ❑ Dual agency disclosure: timing and written consent
  - consent must be obtained before or at the moment the dual agency arises, never after
  - the initial disclosure form must carry the statutory dual agency advisory in all capital letters
  - the initial disclosure must also describe the duties owed under Section 37-51-313, MCA, and define 'adverse material fact'
  - every disclosure must identify the type of relationship and carry the recipient's signature, the licensee's signature, and the date

- ❑ Sex offender registry: not a required disclosure, but a required reference
  - Section 37-51-105, MCA, does not require a licensee to research or report registry contents
  - licensees ARE responsible for telling buyers and tenants how to find the registry themselves
  - direct them to the Montana Department of Justice public registry

- ❑ Other transaction disclosures
  - identify yourself as a licensee at first contact when seeking property information, whether for your own account or as an agent

- a salesperson in a for-sale-by-owner personal transaction must disclose that fact to the other party
- internet advertising of another brokerage's listing must disclose and identify that brokerage
- a broker who receives interest from a trust account must disclose the arrangement to the principal
- a property manager discloses the contractual relationship to owners and tenants; no separate Section 37-51-314 disclosure is required

Handling Documents and Trust Funds

- ❑ Trust fund basics: the broker is always responsible
  - ARM 24.210.426 sets the trust account rules; Section 37-51-324, MCA, authorizes citations for failing to meet them
  - the broker is accountable for all trust funds at all times, including funds handled by salespersons
  - salespersons must place trust funds with the supervising broker in time for the broker to meet the deposit deadline
  - deposit deadline: within 3 business days of receipt, unless the parties have agreed otherwise
  - a firm with more than one broker may use a single trust account, and a broker may keep more than one, each maintained separately
  - delegating trust account authority to a designated broker does not relieve either broker of responsibility

- ❑ Trust account structure
  - must be an insured account at a financial institution located in Montana
  - must be identified by the words 'trust account'
  - funds must be liquid; no sweep accounts, certificates of deposit, or repurchase agreements
  - a broker may keep up to $1,000 of personal funds in the account for maintenance and bank fees; anything more is commingling
  - if personal funds are kept there, the broker must maintain a chronological ledger of those deposits and disbursements
  - interest may be payable to the broker only if a written agreement identifies it as compensation for services performed

- ❑ Getting money out of trust
  - trust funds stay in the account until the transaction closes or terminates, unless disbursed to the closing agent on the written agreement of buyer and seller
  - money that becomes due to the broker must be withdrawn within 10 business days
  - no payment of personal bills, wages, benefits, recreational expenses, or business operating expenses from a trust account
  - no disbursement may be made until the corresponding deposit has been verified

- [ ] Trust account records: what must be documented
    - proof of each deposit with the date, the amount, the source of the money, and where it was deposited
    - monthly bank statements retained on file, and monthly reconciliation of the account
    - numbered trust account checks carrying the broker's business name and address, with voided checks recorded
    - a chronological record of receipts and disbursements with names, dates, amounts, and a running balance after each entry
    - a separate chronological ledger for each transaction, with its own running balance
    - records may be kept electronically so long as they can be audited

- [ ] Board audits
    - the Board may examine trust accounts and real estate documents during normal business hours
    - the broker must fully cooperate; non-cooperation is itself unprofessional conduct
    - a trust account citation carries 5 business days to pay the fine or file a written dispute

- [ ] Document retention
    - trust account records and all real estate documents, including sales contracts, leases, options, agency agreements, and closing statements, must be kept 8 years
    - the 8 years run from the later of the date of receipt or the date the transaction was completed

Listings and Buyer Brokerage Agreements

- [ ] Every brokerage relationship rests on a written agreement
    - acting as a seller agent without a written listing agreement is unprofessional conduct under ARM 24.210.641
    - so is acting as a buyer agent without a written buyer broker agreement
    - a listing negotiated by a salesperson is not valid until the supervising broker reviews, signs, and dates it
    - Montana recognizes exclusive right to sell, exclusive agency, open, and entry-only listings

- [ ] What every listing agreement must address
    - the identity of the seller, the brokerage, and the supervising broker
    - a legal description and street address of the property
    - the asking price and acceptable terms
    - the commission, expressed as a rate or amount, and the conditions under which it is earned
    - any concession the seller will offer a buyer or a cooperating brokerage, and any limits on it
    - a specific duration and the conditions for termination; no open-ended listings
    - any holdover or protection period after the listing term ends
    - authorization for MLS, internet advertising, and cooperation with other brokerages

- conspicuous disclosure that fees and commissions are not set by law and are fully negotiable
- the relationship disclosure required by Section 37-51-314, MCA

❑ What every buyer broker agreement must address

- the identity of the buyer, the brokerage, and the supervising broker
- the geographic area of the search and any property type or price range
- a specific duration and the conditions for termination
- compensation stated as a rate, amount, or clearly described formula, and objectively ascertainable
- a term prohibiting compensation from any source above the agreed amount or rate
- who is expected to pay the compensation and how any shortfall will be handled
- conspicuous language that commissions are not set by law and are fully negotiable
- the relationship disclosure required by Section 37-51-314, MCA
- whether the agreement is exclusive, and the consequences of using another brokerage during the term
- the agreement must be signed before the buyer tours a home, in person or by live virtual tour

❑ Contacting clients already under contract with another broker

- negotiating directly with a seller or buyer known to be under a written exclusive agreement with another broker is unprofessional conduct
- the parties may consent to direct communication, but the consent must be documented
- a buyer who wants to switch brokers must first terminate the existing agreement or obtain a written release

❑ Termination and cooperation

- when a listing or buyer broker agreement ends, any cooperating relationship created under it ends too, unless the parties agreed otherwise in writing

Ethics and Illegal Inducements

❑ Lotteries, raffles, and contests: not allowed to close deals

- soliciting or selling property through a lottery, raffle, or contest to influence a purchaser is unprofessional conduct under Section 37-51-321, MCA
- the rule targets incentives that condition the real estate decision on a game of chance

❑ Door prizes: when they are and aren't allowed

- permissible: a drawing anyone may enter free, with no consideration and no further commitment required
- not permissible: any prize that requires attending a listing presentation, signing a buyer agreement, or making an offer
- the dividing line is free participation with no strings attached

- ❑ False promises
  - making false promises likely to influence, persuade, or induce a party is unprofessional conduct
  - promising a particular price, financing rate, or concession without a basis in fact is improper even when well intended

- ❑ Referrals, RESPA, and disclosure
  - a referral relationship that pays the licensee is not improper by itself, but it must be disclosed
  - RESPA prohibits giving or receiving a fee, kickback, or thing of value for referring a settlement service in a federally related mortgage
  - a covered referral arrangement risks both federal liability and a Montana discipline finding

- ❑ The NAR Code of Ethics
  - applies to Montana licensees who are members of the Montana Association of REALTORS or a local board
  - 17 Articles with supporting Standards of Practice, enforced by local grievance committees and professional standards panels
  - a single act can violate both the Code and Board rules, generating parallel proceedings
  - local boards must share final ethics decisions involving public-trust violations with the Board of Realty Regulation
  - a licensee who is not a REALTOR remains bound by Section 37-51-321, MCA, ARM 24.210.641, and fair housing law

Part Four: Montana Agency Regulation

Agency: Authorized Relationships in Montana

- ❑ Montana agency is defined by statute, not common law
  - Section 37-51-313, MCA, replaces the common law of agency for these relationships
  - there are exactly five authorized relationships; nothing outside that list applies
  - the statutory terms are defined in Section 37-51-102, MCA, and are not the general term 'agent' used elsewhere in Montana law

- ❑ The five authorized relationships
  - seller agent: represents the seller under a written listing agreement
  - buyer agent: represents the buyer under a written buyer broker agreement
  - dual agent: represents both parties with the signed, written consent of each
  - statutory broker: assists with a transaction without representing either party
  - property manager: manages property for an owner under Sections 37-56-105 through 37-56-107, MCA

- ❑ The statutory broker is the default role
  - a licensee is presumed to be a statutory broker until a written agreement is signed or a different relationship is disclosed
  - the statutory broker is not the agent or representative of anyone in the transaction
  - many Montana transactions begin as statutory broker and ripen into agency when the written agreement is signed

- ❑ Subagency: not automatic, it takes an offer and an acceptance
  - a buyer or seller agent may offer subagency to another broker, who must accept it
  - without an explicit acceptance the cooperating broker is a statutory broker, not a subagent
  - a subagent owes the principal the same duties the original agent owes
  - a subagent has no independent agency relationship with the other party

- ❑ In-house designates: solving the dual agency problem inside one office
  - when two agents in one brokerage end up on opposite sides, the supervising broker may name an in-house seller agent designate and an in-house buyer agent designate
  - each designate represents only the designated party and is NOT a dual agent
  - the supervising broker does not become a dual agent by overseeing both designates
  - the arrangement still requires information barriers so one principal's protected information does not reach the other

- ❑ When dual agency cannot be used
  - a licensee who is a principal in the transaction, buying or selling for the licensee's own account, cannot be a dual agent
  - acting in the dual capacity of broker and undisclosed principal is unprofessional conduct under Section 37-51-321, MCA

- plan ahead by addressing dual agency consent in both the listing agreement and the buyer broker agreement
- if a principal declines dual agency in advance, in-house designates may still be available

❑ Written agreement requirement: the 2023 statutory change

- a 2023 amendment to Section 37-51-313, MCA, requires the written agreement before acting as a buyer agent or a seller agent
- the amendment raised a long-standing Board rule in ARM 24.210.641 to the level of statute
- acting without the required agreement does not eliminate the duties; the licensee still owes them

❑ When agency ends

- at the earliest of completed performance, the agreed expiration date, or an authorized termination
- a statutory broker relationship continues until the transaction is completed, abandoned, or terminated
- two duties survive termination: accounting for the principal's money and property, and confidentiality

Agency Duties and Responsibilities

❑ Seller agent duties to the seller

- act solely in the best interests of the seller
- obey promptly and efficiently all lawful instructions of the seller
- disclose all relevant and material information known to the agent and not known or discoverable by the seller
- safeguard the seller's confidences
- exercise reasonable care, skill, and diligence in pursuing the seller's objectives
- fully account for any funds or property of the seller that comes into the agent's possession
- comply with all applicable federal and state laws, rules, and regulations
- with written disclosure and the seller's written consent, a seller agent may list competing properties without breaching any obligation

❑ Seller agent duties to the buyer (non-client minimums)

- disclose any adverse material facts about the property that are known to the agent
- disclose when the agent has no personal knowledge of the truth of information about adverse material facts
- act in good faith with the buyer and the buyer agent
- no requirement to inspect the property or to verify what the seller says

❑ Buyer agent duties to the buyer

- these mirror the seller agent duties: loyalty, lawful instructions, disclosure, confidences, care, accounting, and legal compliance

- with written disclosure and the buyer's written consent, a buyer agent may represent multiple buyers interested in the same or similar property

❑ Buyer agent duties to the seller (non-client minimums)

- disclose adverse material facts known to the agent about the buyer's ability to perform on a purchase offer
- disclose when the agent has no personal knowledge of the truth of that information
- act in good faith with the seller and the seller agent

❑ Statutory broker duties: honest and fair, but advocating for no one

- tell the buyer about adverse material facts concerning the property that the broker knows
- tell the seller about adverse material facts concerning the buyer's ability to perform
- exercise reasonable care, skill, and diligence in putting the transaction together
- no duty to inspect the property or to verify anyone's statements

❑ Dual agent duties: both sides, with one critical exception

- the dual agent owes the seller the duties of a seller agent and the buyer the duties of a buyer agent
- the duty to disclose adverse material facts overrides confidentiality; the dual agent must disclose to both parties

❑ What a dual agent may NEVER disclose without written consent

- that the buyer is willing to pay more than the offered purchase price
- that the seller is willing to accept less than the asking price
- the factors motivating either party to buy or sell
- any information a party has indicated in writing is to be kept confidential

❑ Property manager duties

- governed by Sections 37-56-105 through 37-56-107, MCA, and the Department's property manager rules
- the relationship runs from a contract between the property manager and the owner
- disclose the contractual relationship to all customers and clients, including owners and tenants
- no separate Section 37-51-314 relationship disclosure is required

❑ Duty to ascertain pertinent facts (Section 37-51-313(13), MCA)

- every licensee must endeavor to ascertain all pertinent facts about each property in a transaction
- the purpose is to avoid error, exaggeration, misrepresentation, or concealment of pertinent facts
- the standard is reasonable effort; it does not turn the licensee into an inspector or an attorney
- it does foreclose the defense that the licensee was deliberately incurious

❑ Adverse material facts: what the duty to disclose covers

- definition: a fact the licensee should recognize as significant enough to affect a person's decision to buy or sell

- covers facts materially affecting value or structural integrity, a documented health risk to occupants, or the buyer's ability or intent to perform
- property-side examples: foundation settlement, a failing roof, a positive radon test, flooding history, septic failure, unrecorded easements or boundary disputes, title defects
- buyer-side examples: job loss, a bankruptcy filing, or withdrawal of a loan commitment
- does NOT cover the fact that an occupant has or has had a communicable disease, or that the property was the site of a suicide or felony
  - the exclusion does not bar a buyer from asking, and a licensee asked directly must answer truthfully

❑ Confidentiality: broad, lasting, and limited

- the duty is to safeguard the principal's confidences, not every fact the principal happens to mention
- the duty survives termination of the agency relationship
- a former seller agent may not use the former seller's confidential information against that seller in a later transaction
- five exceptions release the licensee from continuing confidentiality
  - subsequent conduct by the principal that authorizes disclosure
  - disclosure of adverse material facts about the property or the principal's ability to perform
  - disclosure required by law or to prevent the commission of a crime
  - the information is being disclosed by someone other than the licensee
  - the disclosure is reasonably necessary to defend the licensee's conduct

❑ Sexual or violent offender registration (Section 37-51-105, MCA)

- the licensee's responsibility is limited to two disclosures
  - that registration information may be maintained, and by whom
  - any actual knowledge the licensee has of registration information pertaining to the property
- the registry is maintained under Title 46, Chapter 23, Part 5, MCA
- no duty to research the registry or report its contents

❑ Vicarious liability (Section 37-51-315, MCA)

- a principal is not liable for an agent's or subagent's misrepresentation unless the principal had actual knowledge of it or it originated with the principal
- a broker is not liable for a subagent's misrepresentation unless the broker had actual knowledge, the subagent is an employee rather than an independent contractor, or it originated with the broker
- an agent is not liable for the principal's misrepresentation unless the agent had actual knowledge of it
- an agent who repeats a seller statement in good faith is protected by disclosing that the agent has no personal knowledge of its truth

Agency Disclosure Recap and Timing Summary

- ❑ Initial disclosure: given to your own client at the start
  - seller or buyer agent: at the time the listing agreement or buyer broker agreement is executed
  - statutory broker: when the broker first endeavors to locate property for the buyer
  - anticipated dual agent: use the initial disclosure form and obtain written consent before dual agency begins

- ❑ Subsequent disclosure: given to the other side when negotiations commence
  - seller agent gives it to the buyer or buyer agent; a seller subagent also gives one to the seller
  - buyer agent gives it to the seller or seller agent; a buyer subagent also gives one to the buyer
  - statutory broker gives it to the seller or seller agent
  - a licensee becoming a dual agent adds the other party's written consent if it was not given earlier

- ❑ What 'negotiations' means here
  - efforts to act as an intermediary and to facilitate or participate in contract discussions
  - completing forms for offers, counteroffers, addendums, and other writings
  - presenting offers and counteroffers
  - the subsequent disclosure must precede or coincide with these activities, never follow them

- ❑ What the initial disclosure must contain
  - a description of the duties owed under Section 37-51-313, MCA
  - the statutory dual agency advisory, reproduced in all capital letters
  - a definition of 'adverse material fact'
  - identification of the type of relationship disclosed
  - the signature of the seller or buyer receiving it, the signature of the licensee, and the date

- ❑ The statutory dual agency advisory, word for word
  - IF A SELLER AGENT IS ALSO REPRESENTING A BUYER OR A BUYER AGENT IS ALSO REPRESENTING A SELLER WITH REGARD TO A PROPERTY, THEN A DUAL AGENCY RELATIONSHIP MAY BE ESTABLISHED.
  - IN A DUAL AGENCY RELATIONSHIP, THE DUAL AGENT IS EQUALLY OBLIGATED TO BOTH THE SELLER AND THE BUYER.
  - THESE OBLIGATIONS MAY PROHIBIT THE DUAL AGENT FROM ADVOCATING EXCLUSIVELY ON BEHALF OF THE SELLER OR BUYER AND MAY LIMIT THE DEPTH AND DEGREE OF REPRESENTATION THAT YOU RECEIVE.
  - A BROKER OR A SALESPERSON MAY NOT ACT AS A DUAL AGENT WITHOUT THE SIGNED, WRITTEN CONSENT OF BOTH THE SELLER AND THE BUYER.

- ❑ What the subsequent disclosure must contain (Section 37-51-314(7), MCA)
  - identification of the type of relationship disclosed

- the signature of the seller or buyer, the signature of the licensee, and the date
- it may stand alone or be included in other transaction documents
- if it carries a new dual agency consent, it must include everything the initial disclosure requires

❑ Permitted optional content

- a disclosure may add a description of the other available relationships and their corresponding duties
- it may include a consent to the creation of dual agency and other definitions or provisions of the chapter
- any addition must be consistent with the required content and the form must clearly identify the relationship disclosed
- many Montana brokerages use one form that walks the principal through every possible relationship

❑ Practice points that come up repeatedly

- the disclosure must precede the activity it covers; giving it after showings does not bring the earlier showings under the disclosed relationship
- it need not be a separate document; it may be combined with the listing agreement or buyer broker agreement
- a licensee who starts as a statutory broker and later signs a written agreement must give a new initial disclosure at that time
- if a disclosed relationship changes during the transaction, a subsequent disclosure documenting the change is required

❑ Timing summary by role

- seller agent: initial to the seller at listing execution; subsequent to the buyer or buyer agent when negotiations start
- seller subagent: initial to the seller at listing execution; subsequent to the seller and to the buyer or buyer agent when negotiations start
- buyer agent: initial to the buyer at buyer broker agreement execution; subsequent to the seller or seller agent when negotiations start
- buyer subagent: initial to the buyer at agreement execution; subsequent to the buyer and to the seller or seller agent when negotiations start
- statutory broker: initial to the buyer when first locating property; subsequent to the seller or seller agent when negotiations start
- dual agent: to both buyer and seller before or at the time dual agency arises
- property manager: disclose the contractual relationship to all customers and clients; no separate subsequent disclosure

Part Five: Additional Montana Laws and Practices

Errors and Omissions Insurance

- E&O insurance is mandatory for every active Montana licensee
  - enacted in 2019 under Section 37-51-325, MCA; no exceptions for active licensees
  - coverage must be continuous for the entire period of active licensure
  - even one day without coverage while active is treated as a continuing violation
  - inactive licensees are exempt, but must place coverage in force before returning to active status

- Three ways to satisfy the requirement
  - enroll in the Board's group policy, currently administered by Rice Insurance Services Center; the simplest option
  - purchase an individual policy from any carrier that meets the statutory minimums
  - be covered under a policy the firm obtains, provided the licensee is named on it or covered by endorsement
  - under the group policy the coverage is specific to the licensee, so it follows the licensee to a new supervising broker

- Minimum policy standards
  - an automatic 60-day extended reporting period if the policy is cancelled or not renewed for any reason other than nonpayment
  - an optional extended reporting period of at least 365 days, requested and paid for within 60 days after expiration or cancellation

- Proof of coverage
  - proof is required when applying for a license and at every annual renewal
  - failure to produce proof on request exposes the licensee to administrative suspension or discipline

Landlord and Tenant Relationship

- Montana residential landlord-tenant law: three statutes to know
  - Title 70, Chapter 24, MCA: the Residential Landlord and Tenant Act of 1977, covering houses, apartments, condominiums, and townhouses
  - Title 70, Chapter 33, MCA: mobile home lot rentals, covered by their own separate act
  - Title 70, Chapter 25, MCA: security deposits, with separate rules for holding and returning them

- Who is exempt from the main Act
  - hotels, motels, and similar transient lodging
  - institutional residency for medical, educational, or correctional purposes

- occupancy by an owner of a condominium unit or a holder of a proprietary lease in a cooperative
- occupancy by a member of a fraternal or social organization in a building the organization operates
- occupancy by a buyer in possession under a contract of sale before closing
- mobile home lot rentals, which are covered by Chapter 33 instead

❑ Disclosures the landlord must make

- the name and address of the person authorized to manage the property
- the party authorized to accept service of process and to receive demands and notices
- a written list of existing damages before the tenant pays a security deposit; the tenant may inspect and correct the list
- federal lead-based paint disclosure applies to pre-1978 rentals, and Montana radon disclosure applies when the landlord has test results

❑ Key landlord duties under the Act (cannot be waived)

- maintain the premises to applicable building and housing code standards
- make all repairs needed to keep the unit fit and habitable
- keep all common areas clean and safe
- maintain electrical, plumbing, heating, ventilating, and air conditioning facilities in good and safe working order
- provide for removal of garbage and supply running water, hot water, and heat

❑ Key tenant duties (also non-waivable)

- keep the unit clean and safe and dispose of garbage properly
- comply with building and housing codes applicable to tenants
- use all facilities and appliances in a reasonable manner
- avoid deliberate or negligent damage beyond ordinary wear and tear
- do not disturb a neighbor's peaceful enjoyment of the premises

❑ Security deposits: timing is everything

- no statutory cap on the deposit amount; it is a negotiated term
- the deposit may be applied only to unpaid rent, damage beyond ordinary wear and tear, and cleaning or restoration the tenant made necessary
- no deductions: return the entire deposit within 10 days after the tenant terminates and vacates
- deductions proposed: deliver the balance with a written itemized list within 30 days
- missing the deadline or the itemization exposes the landlord to the withheld amount plus reasonable attorney fees

❑ Termination notices

- month-to-month tenancy: 30 days written notice from either side
- nonpayment of rent: 3-day written notice to pay or vacate
- if the tenant pays in full within the 3 days the tenancy continues; otherwise the landlord may file for eviction
- other lease violations take a 14-day or 30-day notice depending on whether the violation can be cured

- a clear and present danger to others, damage above the statutory threshold, or unlawful activity may justify a shorter notice

Foreclosure and Redemption in Montana

- ❑ Montana's two foreclosure tracks
    - trust indenture under the Small Tract Financing Act (Title 71, Chapter 1, Part 3, MCA): used for most residential loans, foreclosed non-judicially
    - mortgage under general mortgage law: used for larger parcels and commercial property, foreclosed judicially
    - a trust indenture may be used only where the property is 40 acres or less; exceeding the limit makes the instrument a mortgage
    - under a trust indenture the borrower conveys title to a trustee, who holds it for the lender until the debt is satisfied or the power of sale is exercised

- ❑ Non-judicial foreclosure: how it works
    - the trustee records a notice of sale and mails it to the grantor at least 120 days before the sale date
    - the notice must be posted conspicuously on the property at least 20 days before the sale
    - the notice must be published weekly for 3 successive weeks, with the last publication at least 20 days before the sale
    - the property is sold at public auction to the highest bidder; anyone except the trustee may bid, including the lender
    - the grantor may reinstate at any time before the sale by paying all amounts due and curing the default

- ❑ Two major protections for borrowers under non-judicial foreclosure
    - no deficiency judgment (Section 71-1-317, MCA): if the sale price does not cover the loan, the shortfall is discharged and the borrower is not personally liable
    - a deficiency is also unavailable in a judicial foreclosure of a trust indenture on an occupied single-family residence
    - no redemption right (Section 71-1-318, MCA): the sale is final and the purchaser takes title free of the grantor's interest

- ❑ Judicial foreclosure and mortgage redemption
    - the lender files a complaint, the court enters a judgment and decree of sale, and the sheriff conducts the public sale
    - the borrower has a 1-year right of redemption running 365 days from the date of sale
    - redemption requires paying the purchase price plus statutory interest, foreclosure costs, and any taxes or assessments the purchaser paid
    - if the property is a residence, the borrower may remain in possession during the redemption period

- ❑ After the sale: possession timeline
    - non-judicial (trust indenture): the purchaser is entitled to possession on the 10th day after the sale under Section 71-1-319, MCA
    - judicial (mortgage): possession follows expiration of the 1-year redemption period

- buyers at foreclosure sales need to understand this distinction before bidding

Place of Business and Officing Regulations

- ☐ Every broker must maintain a real physical address (Section 37-51-308, MCA)
  - a post office box or a virtual office does not qualify as a designated address
  - the address must be accessible so the Board can visit it for an audit
  - the broker's license, or a current copy, must be displayed there
  - copies of every affiliated salesperson's current license must also be displayed there

- ☐ Home offices, virtual brokerages, and remote work
  - a home office qualifies if it is a physical street address that supports the display, audit, and record-keeping obligations
  - a fully virtual brokerage with no physical location does not satisfy the statute
  - remote work by salespersons does not relax the broker's office obligation or the supervision rules of ARM 24.210.605 and 24.210.606

- ☐ Moving? Notify the Board first, or within 10 days
  - update the designated address on the license and pay the required fee
  - the Department then issues a license for the new location for the unexpired period

- ☐ Trust account location and records
  - the trust account must be at an insured financial institution located in Montana
  - records must be kept at the place of business and be available for audit
  - retain trust account records and all real estate documents for 8 years under ARM 24.210.601
  - the retention period survives a move, an office closing, or a transfer of the supervisory role

Montana Fair Housing

- ☐ Montana adds three classes beyond the federal seven
  - the Montana Human Rights Act, Title 49, Chapter 2, MCA, is the state law; Section 49-2-305 is the principal housing provision
  - federal protected classes: race, color, religion, sex, national origin, familial status, and disability
  - Montana adds age, creed, and marital status
  - a Montana licensee must treat all ten classes as off-limits for housing decisions
  - familial status means having a child or children who live or will live with a person

- ☐ What is prohibited
  - refusing to sell or rent, and refusing to negotiate
  - imposing different terms or conditions, or discriminating in services or facilities
  - advertising that indicates a preference or limitation

- denying that housing is available, steering, and blockbusting
- a licensee may not follow discriminatory instructions; client direction is not a defense

❑ Limited exemptions, but advertising is never exempt

- age and familial status prohibitions do not apply to a dwelling for no more than two families where the owner occupies one unit
- an owner-occupied private residence renting three or fewer rooms is exempt from many prohibitions
- housing for older persons may be exempt from the age and familial status provisions
  - occupied solely by persons 62 or older, or
  - 80 percent of occupied units have at least one resident 55 or older, with a published written policy
- no exemption excuses discriminatory advertising

❑ Filing a complaint

- Montana Human Rights Bureau: file within 180 days of the discriminatory act
- HUD: file within 1 year; many complaints are dual-filed
- remedies include injunctive relief, actual damages, and reasonable attorney fees
- a substantiated complaint also triggers Board discipline under Section 37-51-321, MCA

Land Description

❑ Three legal description methods used in Montana

- rectangular survey system (the federal Public Land Survey System): used for most of the state
- metes and bounds: used for irregular parcels that do not fit the rectangular grid
- lot-and-block: references a recorded subdivision plat

❑ The rectangular survey system: how Montana land is divided

- based on the Montana Principal Meridian and its baseline, surveyed after 1867
- a township is 6 miles by 6 miles, divided into 36 sections of one square mile each
- sections are numbered 1 through 36 starting in the northeast corner, working west across the top row, then east on the next
- each section contains 640 acres

❑ Breaking a section down: aliquot parts

- a section divides into halves of 320 acres, quarters of 160 acres, quarter-quarters of 40 acres, and smaller
- example: the southwest quarter of the northeast quarter of Section 12, T2N, R5E, Montana Principal Meridian, is 40 acres
- government lots are used where regular section corners could not be set because of water or other features, and are identified by number rather than aliquot part

❑ Metes and bounds and lot-and-block

- metes and bounds: starts at a point, traces the boundary by bearing and distance through each turn, and returns to the start

- lot-and-block: references a recorded plat, such as Lot 4, Block 7, Mountainview Subdivision, on file with the county clerk and recorder
- verify that the plat referenced is the recorded version and that any amendments are accounted for
- every contract, deed, and listing must carry a legal description sufficient to identify the parcel with certainty

Common Interest Ownership and Condominiums

- ❑ Montana uses the Unit Ownership Act, not the uniform act
  - Title 70, Chapter 23, MCA, is the Unit Ownership Act; Montana has not adopted the Uniform Common Interest Ownership Act
  - a condominium is ownership of single units together with common elements on property submitted to the Act
  - under current law the term condominium does not include a townhome or a townhouse
  - property comes under the Act only when the owner records a declaration in the county where the property is located

- ❑ Creating a condominium: what must be recorded
  - the declaration must describe the land, name the property, identify each unit, and state each owner's percentage interest in the common elements
  - it must describe the limited common elements and name a person within the county to receive service of process
  - it must carry local government certification that the project is exempt from subdivision review under Section 76-3-203, MCA, or was approved under Title 76, Chapter 3
  - the Department of Revenue must approve the declaration before it may be recorded
  - floor plans certified by a registered architect, engineer, or land surveyor are recorded at the same time
  - bylaws are recorded with the declaration; amending them takes 75% of the unit owners

- ❑ The ownership interest in units and common elements
  - each owner takes exclusive ownership of the unit plus an undivided percentage interest in the common elements
  - the percentage is fixed in the declaration by the unit's value at the date of the declaration relative to all units, and need not conform to market value
  - changing a percentage requires the agreement of every owner with an interest in that common element, plus a recorded amendment
  - the undivided interest cannot be separated from the unit and passes with it even if the deed does not mention it
  - common elements stay undivided; an action for partition is prohibited

- ❑ Liens and common expenses
  - once the declaration is recorded, liens attach only to individual units, never to the property as a whole
  - the association's lien for common expenses outranks all other liens except tax and assessment liens and a first mortgage or trust indenture of record

- a buyer at a first mortgage or trust indenture foreclosure takes free of common expenses that came due before the purchase, and the shortfall becomes a common expense of all owners
- in a voluntary sale the grantee is jointly and severally liable for the grantor's unpaid common expenses, unless the manager furnishes a statement of the amount owed

❑ The condominium disclosure and the 72-hour rule

- when the seller constitutes a majority of the unit owners, the seller must disclose that fact before any buy-sell agreement is signed
- on request the seller must furnish a copy of the Unit Ownership Act, the bylaws, and the administrative regulations
- the buy-sell agreement is not effective until 72 hours after the buyer receives those documents
- the buyer may withdraw the offer without penalty during that 72-hour window

❑ Removing property from the Act

- all unit owners may remove the property with the consent of all lienholders
- 90% of the owners may declare the property obsolete and vote to restore it or sell it
- if the association does not decide to rebuild within 60 days of damage or destruction, the property is removed from the Act
- after removal the owners hold the property in common and it becomes subject to partition

The Statute of Frauds in Montana

❑ Two statutes do the work in Montana

- Section 28-2-903, MCA, lists the agreements that are invalid unless in writing and subscribed by the party to be charged
- Section 70-20-101, MCA, requires a written instrument to create, grant, assign, surrender, or declare an estate or interest in real property
- the general contract rule sits in Title 28; the property transfer rule sits in Title 70

❑ What must be in writing under Section 28-2-903, MCA

- an agreement that by its terms cannot be performed within one year of its making
- a lease of real property for longer than one year
- an agreement for the sale of real property or of an interest in real property
- an agreement authorizing or employing an agent or broker to buy or sell real estate for compensation or a commission
- a promise to answer for the debt or default of another, and loan and credit agreements

❑ The point licensees miss most often

- the listing agreement and the buyer broker agreement are themselves within the statute of frauds
- an oral listing will not support a suit for a commission in Montana, and the case law on the point is long settled
- this is a second, independent reason for the written agreement requirement of Section 37-51-313, MCA, and ARM 24.210.641

- an agent signing a contract for a principal must hold written authority subscribed by that principal

- ❑ What the writing has to look like
  - it must be subscribed by the party to be charged, meaning the party the agreement is being enforced against
  - a note or memorandum can satisfy the statute; a formal contract is not required
  - it must identify the parties, the property, and the essential terms
  - the property description must be sufficient to identify the parcel with certainty

- ❑ Exceptions and limits (Section 70-20-102, MCA)
  - an estate at will, or a lease for a term not exceeding one year, may be oral
  - the statute does not affect a testator's power to dispose of real property by will
  - it does not prevent a trust from arising or being extinguished by implication or operation of law
  - it does not abridge a court's power to compel specific performance where there has been part performance
  - the statute governs enforceability, not validity; a fully executed oral agreement cannot be undone by invoking it

Section IV: National Practice Tests

Test 1: Rights; Interests and Estates; Ownership

1.1 Which of the following would be defined as real estate as opposed to real property?

a. Wells, driveways, and signs on a parcel of land.
b. Mobile homes temporarily parked on a parcel of land.
c. Timber that has been cut and is lying on a parcel of land.
d. Business equipment an owner or tenant has placed on a parcel of land.

1.2 Which of the following would be considered a property improvement?

a. An alteration to land to make it more useful.
b. An increase in the value of a property.
c. A chicken coop permanently attached to land.
d. A parcel of land that has passed a percolation test.

1.3 Which of the following best describes the physical boundaries of land?

a. The surface of the earth and infinite space above the surface.
b. The center of the earth and infinite space above the earth.
c. The surface of the earth and all water and minerals on or below the surface to the center of the earth.
d. The surface of the earth and the air rights above the surface to the point defined by local zoning.

1.4 The "bundle of rights" refers to a set of rights

a. enjoyed by the owner of a property.
b. that is synonymous with the Bill of Rights.
c. guaranteed to citizens by the Statute of Rights.
d. specified in a deed or land contract.

1.5 Which of the following best describes the legal concept of personal property?

a. Any item which is acquired in a fee simple sale transaction.
b. Any item of property that is not definable as real property.
c. Any movable property owned by an individual, partnership, or corporation.
d. Any item that is not a natural item affixed to the earth.

1.6 The right to encumber a property means that the owner can

a. sell the property to an encumbered party.
b. pledge the property as collateral for debt.
c. lease the property.
d. assign the bundle of rights to another.

1.7 A property owner leases 60 acres of agricultural land for a renewable period of 5 years. In the context of real estate rights, this lease represents a(n)

a. transfer of a portion of the bundle of rights.
b. encroachment on the bundle of rights.
c. conveyance of the complete bundle of rights.
d. encumbrance of the tenant's rights.

1.8 A homeowner is very upset over a drone that a neighbor flies over his house. He takes his case to court to end this possible violation of rights. Does he have a case, and on what basis?

a. No. The neighbor is not physically on his property.
b. No. The drone is in the air, so he cannot exercise any surface rights.
c. Yes. The owner has the right to stop encroachments.
d. Yes. The drones infringe on his air rights.

1.9 Littoral rights apply to which of the following?

a. Boatable ponds entirely contained within the boundaries of an owner's property.
b. Streams and rivers.
c. Navigable lakes, seas, and oceans.
d. Navigable streams and rivers.

1.10 A retired couple has just bought a retirement home with a pier on a large lake. In this case the retirees' water rights extend to

a. the high water mark of the body of water at the shoreline.
b. the low water mark of the body of water at the shoreline.
c. the center of the lake.
d. the end of the pier.

1.11 A waterfront homeowner has just died. What will become of the water rights the owner enjoyed while living in the home?

a. They revert to the state when the property is sold.
b. They are extinguished.
c. They are a personal right belonging to an individual owner, not attaching to the real property.
d. They transfer with the property when the property is sold.

1.12 Riparian rights concern which of the following bodies of water?

a. Lakes.
b. Seas and oceans.
c. Streams and rivers.
d. Navigable lakes.

1.13 Which of the following best describes a "fixture?"

a. Any item of personal property positioned within the boundaries of a parcel of real estate.
b. An item of personal property that has been converted to real property.
c. An item of real property temporarily placed on land for the purpose of conducting a business.
d. An item of personal property that has been left in one location for a period of six months.

1.14 An item may be considered personal property as opposed to real property provided that

a. the owner intended to remove it after a period of time.
b. it can be removed without altering the appearance of the structure.
c. it is unnecessary to the physical integrity of the structure.
d. the owner installed it at some time after acquiring the real property.

1.15 Two people own a house, each having an undivided equal interest. Which of the following best describes what each party owns?

a. Fifty percent of the physical house and the land it rests on.
b One hundred percent of the home and the land.
c. Fifty percent of the estate consisting of the indivisible whole of the real property.
d. Each owns one hundred percent of the estate represented by the real property and fifty percent of the physical house and the land it rests on.

1.16 A real property interest that includes the right to possess is considered

a. an estate in land.
b. a leasehold estate.
c. a fee simple estate.
d. the bundle of rights.

1.17 The right to control land usage by zoning and eminent domain is an example of

a. a public interest.
b. a police interest.
c. an encumbrance.
d. an estate in law.

1.18 If the duration of an owner's rights in an estate is not determinable, the owner has

a. a tenancy at sufferance.
b. a leased fee simple estate.
c. a freehold estate.
d. a leasehold estate.

1.19 The distinguishing feature of a leasehold estate is

a. ownership of an interest by a tenant.
b. temporary ownership of the full bundle of rights in a property.
c. unlimited ownership of one right in the bundle of rights in a property.
d. that the estate is limited by a lease term.

1.20 A landowner conveys a parcel of property with the provision that the land cannot be developed for retail purposes. The new owner immediately begins to develop a retail shopping outlet, the grantor finds out and takes the property back. What kind of estate did this landowner convey?

a. Fee simple absolute.
b. Life estate with reversion.
c. Life estate with condition subsequent.
d. Fee simple defeasible.

1.21 Ned grants his sister Alice an estate for as long as she lives. Her descendants, however, cannot inherit the estate. What kind of estate is it?

a. An estate pur autre vie.
b. An estate for years.
c. An ordinary life estate.
d. A legal life estate.

1.22 Homestead estates are examples of

a. a conventional life estate.
b. a legal life estate.
c. an estate created by an owner's agreement.
d. a fee simple absolute.

1.23 Louis owned a boat and a house before marrying Barbara. While she was single, Barbara owned a new car. The two got married and bought a second home. As a wedding present, Barbara's father bought Louis a motorcycle. Under the law of community property, what property can Louis sell without his wife's consent or signature?

a. The boat and house.
b. The boat, house, and motorcycle.
c. The second home and the motorcycle.
d. The boat and motorcycle.

1.24 Katelyn rents an apartment for one year. What rights has she acquired under the leasehold?

a. The right to exclude everyone from the premises.
b. The right to encumber the fee interest.
c. The right to sell the premises.
d. The right to possess and use the premises.

1.25 An estate from period-to-period will continue as long as

a. the tenant makes, and landlord accepts, regular rent payments.
b. the term specified in the lease.
c. the period is less than a year.
d. the landlord has not sold the property.

1.26 An estate at will

a. cannot be terminated.
b. is terminated only if so stated in the lessee's last will and testament.
c. terminates on the death of lessor or lessee.
d. terminates on the date specified in the lease agreement.

1.27 A tenant continues to occupy an apartment after lease expiration without the consent of the landlord. This type of estate is called

a. an estate at sufferance.
b. a holdover estate.
c. a canceled leasehold.
d. a hostile leasehold.

1.28 A tenant without a lease has been sending the landlord monthly rent checks, and the landlord continues to accept the payments. What kind of leasehold estate exists?

a. Estate for years.
b. Estate from period to period.
c. Estate at will.
d. Estate at sufferance.

1.29 A fee or life estate is held by an individual. This form of estate is referred to as a(an)

a. tenancy in severalty.
b. tenancy by the entireties.
c. absolute fee simple.
d. legal fee simple.

1.30 Six people have identical rights in a property and enjoy an indivisible interest. However any of the owners may sell or transfer his/her interest without consent of the others. This form of ownership is a

a. joint tenancy.
b. homestead ownership.
c. tenancy in common.
d. estate in severalty.

1.31 The "four unities" required to create a joint tenancy include which of the following conditions?

a. Parties must acquire respective interests at the same time.
b. Parties must be residents of the same state at the time of acquiring the interest.
c. Parties must be family members.
d. Parties must have joint financial responsibility.

1.32 Unlike tenants in common, joint tenants

a. own distinct portions of the physical property.
b. cannot will their interest to a party outside the tenancy.
c. may own unequal shares of the property.
d. cannot encumber their interest to outside parties.

1.33 Which of the following life estates is created by operation of law rather than by the owner?

a. Conventional life estate.
b. Ordinary life estate.
c. Legal life estate.
d. Community property life estate.

1.34 Which of the following is true of a homestead?

a. A homestead interest cannot be conveyed by one spouse.
b. A homestead interest cannot be passed to the children of the head of household.
c. A homestead interest is a form of conventional life estate.
d. A homestead is a primary or secondary residence occupied by a family.

1.35 A tenant in common can

a. sell or transfer his interest without the consent of the other tenants in common.
b. use his or her interest in the estate to encumber the entire estate.
c. sell, encumber or transfer his or her interest only to the other tenants in common.
d. sell, encumber or transfer his or her interest only with the consent of all the other tenants in common.

1.36 Which of the following would be considered community property?

a. Property acquired before marriage
b. A motorcycle bought after the marriage with separate property funds
c. Income derived from community property
d. A mother's heirloom wedding ring gifted to the wife after her wedding

1.37 When real property is held in a land trust, who controls the property?

a. The trustor
b. The trustee
c. The beneficiary
d. The mortgagee

1.38 In a community property state, John marries Patricia. Prior to the marriage John owned an SUV. During the marriage, John bought a Buick, John and Patricia bought a second property with money earned from Patricia's job, and each individual received a motorcycle from Patricia's uncle as a gift. What property is community property in this marriage?

a. The SUV, the Buick, and the second property.
b. The SUV, the Buick, the second property, and the motorcycles.
c. The Buick and the second property.
d. The Buick, the second property, and the motorcycles.

1.39 Which of the following is true of a cooperative?

a. A cooperative may hold an owner liable for the unpaid operating expenses of other tenants.
b. The owners have a fee simple interest in the airspace of their respective apartments.
c. Owners may sublease their apartments even if they sell their stock in the cooperative.
d. The proprietary lease is guaranteed to have a fixed rate of rent over the life of the lease term.

1.40 Which of the following is true of a tenancy in common?

a. The co-owners must be related.
b. The owners enjoy an indivisible interest.
c. The tenants must acquire their interests at the same time.
d. The tenants must pay equal amounts for their interest in the estate.

1.41 Carissa and Robert acquire a condominium as tenants in common. In this circumstance, Carissa can

a. sell her interest to a third party without the consent of Robert.
b. use her interest in the estate to mortgage the entire estate.
c. sell her interest only to Robert.
d. sell encumber or transfer her interest only with the consent of Robert.

1.42 When a tenant in common dies, what happens to the tenant's interest in the estate?

a. It is divided equally among the surviving tenants in common.
b. The surviving tenants must buy the interest from the deceased tenant's heirs or sell their interests to the heirs.
c. It becomes a joint tenancy.
d. It passes by probate to the deceased tenant's heirs.

1.43 Which of the following is true of a joint tenancy?

a. The tenants can determine the size of the share owned by each tenant.
b. The size of the tenant's shares is determined by the amount of equity each has invested in the property.
c. The tenants have an equal and indivisible ownership interest.
d. There can be no more than two co-owners, and each has a fifty percent interest.

1.44 In contrast to a tenancy in common, in a joint tenancy

a. there is a single title to the property.
b. there are as many titles to the property as there are co-owners.
c. title is held by a trustee.
d. co-owners who are married hold separate titles.

1.45 If a joint tenant sells his or her interest to an outside party,

a. the new owner becomes a tenant in common with the other owners, who continue to hold a joint tenancy with each other and a tenancy in common with the new owner.
b. the joint tenancy continues with the new owner as the third joint tenant.
c. the joint tenancy terminates and all owners become tenants in common.
d. the joint tenancy terminates and the owners must create a new joint tenancy to include the new owner.

1.46 When a joint tenant dies, what happens to the tenant's interest in the estate?

a. It passes to the decedent's heirs, who become joint tenants.
b. It passes as a tenancy in common to the decedent's heirs.
c. The joint tenancy terminates and becomes a tenancy in common with the decedent's heirs and the surviving tenants as co-owners.
d. It passes to the surviving joint tenants.

1.47 Under what conditions can two individuals own a property as tenants by the entireties?

a. If they so elect at the time of acquiring title.
b. If they are blood relatives.
c. If they are married.
d. If they incorporate.

1.48 When an estate is held in a trust, which party holds legal title?

a. The beneficiary.
b. The trustor.
c. The trustee.
d. The grantor.

1.49 Tanya buys a 4-bedroom condominium. As the new owner, she has the right to

a. sell or mortgage the unit without impediment from individual owners of neighboring units.
b. sell the interest in the physical unit separately from the interest in the common elements.
c. prevent non-owners from using the unit owner's portion of the common elements.
d. exclusively possess and use those portions of the common areas structurally or functionally necessary for the operation of the unit.

1.50 A condominium owner's share of maintenance and operations expenses are based on

a. the unit's pro rata share of floor space.
b. the unit's pro rata share of the property value as defined in the declaration.
c. the number of shares the owner purchased in the condominium association.
d. the assessed value of the condominium unit.

1.51 By contrast to a condominium, the owner of a cooperative owns

a. shares in a corporation or association and a proprietary lease in a physical unit.
b. a fee simple interest in a physical unit plus a tenancy in common in common elements.
c. a tenancy in common in a physical unit and the common areas.
d. a ground lease in the physical unit's pro rata share of land and a proprietary lease in the unit.

1.52 In a cooperative, real property is owned only by

a. the individual unit owners.
b. the individual unit owners and the cooperative association.
c. the cooperative developer.
d. the corporate entity of the cooperative association.

1.53 In a time-share freehold, owners acquire

a. undivided interests in the property as tenants in common.
b. a renewable periodic tenancy from for a portion of a year.
c. a pro rata share of a leased fee.
d. a tenancy in severalty for a portion of a year.

1.54 A party has just purchased a manufactured housing unit. When is this property considered real property?

a. As soon as it is purchased
b. As soon as it is constructed
c. As soon as it is affixed to the ground.
d. This form of property is considered personal property at all times.

1.55 Kiki's annual lease expires on December 31st. On January 7th, Kiki has still not vacated the premises. In this case, what happens to this person's tenancy and what is the resulting leasehold estate called, if anything?

a. The tenancy becomes a leasehold by prescription.
b. The estate becomes a holdover tenancy, a periodic leasehold estate.
c. The estate becomes a delinquent estate for years tenancy subject to immediate eviction.
d. There is no subsequent tenancy; the tenant must vacate immediately.

Test 2: Encumbrances; Liens; Title Transfer and Recording; Leases

2.1 Which of the following describes an encumbrance?

a. A third party's right to encroach upon a property without the permission of the property owner.
b. A third party's right to claim the sale proceeds of a property that has been mortgaged as collateral for a loan.
c. A third party's interest in a real property that limits the interests of the freehold property owner.
d. Another's right to acquire a freehold interest in a property against the property owner's wishes.

2.2 Which of the following is true of easements in general?

a. They involve the property that contains the easement and a non-owning party.
b. They apply to a whole property, not to any specific portion of the property.
c. They only involve the legal owner of the property.
d. They may require a specific use, but cannot prohibit one.

2.3 Mr. King wants to offer 100 acres of his property for sale. Since the property is landlocked, he will have to put in a driveway to the road that will run across his remaining property. What kind of easement will he have to grant?

a. An easement in gross.
b. A commercial easement.
c. A personal easement.
d. An easement appurtenant.

2.4 If property Alpha has a court-ordered easement across property Beta in order for Alpha to have access to a public road, the easement is a(n)

a. easement by prescription.
b. personal easement.
c. easement by necessity.
d. easement in gross.

2.5 An encroachment is

a. an easement that has not been recorded on the title of the burdened property.
b. an unauthorized physical intrusion of one property into another.
c. a right granted by a property owner to the owner of an adjoining property to build a structure that protrudes across the property boundary.
d. a structure that does not comply with a zoning ordinance.

2.6 A court might grant an easement by prescription if

a. a town needs to dig a trench across an owner's property to install a sewer line to a neighboring property, and the owner refuses permission.
b. a property owner sells the front half of a lot and wants to continue using the driveway to access the rear of the lot.
c. a trespasser has been using an owner's property for a certain period with the owner's knowledge but without permission.
d. a property owner wants to prevent the owner of an adjoining property from building a an improvement that blocks her view.

2.7 The purpose of a deed restriction is to enable an owner to specify

a. the form of ownership in which a property may be held.
b. how long a property must be owned before it can be legally transferred.
c. what groups of people are legally excluded from future ownership of a property.
d. how a property may be used and what improvements may be built on it.

2.8 Melinda purchases a house and finances it. The lender in turn places a lien on Melinda's title. The lien in this mortgage transaction is

a. evidence of debt incurred by a property owner.
b. a promissory note granted by a property owner as security for a debt.
c. the creditor's claim against the property as collateral security for the loan.
d. the document required to clear clouded title.

2.9 In a lien-theory state, what kind of interest does a mortgage lender have in the liened property?

a. A possessory interest.
b. A tenancy-by-mortgagee interest.
c. A legal interest in a pro rata share of the property.
d. An equitable interest.

2.10 How is a lien terminated?

a. Payment of the debt that is the subject of the lien and recording of the satisfaction.
b. Transfer of the property that has the lien.
c. Recording of another lien that is superior.
d. Death of the lienor or lienee.

2.11 A judge rules in favor of the creditor in a court proceeding and places a judgment lien against all the debtor's assets, including his real property. This is an example of a(n)

a. voluntary junior lien.
b. involuntary superior lien.
c. involuntary specific lien.
d. involuntary general lien.

2.12 A real estate tax lien, a federal income tax lien, a judgment lien, and a mortgage lien are recorded against a property. Which lien will be paid first when the property is sold?

a. Real estate tax lien.
b. Federal income tax lien.
c. Judgment lien.
d. Mortgage lien.

2.13 A lien holder can change the lien priority of a junior lien by agreeing to

a. change the date of recording.
b. lower the amount of the claim.
c. cancel the lien.
d. subordinate the lien.

2.14 Which of the following accurately describes the act of foreclosure?

a. A court-ordered acceleration of loan payments.
b. The final step in a bankruptcy filing.
c. A proceeding to enforce a lien by forcing the sale or transfer of a secured property.
d. A proceeding to take equitable title to a property that was liened as security for a mortgage loan.

2.15 A property is secured by a mortgage that does not contain a "power of sale" clause. To foreclose, the lien holder will have to

a. file a deficiency suit.
b. file a foreclosure suit.
c. file a suit to quiet title.
d. obtain a quit claim deed.

2.16 A homeowner defaults on his mortgage loan. In the subsequent foreclosure action, the lender takes title to the liened property directly instead of initiating a court-ordered public sale. This is an example of

a. strict foreclosure.
b. judicial foreclosure.
c. non-judicial foreclosure.
d. deed in lieu of foreclosure.

2.17 A property owner gives Deanna permission to cross his property as a shortcut to her kindergarten school bus. One day the property owner dies. What right was Deanna granted originally, and will it survive the owner's death?

a. A personal easement in gross, which continues after the owner's death.
b. An easement by prescription, which continues after the owner's death.
c. A license, which continues after the owner's death.
d. A license, which terminates upon the owner's death.

2.18 On two adjacent properties, there is an easement that allows property A to use the driveway that belongs to property B. Here, property A is said to be which of the following in relation to property B?

a. Subservient estate.
b. Servient tenement.
c. Senior tenant.
d. Dominant tenement.

2.19 A property owner who is selling her land wants to control how it is used in the future. She might accomplish her aim by means of

a. an injunction.
b. a deed restriction.
c. an easement.
d. a land trust.

2.20 What distinguishes a lien from other types of encumbrance?

a. It involves a monetary claim against the value of a property.
b. It lowers the value of a property.
c. It is created voluntarily by the property owner.
d. It attaches to the property rather than to the owner of the property.

2.21 Which of the following defines actual notice?

a. It is notice published in a newspaper.
b. It is knowledge one could have or should have obtained.
c. It is notice explicitly stated in a legal document.
d. It is knowledge received or imparted through direct experience.

2.22 Which of the following defines constructive notice?

a. It is notice published in a newspaper.
b. It is knowledge one could have or should have obtained.
c. It is notice explicitly stated in a legal document.
d. It is knowledge received or imparted through direct experience.

2.23 Ownership of real estate can be transferred voluntarily or involuntarily. The three ways title can be transferred voluntarily are by

a. grant, deed, and will.
b. escheat, deed, and covenant.
c. title certificate, will, and deed.
d. sale contract, deed, and warrant of seizin.

2.24 What is the function of recording a deed?

a. It makes the deed valid.
b. It causes title to pass.
c. It gives constructive notice of ownership.
d. It removes all prior recorded encumbrances.

2.25 The only clause that is actually required in a deed is the

a. habendum clause.
b. granting clause.
c. reserving clause.
d. tenendum clause.

2.26 The type of deed that offers the grantee the fullest protection against claims to the title is the

a. general warranty deed.
b. special warranty deed.
c. quitclaim deed.
d. bargain and defend deed.

2.27 What is one of the purposes of a lawsuit to "quiet title"?

a. To force the grantor to defend the title against a third party claim.
b. To terminate a co-ownership estate when one co-owner is unwilling.
c. To keep the owner's name out of the title records.
d. To have an encumbrance removed if the lienholder cannot prove its validity.

2.28 Which of the following best describes the documentary stamp tax?

a. A transfer tax based on the price of the property being conveyed.
b. A tax a title company must pay in order to examine title records in the recorder's office.
c. A tax collected by attorneys and paid to the state when transfer documents are prepared.
d. A tax on stamps used to certify the authenticity of a conveyance.

2.29 The court proceeding that generally settles a decedent's estate is called

a. testate.
b. probate.
c. escheat.
d. distribution.

2.30 If an owner of real property dies intestate and has no legal heirs, what will happen to the property?

a. It will escheat to the state or county.
b. It will transfer to the decedent's executor.
c. It will be divided equally among adjoining property owners.
d. It will become a public easement.

2.31 A municipality wants to build a sewage treatment facility which will require the acquisition of several parcels of privately owned land. What legal power enables the municipality to buy the necessary properties, even against the owners' wishes?

a. Estoppel.
b. Escheat.
c. Alienation.
d. Eminent domain.

2.32 An adverse possessor must be able to successfully demonstrate that he or she has been

a. openly possessing and claiming the property without the owner's consent.
b. occupying the property without an occupancy permit.
c. using the property intermittently and without permission over a period of years.
d. building a permanent structure on the property.

2.33 A buyer has signed a contract to purchase a property, but is uncertain of the condition of the title. Which of the following parties is legally responsible for knowing the condition of the title?

a. The County Recorder.
b. The seller's agent.
c. The buyer.
d. The mortgage lender.

2.34 A break in the chain of title to a property results in

a. a clouded title.
b. a title plant.
c. a lien of indeterminate ownership.
d. a duplicate title.

2.35 Wayne and Leota obtain an insurance policy that protects them from liabilities and losses resulting from title defects. The kind of policy they bought is a

a. homeowner's insurance policy.
b. standard owner's title insurance policy.
c. lender's title insurance policy.
d. private mortgage insurance policy.

2.36 An owner transfers title to a property to a buyer in exchange for a motorcycle. This is an example of

a. voluntary alienation.
b. involuntary liquidation.
c. hypothecation.
d. 1031 exchange.

2.37 A person wishes to convey any and all interests in a property to another without assurance of the property's marketability. This party would most likely use which of the following types of deed?

a. A sheriff's deed.
b. A special warranty deed.
c. A partition deed.
d. A quitclaim deed.

2.38 Jennifer owns a one-half interest in a condominium as a tenant in common with her business partner. If Jennifer has several heirs and dies without a will, the property will

a. pass to the heirs by the laws of descent and distribution.
b. escheat to the state.
c. pass to the surviving spouse based on homestead law.
d. pass to the surviving heirs according to the provisions of the will.

2.39 A drifter secretly lives in an abandoned shack on a large ranch property. After twenty years, the person makes a claim of ownership to the shack and the land immediately surrounding it that he had cleared. This claim will likely be

a. upheld through adverse possession.
b. upheld because of the length of possession.
c. declined through the doctrine of prior appropriation.
d. declined because possession was secretive.

2.40 To be marketable, title must be

a. insured.
b. free of undisclosed defects and encumbrances.
c. abstracted by an attorney.
d. guaranteed by a title certificate.

2.41 Which of the following types of leasehold estate lacks a specific term?

a. Estate for years.
b. Estate from period-to-period.
c. Estate at will.
d. Estate by the entireties.

2.42 A landlord generally has the right to enter the leased premises

a. at any time without notice.
b. for specified reasonable purposes.
c. provided the tenant gives prior permission.
d. only thirty days prior to lease expiration.

2.43 When a tenant rents an apartment, he or she is usually responsible for

a. compliance with the rules and regulations of the building.
b. payment for any alterations to the leased space.
c. recording the lease in title records.
d. occupying the premises throughout the lease term.

2.44 Under landlord-tenant laws, landlords must treat tenants fairly and honestly. In a residential leasehold, this requirement would include

a. insuring the tenant against loss of personal property.
b. providing required building support and services.
c. guaranteeing that a fair rent is being charged.
d. insuring the property for the value of the leasehold.

2.45 While a one-year lease is in effect, the tenant dies of a sudden illness. In this situation,

a. the lease automatically terminates.
b. the tenant's estate has the option of canceling the contract.
c. the landlord can record a lien against the leased fee interest.
d. the tenant's estate is still obligated under the lease.

2.46 Three students rent a house together, and all three sign a one-year lease. Six months later, two students move out. Which of the following is true of the remaining rent obligation?

a. The remaining tenant is responsible for the full rent obligation.
b. The remaining tenant is responsible for one third of the rent obligation.
c. The lease is cancelled due to abandonment. Therefore, the rent obligation is extinguished.
d. The departing tenants have no further rent obligation.

2.47 A tenant transfers a portion of the leasehold interest to another party. The instrument that accomplishes this transfer is a(n)

a. deed.
b. novation.
c. sublease.
d. reconveyance

2.48 Vijay enters into a lease for his new store. The provisions of the lease require Vijay to pay the operating expenses of the premises such as janitorial and repair expenses. This is an example of a

a. gross lease.
b. percentage lease.
c. land lease.
d. net lease.

2.49 A tenant obtains a full-service lease where the landlord agrees to pay all operating expenses in exchange for an additional $5.00 rent per square foot. Another term for this lease is a(n)

a. gross lease.
b. proprietary lease.
c. exchange lease.
d. full service net lease.

2.50 Which of the following circumstances is the most likely scenario for a ground lease?

a. A developer wants to acquire a necessary parcel that separates two parcels she already owns.
b. An owner-developer wants to retain ownership of the land portion of the improved real property.
c. A fast food company wants to place a restaurant in an existing building without buying either land or improvement.
d. A farmer wants to sell his property to a mining company.

2.51 A tenancy at will can usually be terminated by

a. either party giving proper notice.
b. either party without notice.
c. a sublease, with the lessor's approval.
d. an assignment by the lessor.

2.52 Under the Uniform Residential Landlord and Tenant Act, if a lease does not state a clear expiration date, the lease is regarded as

a. invalid.
b. a tenancy from period-to-period.
c. a tenancy at will.
d. a tenancy for years.

2.53 The Uniform Residential Landlord and Tenant Act generally does not apply to

a. a hotel.
b. a single-family residence.
c. a unit in an apartment building that has fewer than ten units.
d. a duplex in which the owner occupies one of the units.

2.54 In executing a condominium lease, a tenant has acquired

a. a temporary transfer of legal title.
b. a limited freehold interest in the air space of her unit.
c. a temporary possessory interest.
d. a title conveyance in exchange for rent.

2.55 When a tenant acquires a leasehold estate through a lease, what does the property owner acquire?

a. A freehold estate for years.
b. A reduced leasehold estate.
c. A defeasible estate.
d. A leased fee estate.

2.56 When an owner leases her property, she temporarily relinquishes the right to

a. transfer the property.
b. encumber the property.
c. occupy the property.
d. maintain the property.

2.57 Which of the following happens when a leased property is sold?

a. The buyer acquires title subject to the lease, which remains in effect.
b. The lease is cancelled.
c. The lease expires within thirty days unless renewed.
d. A new lease is automatically executed.

2.58 If a lease does not state a specific ending date, when does it terminate?

a. Immediately, since it is an invalid lease.
b. After one year.
c. When either party gives proper notice.
d. Whenever the property is sold.

2.59 In accordance with the statute of frauds,

a. leases in excess of one year must be recorded to be enforceable.
b. oral leases are not enforceable.
c. a five-year lease must be in writing to be enforceable.
d. an unwritten lease is fraudulent.

2.60 Which of the following is true of a sublease?

a. The subtenant takes over sole responsibility for performance of the original lease contract.
b. The original tenant retains primary responsibility for performance of the original lease contract.
c. It does not convey any of the leasehold interest.
d. It conveys the entire leasehold interest.

2.61 A homeowner goes bankrupt and the lender forecloses on her residence. In the foreclosure sale, the proceeds are insufficient to pay off the loan, and the court orders other property sold to cover the shortfall. This action is called a(n)

a. strict foreclosure.
b. suit for specific performance.
c. equity foreclosure judgment.
d. deficiency judgment.

2.62 To make a successful claim of adverse possession, the adverse possessor must satisfy which of the following criteria?

a. The possession must have been concealed, without permission, and for a statutory period of time.
b. The possession must have been unconcealed, for the necessary length of time, and without permission.
c. The possession must be with intent, secretive, notorious and hostile.
d. The possession must be open, without permission, for the statutory period of time, and within the number of permitted intervals.

2.63 One of the primary benefits of recording conveyances is to give evidence to the public that the new owner actually owns the property. What is another benefit of recording to the homeowner?

a. Recording instruments establishes the title's marketability.
b. Recording the deed prevents any future clouds on title.
c. Recording prevents lienholders from illegal credit practices.
d. Recording the deed of conveyance nullifies any and all claims of adverse possession.

2.64 Broker Yvonne successfully closed on her listing, but the seller refused to pay the commission. What is one legitimate course of action available to Yvonne?

a. A vendor's lien
b. An intangible lien
c. A broker's lien
d. A mechanic's lien

2.65 One of the key characteristics of a short sale is that the transaction typically takes much longer to close. What is another anomaly of a short sale that makes it a unique conveyance alternative?

a. The lender must approve of the modified loan and selling terms.
b. The Real Estate Commission may intervene to protect the broker from seller default.
c. The broker must take a discount on the conventional commission scale.
d. The IRS must audit any loan modification.

Test 3: Land Use; Legal Descriptions; Contract Law

3.1 Which of the following is true regarding master planning and zoning?

a. The aggregate of zoning ordinances is the master plan.
b. A master plan eliminates the need for zoning ordinances.
c. Master planning is a county-level function; zoning is limited to the city level.
d. Zoning ordinances are a primary means of keeping land use in harmony with the master plan.

3.2 The basic intent of zoning ordinances is to

a. establish the basis for public ownership of land for the common good.
b. establish subdivision rules and regulations.
c. specify usage for every parcel within the zoning authority's jurisdiction.
d. restrict development in unincorporated areas.

3.3 Why do zoning authorities create different types of zones?

a. To ensure that a variety of building structures are available in the community.
b. To separate land uses so that they do not interfere with each other.
c. To preserve high density land uses.
d. To discourage industrial and commercial users from relocating.

3.4 The key consideration in granting a zoning exception known as a special exception is which of the following?

a. Hardship
b. Change of zones
c. The public interest
d. The use was legal prior to the new zone creation

3.5 The intensity of land usage generally refers to what?

a. The number of residential building lots per acre.
b. The number of people per square mile.
c. The number of building permits issued per year within a zoning jurisdiction.
d. The area of a commercial or industrial facility in relation to the size of the site.

3.6 How does Planned Unit Development zoning vary from ordinary zoning?

a. It applies only to office parks.
b. It incorporates a number of different zones within a single property boundary.
c. It requires that multiple tracts of land be developed according to a single design.
d. It requires developers to obtain a separate building permit for every structure.

3.7 Which of the following situations is most likely to represent an illegal nonconforming use?

a. A homeowner in a residential zone converts her residence to a private school.
b. A homeowner builds a toolshed in a neighborhood where there are no toolsheds.
c. A storeowner remodels a storefront in accordance with regulations, and then the zoning is changed to residential.
d. A new zoning ordinance outlaws two-story additions after a homeowner completes an addition.

3.8 What is the difference between a variance and a nonconforming use?

a. A variance, once granted, is unconditional and permanent.
b. A variance is granted by the zoning board if the owner has a justifiable reason.
c. A nonconforming use is allowed if the owner requests it in advance of building.
d. A nonconforming use violates current zoning, but a variance does not.

3.9 A document certifying that a structure complies with building codes and is ready for use is referred to as a(n)

a. inspection report.
b. satisfaction bond.
c. certificate of occupancy.
d. user permit.

3.10 Which of the following is true of an eminent domain proceeding?

a. It cancels the property owner's mortgage loan balance.
b. It leaves the property owner with equitable title in place of legal title.
c. It conveys legal title to the acquiring entity.
d. It clouds the chain of title by canceling the original grant.

3.11 Among other provisions, the Superfund Act (CERCLA) and Superfund Amendment and Reauthorization Act of 1986 provided that

a. large development projects undergo an environmental impact survey immediately after completion of construction.
b. industrial users of real estate comply with air quality standards.
c. the EPA would give financial help to homeowners to remedy any hazardous situation resulting from radon, asbestos, or lead-based paint.
d. parties responsible for improper disposal of hazardous waste could be charged for the cleanup costs.

3.12 Public land use planning strives to balance which of the following potentially conflicting interests?

a. Individual property rights and the public's interest.
b. Public policy makers and community business leaders.
c. Tenant occupancy specifications and construction contractors.
d. Individual property owners and municipal planning agencies.

3.13 Zoning, building codes, and environmental restrictions are forms of local land use control known as

a. master planning.
b. preemption.
c. police power.
d. concurrency.

3.14 If a municipality exerts its power of eminent domain against a certain property owner, what happens?

a. The owner must pay higher property taxes or give up the property.
b. The owner must cede an easement without receiving any compensation.
c. The municipality annexes the property.
d. The owner must sell the property in exchange for market-value compensation.

3.15 To be valid, a local zoning ordinance must

a. reasonably promote community health, safety and welfare.
b. comply with federal zoning laws.
c. apply only to unique properties.
d. published periodically in the local newspaper.

3.16 Why do communities require building permits?

a. To promote development.
b. To establish the basis for an inspection.
c. To promote certificates of occupancy.
d. To ensure that improvements comply with codes.

3.17 What is the purpose of residential zoning?

a. To increase home values in a neighborhood.
b. To regulate the density of dwellings in the residential zone.
c. To prevent families from residing in commercial and industrial sites.
d. To maximize intensity of usage.

3.18 A non-profit organization wants to erect an urgent care facility in a residential zone. Given other favorable circumstances, the local authorities may grant permission by allowing

a. a special exception.
b. an illegal nonconforming use.
c. an easement.
d. a license.

3.19 A property that conformed with zoning ordinances when it was developed but does not conform to new ordinances is said to be

a. an illegal special exception.
b. a variance.
c. a legal nonconforming use.
d. unmarketable.

3.20 The approval process for development of multiple properties in an area includes submission of

a. a covenant of restriction.
b. a plat of subdivision.
c. a court order.
d. a developer's pro forma.

3.21 A legal description of a property is one which

a. accurately identifies the boundaries of the property as distinct from all other properties.
b. accurately describes the location and dimensions of the lot and improvements on the property.
c. is accepted by a licensed surveyor as suitable for inclusion in a survey of the property.
d. is written by an attorney licensed to practice real estate law in the state in which the property is located.

3.22 The essential elements of the metes and bounds system are

a. parallels, base lines, and meridians.
b. boundaries, distances, and a base line.
c. reference points, angles, and distances.
d. lot numbers, sections, and ranges.

3.23 In the Rectangular Survey System, a range is the area in between

a. any row of sections in a township.
b. two consecutive meridians.
c. a principal meridian and a base line.
d. a parallel and a meridian.

3.24 In the Rectangular Survey System, a tier is defined by

a. six consecutive sections of a township.
b. two consecutive meridians.
c. two consecutive parallels.
d. a parallel and a meridian.

3.25 In the Rectangular Survey System, what are the dimensions of a township?

a. One mile square.
b. Six miles by six miles, or 6 miles square.
c. Thirty-six miles square.
d. The north and south boundaries are one mile apart; the east and west boundaries are indeterminate.

3.26 What portion of a section is ten acres?

a. 1/8.
b. 1/16.
c. 1/32.
d. 1/64.

3.27 The lot and block system of legally describing property is used for

a. farm properties.
b. any property in an unincorporated area.
c. properties where metes and bounds is not acceptable.
d. properties in a subdivision.

3.28 A certain legal description contains the phrase, "...northwesterly along Erie Road to the POB...". What kind of description is this?

a. Plat survey.
b. Government grid.
c. Metes and bounds.
d. Rectangular survey.

3.29 How many sections are there in a township?

a. One.
b. Six.
c. Twelve.
d. Thirty-six.

3.30 In the Rectangular Survey System, a section contains how many acres?

a. 640.
b. 320.
c. 160.
d. 40.

3.31 The valuable consideration necessary to make a contract valid must be

a. money.
b. something tangible.
c. something of value traded in exchange for something of value.
d. something of equal value with whatever is received in exchange.

3.32 A real estate sales contract, to be enforceable, must

a. contain a legal description of the property.
b. be written on a form approved by the state bar association.
c. be acknowledged by three witnesses.
d. be recorded within three days to be enforceable.

3.33 How much time does a seller have to accept a buyer's offer?

a. Forty-eight hours from the time of the offeror's signing of the offer.
b. Twenty-four hours from the time of the offer's delivery to the seller.
c. Within 24 hours following the stated expiration.
d. A reasonable time, or until the expiration date on the offer.

3.34 A buyer submits an offer to a seller and then dies in a car accident. Before learning of the buyer's death, the seller accepts the offer. Which of the following is true?

a. The seller can force the buyer's estate to go through with the purchase.
b. The buyer's death terminated the offer.
c. The seller must make a new offer with the same terms to the buyer's heirs.
d. The buyer's heirs have the option of enforcing the contract.

3.35 Which of the following contracts can be assigned to another party?

a. An exclusive listing agreement.
b. A personal services agreement.
c. A contract for the sale of undeveloped land.
d. An employment contract between a broker and a salesperson.

3.36 An implied agency relationship may be deemed to exist if

a. the parties do not disavow an express contract that has expired.
b. the parties act is if there is a contract.
c. an offering party does not receive written notice that the offer has been rejected.
d. the parties promise to perform their part of the agreement if the other party performs.

3.37 Which of the following is an executory contract?

a. An expired lease.
b. A sale contract before closing.
c. A recorded sale contract.
d. An option to buy after it is exercised.

3.38 A bilateral contract is one in which

a. both parties promise to do something in exchange for the other party's performance.
b. both parties receive equal consideration.
c. two parties agree to perform a service together.
d. both parties promise to do something if the other party performs first.

3.39 A homeseller signs a listing agreement with a broker then subsequently revokes the listing. Which of the following is true?

a. The seller continues to have contractual obligations to the broker.
b. The contract remains in full force until the expiration date.
c. The broker may have a claim for marketing expenses expended during the listing term.
d. The seller cannot sign a listing agreement with another broker.

3.40 A breach of contract is

a. a termination of the contract by the mutual consent of the parties.
b. financial damage suffered by a party because another party has nullified a contract provision.
c. a lawsuit to force a party to discharge the contract.
d. the failure of a party to perform according to the terms of the contract.

3.41 What is rescission?

a. The act of withdrawing an offer before it has been accepted.
b. The act of declaring that a contract is no longer in effect for a given party.
c. The act of declaring a contract unenforceable.
d. The act of modifying the terms of an offer.

3.42 To be valid, a valid contract must

a. reflect a mutual understanding or agreement.
b. use precise wording in a document.
c. not be executable.
d. be created only by an attorney.

3.43 Two parties enter into a contract. The agreement fulfills all the requirements for a valid contract, with no disqualifying circumstances. Given this situation, it is still possible that the contract may be

a. void.
b. illegal.
c. unenforceable.
d. voidable.

3.44 The guardian for a mentally incompetent party enters into an oral contract with another party to buy a trade fixture on behalf of the incompetent party. This contract

a. does not meet validity requirements.
b. is possibly valid and enforceable.
c. must be in writing to be valid.
d. is valid but unenforceable.

3.45 A prospective homebuyer submits a signed offer with the condition that the seller pay for the inspection at closing. The seller disagrees, crosses out the provision, then signs and returns the document to the buyer. At this point, assuming all other contract validity items are in order, the original offer is now

a. an accepted offer, therefore a valid contract.
b. an executable option.
c. a counteroffer.
d. an invalid offer.

3.46 A construction contractor executes a contract with a buyer. In the agreement, the contractor promises to complete construction by November 20. This promise can be construed as

a. an option.
b. mutual consent.
c. a meeting of the minds.
d. valuable consideration.

3.47 A seller contracts to sell a property that she does not own. The sale contract for this transaction

a. is executable.
b. must be in writing.
c. is void.
d. is illegal yet potentially enforceable.

3.48 The statute of limitations requires that parties to a contract who have been damaged or who question the contract's provisions

a. must act within a statutory period.
b. must select a specific, limited course of action for recouping their losses.
c. must arbitrate prior to taking court action.
d. must wait a statutory period before they may take legal action.

3.49 The purpose of the statute of frauds is to

a. invalidate certain oral contracts.
b. require certain conveyance-related contracts to be in writing.
c. nullify oral leases and listing agreements.
d. eliminate fraud in real estate contracts.

3.50 A seller immediately accepts a buyer's offer but waits ten days before returning the accepted document to the buyer. Meanwhile, the offer has expired. Which of the following is true?

a. The buyer is bound to the contract since it was accepted immediately.
b. The buyer has no obligations to the seller whatsoever.
c. The buyer may not rescind the expired offer.
d. The seller may sue for specific performance.

3.51 A deed restriction limits how owners may use a property within a given subdivision. One key characteristic of a deed restriction is that it

a. may be revoked by an owner.
b. may be exempt from ADA restrictions.
c. may not be discriminatory.
d. may not apply to protected classes, vis a vis fair housing laws.

Test 4: Agency; Listing Agreements

4.1 The agency relationship is defined by

a. the Realtor Code of Ethics.
b. the laws of agency, or in some states, by statute.
c. the law of real estate contracts.
d. the agreement between a principal and an agent.

4.2 Which of the following is true of the connection between compensation and the agency relationship?

a. An agreement to give and receive compensation creates an agency relationship.
b. If an agency relationship exists, the principal must provide valuable consideration to the agent.
c. The relationship is independent of any compensation arrangement.
d. If an agency relationship exists, the agent is entitled to compensation.

4.3 One of the parties to an agency relationship defaults, and the agreement terminates. Which of the following is true?

a. All obligations are extinguished.
b. Both parties must continue to perform all other obligations of the agreement.
c. The defaulting party may have a financial consequence.
d. The damaged party has no claim against the defaulting party.

4.4 Among the fiduciary duties imposed on a real estate agent is the requirement to

a. refuse offers the agent knows will be unacceptable to the principal.
b. present all offers to the principal regardless of their amount.
c. advise the principal against accepting an offer that is below full price.
d. advise a prospect that the principal will not accept the prospect's offer in order to elicit a better offer.

4.5 One of the agent's fiduciary duties that continues even after a listing agreement expires is

a. obedience.
b. diligence.
c. confidentiality.
d. disclosure.

4.6 The standard of care and competence that a principal can expect from an agent is generally that which is

a. specified in the agency agreement.
b. necessary to earn the promised compensation.
c. necessary to procure a customer.
d. comparable to that of other practitioners in the area.

4.7 Agent Michael is showing his new listing to a buyer who informs him that he has just inherited five million dollars. Michael is now bound by fiduciary duty to

a. keep the information in confidence.
b. disclose the information to the buyer's agent.
c. disclose the information to the seller.
d. verify the buyer's statements before disclosing them to the client.

4.8 Agent Gerry has executed an exclusive buyer broker agreement with the Andersons. The agent subsequently places an offer with Melinda, the exclusive selling agent for the Lincolns, to buy their lakefront property. The offer contains provisions for the Lincolns to pay the brokerage commission, which the Lincolns agree to. Given this set of circumstances, Gerry owes the full set of fiduciary duties to

a. the Andersons.
b. the Lincolns.
c. Gerry's broker.
d. Melinda's broker.

4.9 A subagent is the agent of

a. the seller.
b. the buyer.
c. a broker who has an agency relationship with a client.
d. the client's and the customer's agents.

4.10 Which of the following is a dual agency situation?

a. Two agents share the exclusive right to represent the same client on all transactions.
b. One agent represents both sides in a transaction.
c. A selling agent from one brokerage works with a listing agent from another brokerage to complete a transaction.
d. One agent represents two sellers at the same time.

4.11 The duties of a transaction broker or facilitator include

a. preserving the confidentiality of information received from either party.
b. helping the two parties achieve their respective objectives.
c. disclosing material facts that affect the value of the property to both parties.
d. choosing to obey the instructions of one party and informing the other party of the decision.

4.12 In which of the following contact situations would a seller's agent be expected to disclose his agency relationships?

a. The agent is showing the client's property to a prospective buyer.
b. The agent tells an acquaintance at a party about the client's property.
c. The agent answers questions about the client's property for a telephone caller responding to a newspaper ad.
d. The agent is showing a potential buyer houses in a certain price range in the multiple listing book.

4.13 The essential foundation of the agency relationship consists of

a. mutual respect, compensation, and confidentiality.
b. diligence, results, and compensation.
c. service, marketing, and respect.
d. good faith, trust and confidence.

4.14 Audrey wants to take a vacation. To do so, she authorizes an agent to conduct the operations of one of her business enterprises. The kind of agency she has established is

a. limited.
b. general.
c. universal.
d. special.

4.15 A property seller empowers an agent to market and sell a property on his behalf. The kind of agency represented is

a. general.
b. special.
c. universal.
d. no agency.

4.16 Implied agency arises when

a. an agent accepts an oral listing.
b. a principal accepts an oral listing.
c. a party creates an agency relationship outside of an express agreement.
d. a principal agrees to all terms of a written listing agreement, whether express or implied.

4.17 An agency relationship may be involuntarily terminated for which of the following reasons?

a. Condemnation of the property.
b. Mutual consent.
c. Full performance.
d. Renewal of the agent's license.

4.18 A principal discloses that she would sell a property for $500,000. During the listing period, the house is listed and marketed for $530,000. No offers come in, and the listing expires. Three weeks later, the agent confides to a customer that the seller would have sold for less than the listed price. Which of the following is true?

a. The agent has violated the duty of confidentiality.
b. The agent has fulfilled all fiduciary duties, since the listing has expired.
c. The agent is violating the duties owed this customer.
d. The agent has created a dual agency situation with the customer.

4.19 A principal instructs an agent to market a property only to families on the west side of the university campus. The agent refuses to comply. In this case,

a. the agent has violated fiduciary duty.
b. the agent has not violated fiduciary duty.
c. the agent is liable for breaching the listing terms.
d. the agent should obey the instruction to salvage the listing.

4.20 An owner's agent is showing a buyer a residential property for sale. The buyer notices water stains on the foundation walls and floor, and informs the agent. The appropriate course of action for the agent is to

a. immediately contract to paint the ceiling.
b. immediately contract to repair the roof.
c. suggest the buyer make a lower-price offer.
d. inform the seller.

4.21 The meaning and salient characteristics of the agency relationship should be disclosed to the client

a. prior to completing a listing agreement.
b. prior to or upon completion of an offer.
c. upon the initial contact with the person.
d. prior to showing properties.

4.22 When must a listing agent disclose his or her agency relationship to prospective tenants or buyers?

a. Immediately prior to the initial contact.
b. Upon initial contact.
c. Whenever substantive communication is made beyond casual conversation.
d. Immediately following any offer executed by the customer.

4.23 A buyer agent or tenant representative should disclose his or her agency relationship to the owner's agent

a. immediately prior to the initial contact.
b. upon initial contact.
c. immediately prior to substantive contact.
d. immediately following any offer executed by the landlord.

4.24 An agent is operating as a disclosed dual agent on a transaction. In this case, the agent

a. may not represent one party's interests to the detriment of the other.
b. must operate without a listing agreement.
c. must be obedient and loyal to both parties.
d. must require that the principals refrain from disclosing any material facts to him.

4.25 An agent informs a buyer that a provision in a contract is very commonplace. After explaining the clause, the agent assures the buyer that the clause does not mean anything significant. If something goes wrong with the transaction, the agent could be liable for

a. violating duties owed a customer.
b. misinterpreting the clause.
c. intentional misrepresentation.
d. practicing law without a license.

4.26 When a broker enters into a listing agreement, the broker has agreed to accept which of the following?

a. Fiduciary and contractual obligations with the client.
b. Fiduciary relationships with client and customer.
c. Contractual obligations with cooperating brokers.
d. Fiduciary obligations with the customer.

4.27 The degree of authority granted by a residential brokerage listing agreement generally allows the agent to

a. create contractual obligations for the client.
b. negotiate the selling price between client and customer.
c. hire inspectors, and other individuals to prepare the property for marketing.
d. market, sell and show the property.

4.28 A salesperson, without an oral or written listing agreement, brings potential buyers to the seller. The seller says, "You can bring me buyers if you want, but I'm not paying you a commission." The salesperson then continues to direct buyers to the property. Which of the following is true about this situation?

a. There is no agency relationship, and therefore the seller will owe no commission if one of the salesperson's buyers buys the property.
b. An implied agency may have been created, with obligations to perform for both seller and agent.
c. The seller and agent have an illegal, undisclosed agency relationship.
d. The agent has an open exclusive agency listing with no commission agreement, and therefore owes no fiduciary duties to the seller.

4.29 An agent enters into a listing agreement with a homeseller, but then becomes too busy to professionally fulfill the terms of the agreement. To solve the dilemma, the agent assigns the agreement to another licensee in the office. Which of the following is true about this situation?

a. The agent cannot assign the listing agreement.
b. The new listing agent acquires the full set of fiduciary duties owed to the client.
c. The new broker has to split any commission that results with the assigning broker.
d. The original broker has to disclose the assignment to the seller.

4.30 From an agent's point of view, the most desirable form of listing agreement is a(n)

a. exclusive agency.
b. exclusive right to sell.
c. open listing.
d. net listing.

4.31 What is a multiple listing?

a. A listing shared by a listing agent and a selling agent.
b. A listing that a listing agent delegates to a subagent.
c. A listing that is entered in a multiple listing service.
d. A listing that authorizes a listing agent to market more than one property for a seller.

4.32 Which of the following conditions is necessary for a customer to qualify as "ready, willing, and able" in the context of a commissionable transaction?

a. The customer's offer must be accepted.
b. The customer must be legally competent to undertake the transaction.
c. The customer must have a commitment from a lender.
d. The customer must have no business relationship with the agent.

4.33 Although a listing broker may delegate listing tasks to an employed licensee, the broker may not delegate the authority to

a. obtain and distribute compensation.
b. provide cooperating brokers with information about the property.
c. advertise the property.
d. inspect the property for hazardous substances.

4.34 Agent Peter has an open listing with Frank. Paul is Peter's broker. Agent Perry's customer buys Frank's house. Patrick has a commission agreement with Frank. Who is most likely to be compensated in this scenario?

a. Peter, since he has a written listing agreement.
b. Paul, since he is Peter's broker
c. Perry, since he found the customer.
d. Patrick, since he has a commission agreement.

4.35 If an agent has an exclusive listing to sell a property, and the property is then taken by eminent domain, what is the status of the listing?

a. The seller's obligations under the listing are assigned to the agency that takes the property.
b. It becomes a voidable contract.
c. The commission clause of the agreement is canceled.
d. It may be terminated against the agent's will.

4.36 A broker obtains an exclusive listing to sell a house, but after two months, he abandons the listing because the seller is too demanding and hot-tempered. What can the seller do in this situation?

a. Have the licensee's license revoked for negligence.
b. Sue the broker for money damages.
c. Sign a listing agreement with another broker and force the first broker to pay the commission.
d. Force the broker to perform the contract without compensation.

4.37 An owner agrees to pay a broker for procuring a tenant unless it is the owner who finds the tenant. This is an example of a(n)

a. exclusive right-to sell agreement.
b. exclusive agency agreement.
c. open listing.
d. net listing.

4.38 A landlord promises to compensate a broker for procuring a tenant, provided the broker is the procuring cause. This is an example of a(n)

a. exclusive right-to rent agreement.
b. exclusive agency agreement.
c. open rental listing.
d. net lease listing.

4.39 A property owner agrees to pay a broker an open-ended commission as the difference between the sale price and a net amount, provided the owner receives a minimum amount of proceeds from the sale at closing. This is an example of a(n)

a. exclusive right-to sell agreement.
b. exclusive agency agreement.
c. open listing.
d. net listing.

4.40 In the context of agency law, the legal difference between an owner representation agreement and a buyer representation agreement is

a. the client.
b. the commission amount.
c. fiduciary duties.
d. regulatory approvals.

4.41 A multiple listing authorization gives a broker what authority?

a. To list the owner's property in a multiple listing service.
b. To sell several properties for the owner at once.
c. To represent both seller and buyer, if necessary, in selling the property.
d. To delegate the listing responsibilities to other agents.

4.42 Which of the following relationships characterizes a designated agency relationship?

a. A broker assign a preferred subagent from other firms to represent each party.
b. There is no such duty as maintaining confidentiality.
c. The broker primarily represents the seller.
d. The broker assigns who is to represent the buyer and seller.

Test 5: Brokerage Business; Sale Contracts

5.1 Which of the following business entities is generally prohibited from brokering real estate?

a. Sole proprietorship.
b. Partnership.
c. Corporation for profit.
d. Non-profit corporation.

5.2 A joint venture may generally broker real estate if the co-venturers

a. form a business trust.
b. form a co-operative association.
c. are properly licensed.
d. are limited partners.

5.3 A licensed salesperson may work only for

a. a client who has signed a listing agreement with a licensed broker.
b. a single employing broker who has an active broker's license.
c. a client who has signed an authorization agreement with a licensed salesperson.
d. an employer who has an active or inactive broker's license.

5.4 Which of the following activities is a licensed salesperson allowed to engage in?

a. Accept a listing that is in an associate's name.
b. Accept a commission directly from the MLS.
c. Offer a property for lease on behalf of the employing broker.
d. Sign a contract with a management company on behalf of a client.

5.5 If a salesperson has worked on a completed transaction that involved a listing agent, a selling agent, and several subagents for each of these, from whom will the salesperson receive any compensation that is due?

a. The listing agent.
b. The selling agent.
c. The seller.
d. The employing broker.

5.6 A property has sold for $380,000. The listing agreement calls for a commission of 6.5%. The listing broker and seller have agreed the listing broker will share the commission equally with the buyer broker. What will the listing agent receive if the agent is scheduled to get a 40% share?

a. $4,445.
b. $3,556.
c. $2,667.
d. $4,940.

5.7 A real estate salesperson finds a buyer to a For Sale By Owner property. The home sells for $245,000, and the seller agrees to pay a commission of 3%. The salesperson is on a 65% commission schedule with her broker, who pays her 65% minus office expenses of $500. How much will the salesperson receive from this transaction?

a. $4,778.
b. $4,452.
c. $4,278.
d. $3,175.

5.8 A salesperson makes a listing presentation to a homeseller and obtains a signed listing agreement. The first thing the salesperson must now do is

a. make a final pricing determination for the property.
b. negotiate the commission with the client.
c. complete the signing of the listing.
d. explain the agency relationship to the client.

5.9 Juan shows a customer a property that is listed by another brokerage firm. He obtains an offer that is $15,000 less than the listing price. How should Juan deal with this offer?

a. Advise the buyer that the offer will be rejected.
b. Present the offer to the seller at the earliest possible moment.
c. Ask the listing broker to lower the listing price.
d. Counter the offer.

5.10 A broker receives an earnest money deposit from a buyer and signs the check over to the listing agent as a partial commission advance. What is wrong with this procedure?

a. Nothing, provided the deposit clears the bank and doesn't bounce.
b. The broker and the agent are guilty of price fixing.
c. The broker has illegally converted security funds for business use.
d. The agent may not be able to return the advance if the transaction falls through.

5.11 Under what circumstance may a property listed for sale with a brokerage be advertised without identifying the broker?

a. When the salesperson is an out-of-state licensee.
b. When the ad is restricted to the brokerage's website.
c. When the advertisement is a silent ad.
d. Never.

5.12 Competing brokers in a county seat agree on a standard commission rate for principals within the county. This is a possible violation of

a. fair trade and anti-trust laws.
b. the Statute of Frauds.
c. contract law.
d. the Uniform Commercial Code.

5.13 What is co-brokerage?

a. An owner agent and a buyer agent combine efforts to complete a sale.
b. Outside brokers assist a listing agent in procuring a buyer.
c. An owner or buyer lists with several brokers to complete a transaction.
d. Agents from a single agency cooperate to generate listings for the broker.

5.14 Which of the following may associate his or her name or title with the term "Realtor®"?

a. Any active or inactive broker in the country.
b. Any duly licensed, active agent or broker.
c. Any member in good standing in a properly chartered real estate trade organization.
d. Only members of the National Association of Realtors®.

5.15 Real estate sales agents are legally authorized to

a. represent their employing broker in procuring clients and customers.
b. act directly on a client's behalf to discharge the broker's listing responsibilities.
c. negotiate and execute contracts for sale on behalf of the client.
d. take on the listing responsibilities for other listings in MLS.

5.16 How does the position of an independent contractor licensee (IC) differ from that of an employee licensee?

a. The IC is responsible for his or her own taxes; the broker does not withhold.
b. The IC must obtain his or her own training; it is not provided by the broker.
c. The employee is not entitled to company benefits.
d. The IC must abide by all office meeting schedules.

5.17 A salesperson's commission rate and structure is established by

a. state regulation.
b. competitive conditions.
c. agreement with other brokers in the market.
d. negotiations with the client.

5.18 In obtaining offers from a buyer, an agent must be careful to

a. pursue only those offers which are at or near the listed price.
b. balance the owner's price expectations with the buyer's opinion of value.
c. avoid disclosing what price the owner will accept.
d. avoid completing offers that are beneath market value.

5.19 Commingling is the practice of

a. blending escrow funds on a number of properties in one escrow account.
b. mixing socially with prospects at open houses or other marketing functions.
c. allocating commission funds from a transaction for use in the agency's business.
d. mixing escrow funds with the broker's operating funds.

5.20 Three leading agencies charge identical commission rates for brokering office properties in Phoenix. Based on this information alone, which of the following is true?

a. There is insufficient evidence of anything other than a normal business practice.
b. The brokers have engaged in legal collusion.
c. The brokers have allocated the Phoenix market.
d. The brokers have illegally fixed prices.

5.21 A real estate sale contract is an executory contract until

a. the completed sale transaction is recorded.
b. the buyer and seller have agreed to all provisions and have signed the contract.
c. all the obligations and promises are performed and the transaction is closed.
d. the loan has been approved, the title insurance has been obtained, and the closing date is set.

5.22 In assisting a buyer or seller to complete an offer to purchase, what should an agent do to reduce the risk of committing an unauthorized practice of law?

a. Use a standard contract promulgated by a state agency or a real estate board.
b. Observe ethical standards promulgated by real estate trade organizations.
c. Offer legal advice only on points of the contract that the agent is absolutely certain about.
d. Write contract terms that are fair to both buyer and seller.

5.23 To be enforceable, a contract for the conveyance of real estate must

a. be acknowledged by witnesses.
b. be written.
c. be recorded.
d. have an expiration date.

5.24 A buyer makes an offer to purchase a house, and the seller accepts the offer. However, before the salesperson can inform the buyer of the seller's decision, the buyer delivers a written notice that she is opting out and cancelling the agreement. At this point, which of the following is true?

a. The contract has been legitimately cancelled and is null and void.
b. The seller must give the buyer an opportunity to make a new offer.
c. The buyer must perform under the terms of the contract
d. The seller must notify the buyer in writing that the buyer is in default.

5.25 Which of the following is an essential element of a valid contract for the sale of real estate?

a. A valid blank form that the contract is written on.
b. A habitable property.
c. An offer and acceptance.
d. A marketable title.

5.26 What kind of interest does the buyer acquire once a real estate sale contract is signed by the principal parties?

a. Legal title.
b. Lienholder interest.
c. Reversionary interest.
d. Equitable title.

5.27 A contingency in a sale contract is

a. a promise by buyer or seller to perform a specific action.
b. a condition that, if unmet, renders the contract unenforceable.
c. one of several alternative actions that buyer or seller may take to satisfy contract requirements.
d. an optional, unilateral action that either party may take at the request of the other party.

5.28 A clause in a sale contract stipulates that the seller must provide evidence that the property is free of active termite infestation. On the day of closing, the buyer learns that inspection service did not provide the required written documentation. The buyer then proceeds to declare that the sale is off. Which of the following is true of this situation?

a. The seller can sue for specific performance.
b. The buyer will be in default, and liable for damages, if he does not complete the transaction.
c. The buyer may be able to have the contract canceled.
d. The contract is automatically void.

5.29 A buyer signs an earnest money agreement and gives it to the broker who showed her the property she is buying. After leaving the broker's office, she reconsiders and decides she prefers a different property. How long does she have to take back her offer?

a. Until the seller communicates acceptance of the offer.
b. Until the earnest money deposit check is cashed.
c. She can take it back at any time, but must forfeit the earnest money.
d. She cannot take it back until after the expiration date of the offer.

5.30 On Wednesday, Fred offers to sell his property to Jack for $275,000, with the offer to remain open until 5 p.m. the next day. On Thursday morning, Sally offers Fred $280,000 for the property and Fred accepts. At 1 p.m. on Thursday afternoon, Jack accepts. Which of the following is true of this situation?

a. The acceptance by Sally creates a contract and terminates Fred's offer to Jack.
b. Fred has entered into contracts with both Jack and Sally to sell the same property.
c. Fred's acceptance of Sally's offer is invalidated by Jack's acceptance, because Fred's offer to Jack was made prior to Sally's offer to Fred.
d. No contract has been created because it is impossible to have two valid sale contracts for the same property.

5.31 Among the items that normally must be disclosed in a sale contract or its addenda is/are the

a. buyer's financial capability.
b. buyer's source of funds for the down payment.
c. seller's acceptable price range.
d. agency relationships and property condition.

5.32 To create an enforceable option-to-buy contract, there must be an exchange of

a. a promise to sell and a promise to buy.
b. valuable consideration and a right to buy.
c. valuable consideration and a promise to buy.
d. a down payment and a post-dated contract for sale.

5.33 Mary Carboy buys a house from Jim Schmidt and at the same time obtains an option to purchase the adjoining vacant lot for $10,000 within one year. A few months later, Carboy informs Schmidt that she is ready to exercise her option, but finds that Schmidt has received an offer of $12,000 from another party. Schmidt states that he will accept the offer unless Carboy is willing to match the $12,000 offer. Which of the following is true of this situation?

a. Schmidt must sell to Carboy for $10,000.
b. Carboy must pay $12,000 or lose the property.
c. Schmidt may sell to Carboy or the other party, but the price cannot exceed $10,000.
d. If the other party delivers payment before Carboy does, the option is canceled.

5.34 Which of the following is true regarding the assignability of an option?

a. It is assignable only if the contract specifically allows assignment.
b. It is never assignable.
c. It is assignable only if the option is exercised.
d. It is always assignable unless the contract prohibits assignment.

5.35 Which of the following is true of a contract for deed transaction?

a. At the end of the contract period, the vendee receives equitable title, provided all required periodic payments have been made.
b. The vendee has no right to possess or occupy the property during the contract period.
c. At the end of the contract period, the vendor conveys legal title, provided the vendee has fulfilled all obligations.
d. The vendor may cancel the contract at any time before the final payment has been received.

5.36 Several buyers are competing for the last available home in a desirable new subdivision. One buyer calls the owner-developer directly on the phone and offers $20,000 over and above the listed price. The developer accepts the offer. At this point,

a. the parties have a valid, enforceable sale contract on the home.
b. the parties have completed a verbal, executory contract.
c. the parties may not cancel their contract.
d. the developer could not entertain other offers on the property.

5.37 An owner completes a sales contract on her property with a buyer. Before closing, the seller runs into financial trouble and assigns the contract to her principal creditor. The buyer cries foul, fearing the property will be lost. Which of the following is true?

a. The buyer can sue the assignee to disallow the illegal assignment.
b. The buyer can take legal action against the assignor.
c. The assignor has completed a legal action.
d. The sale contract is nullified.

5.38. A due-on-sale clause in a sale contract puts parties on notice that

a. the full price of the property is due to the seller at closing.
b. any loans surviving closing become immediately payable.
c. all of the seller's debts must be retired before or upon closing.
d. any conveyance may trigger an acceleration of any loans secured by the property.

5.39 A tenant has an option-to-purchase agreement with the landlord that expires on June 30. On July 1, the tenant frantically calls the landlord to exercise the option, offering the apology that she was busy with a death in the family. Which of the following is true?

a. Since options contain grace periods, the landlord must sell.
b. The tenant loses the right to buy, but can claim the money paid for the option from the landlord.
c. The landlord does not have to sell, but must renew the option.
d. The option is expired, and the tenant has no rightful claim to money paid for the option.

5.40 Two parties enter into a contract for deed agreement. In this form of agreement,

a. title is conveyed to the buyer, but the seller retains possession for a stipulated time period.
b. the buyer contracts to pay all cash at closing in exchange for the deed.
c. the seller retains legal title while the buyer makes partial payments until the contract is fully executed.
d. the buyer immediately acquires legal title and takes possession.

5.41 The federal law that produced the Do-Not-Call list and related protections is referred to as the

a. Solicitation Regulation Act.
b. Telemarketing Prohibition Act.
c. CAN-SPAM Act.
d. Telephone Consumer Protection Act

5.42 New federal regulation in advertising requires email advertisers to give recipients an option to discontinue receiving emails from such advertiser. This legislation is called

a. the CAN-SPAM Act.
b. the Truth-in-Advertising Act
c. the Telephone Consumer Protection Act
d. the Email Advertising Prohibition Act, or EAPA.

5.43 Which of the following is NOT a trust fund violation?

a. Using operating funds to reimburse a tenant's lease deposit if spent by the broker.
b. Keeping enough operating funds in a trust account to cover bank fees.
c. Depositing trust funds in an operating account.
d. Returning trust funds to a buyer if approved by all parties.

5.44 In the village of Bobcat Heights, a group of brokers in the MLS mutually agree to not show broker Nguyen's listings. This would be considered a violation of

a. fair trade practices.
b. redlining.
c. housing discrimination.
d. sandbagging.

Test 6: Economics; Appraisal

6.1 If the price of an item is increasing, one can usually assume that

a. demand for the item is decreasing in relation to supply of the item.
b. demand for the item is increasing in relation to supply of the item.
c. supply of the item is increasing.
d. demand for the item and supply of the item are increasing.

6.2 When the market for an item has achieved market equilibrium, which of the following statements is true?

a. New suppliers will enter the market and drive the price down.
b. Demand will slowly taper off, driving the price down.
c. Unmet demand for the item is directed toward demand for some other item.
d. Supply and demand are equal, and price and value are equal.

6.3 As an economic product, real estate is distinguished by

a. its homogeneity.
b. its variety.
c. the uniqueness of every parcel.
d. its ability to appreciate in value.

6.4 The city of Stevensville has declared a moratorium on new construction. If demand is increasing, what will be the likely effect on real estate prices in the area?

a. Prices level off.
b. Prices continue to follow the trend that preceded the moratorium.
c. Prices fall.
d. Prices rise.

6.5 If Okapi, Inc., a company that markets its sports clothing worldwide, moves into Stevensville and hires 100 employees, it is reasonable to expect that the town will experience

a. an immediate rise in the demand for industrial real estate, but no other changes in the real estate market.
b. an increase in demand for all types of real estate.
c. a housing boom, but no other changes in the real estate market.
d. an immediate increase in the prices for industrial and office real estate, but no impact on the residential market.

6.6 What is "absorption?"

a. The amount of new space that is added to available space over a period of time.
b. The number of houses that are built over a period of time.
c. The amount of space that is occupied at any given time.
d. The number of available units that become occupied over a period of time.

6.7 When vacancies are declining in a real estate market, it is common for the market to experience

a. rising prices.
b. falling prices.
c. falling construction activity.
d. falling absorption.

6.8 The price for any product is a function of four fundamental determinants of value. These are

a. durability, feasibility, mobility, and location.
b. desire, utility, scarcity, and purchasing power.
c. popularity, recognizability, promotion, and rebate.
d. fungibility, costs, convenience, and uniqueness.

6.9 A town is rapidly growing, but all the buildable vacant lots in the most desirable area have already been occupied. In this case, it is likely that the price of existing homes in that area

a. will stabilize, since the population must stabilize.
b. will increase.
c. will decline, since no further building can take place.
d. will not show any predictable movement.

6.10 If there is a significant undersupply of homes in a market, construction will tend to increase. This is an example of

a. supply outstripping demand.
b. demand outstripping value.
c. consumer optimism.
d. the market tending toward equilibrium.

6.11 If commercial real estate rental prices are falling in a market, it is likely that

a. demand has outstripped supply of space.
b. the market is in equilibrium.
c. the market is over-supplied.
d. employment is increasing.

6.12 A construction boom in a market is an indication that prices

a. have been increasing.
b. have been declining.
c. have been in equilibrium.
d. have exceeded supply.

6.13 Why is real estate traditionally considered a relatively illiquid economic product?

a. Its physical form is fixed.
b. Real estate is defined as land, not water.
c. It is often difficult to convert to cash.
d. It cannot be moved.

6.14 What does "base employment" refer to in the context of real estate demand?

a. The lowest category of employment in terms of wages and desirability
b. The number of persons employed in base industries in an area
c. The number of persons employed on military bases in an area
d. The labor pool available for employment in all industries in an area

6.15 What is "vacancy" in real estate market economics?

a. A property that has no owner-occupant
b. The total number of properties of a certain type that are on the market at a given time
c. The absence of certain types of users in a given market area
d. The total existing space of a certain type that is unoccupied at a given time

6.16 A moratorium on new construction is an example of

a. local government influencing the real estate market, regardless of demand.
b. the natural result of demand exceeding supply in a local market.
c. government promotion of the free market concept in the local real estate market.
d. a government policy that aims to restrain a trend of rising prices in the local real estate market.

6.17 Of the following potential influences on a local real estate market, which one would be considered local, rather than regional, national, or global?

a. Changes in money supply
b. Federal Reserve interest rates
c. In- and out-migrations of major employers
d. Trade imbalances with foreign trading partners

6.18 There is a lot of new construction going on in the town of Florence. Which of the following would most likely be the immediate effect on the real estate market?

a. Demand increases and prices rise.
b. Vacancy rises and prices fall.
c. Absorption and vacancy decrease.
d. Supply decreases relative to demand.

6.19 What kind of real estate users are most concerned with neighborhood quality, access to services, property amenities, and quality of life in their demand for real estate?

a. Retail
b. Office
c. Industrial
d. Residential

6.20 One distinguishing feature of real estate as an economic product is

a. its easy convertibility to cash.
b. its quick response to changes in supply-demand balance.
c. its susceptibility to swings in the local economy.
d. the easy substitutability of one item for another.

6.21 Bill Parsons paid $450,000 for a house to operate as a rental property, figuring that he could rent it out at a rate of $2,700 a month. In paying a price based on the property's ability to generate a desired future income, Parsons was motivated by the economic principle known as

a. substitution.
b. anticipation.
c. supply and demand.
d. utility.

6.22 Which of the following situations illustrates the principle of contribution?

a. A homebuyer makes a down payment of 20% instead of the 10% the lender requires.
b. A homeowner adds a third bathroom to a house and thereby increases the appraised value by $10,000.
c. The appraised value of a house goes up by $20,000 over a two-year period because of the prices recently paid for other houses in the neighborhood.
d. Because of a decline in mortgage interest rates, a homeowner in a certain market is able to list her house at a higher price.

6.23 When a property owner combines two adjacent properties to create a single property with a higher value than the sum of the values of the two separate properties, the applicable principle of value is called

a. assemblage.
b. accretion.
c. progression.
d. subdivision.

6.24 What is the difference between market value and market price, if any?

a. There is no difference.
b. Market value is a broker's estimate; market price is a precise number derived by a licensed appraiser.
c. Market value is an average price derived from comparable sales; market price is a price based on the cost of creating the property.
d. Market value is an estimate; market price is the price at which a property sold.

6.25 Which of the following is a valid requirement for defensibly characterizing a property's living area?

a. Countable living area must be attached to the main house.
b. Closets must be excluded from gross living area.
c. The property must be finished, i.e., have completed studwork and sub-flooring.
d. Enclosed porches and stairways cannot be counted as living area.

6.26 How is a property's gross living area generally measured?

a. From the lot's area, minus the area of improved buildings
b. From the exterior walls, above grade, excluding open areas
c. By measuring the interior rooms
d. By measuring area of all enclosed rooms, minus the basement and attic

6.27 Which of the following statements properly describes the central concept of the sales comparison approach?

a. Find the median price of recently sold comparable properties and add or subtract dollar amounts in the subject property to account for competitive differences.
b. Make dollar adjustments to the sale prices of comparable properties to account for competitive differences with the subject.
c. Find at least three comparable properties that are currently for sale and make dollar adjustments to the listing prices to account for competitive differences with the subject.
d. Apply an appreciation factor to the price at which the subject property most recently sold and make dollar adjustments to account for competitive differences with comparable properties currently for sale.

6.28 One of the strengths of the sales comparison approach is that it

a. takes into account the subject property's investment value.
b. reveals the profit margin of the builder or developer of the subject property.
c. discovers the underlying value of the subject property apart from the influence of competing properties.
d. takes into account the competitive value of specific amenities of the subject property.

6.29 In making dollar adjustments in the sales comparison approach, the appraiser

a. adds value to a comparable that is inferior to the subject property.
b. adds value to the subject property if it is inferior to a comparable.
c. subtracts value from a comparable that is inferior to the subject property.
d. subtracts value from the subject property if it is inferior to a comparable.

6.30 The best comparable property for use in the sales comparison approach is the one that

a. requires the most and largest adjustments.
b. requires the fewest and smallest adjustments.
c. sold most recently at the highest price.
d. is located closest to the subject property.

6.31 A house is being appraised using the sales comparison approach. The house has three bedrooms, two bathrooms, and a patio. The appraiser selects a comparable house that has three bedrooms, 3 bathrooms, and no patio. The comparable house just sold for $400,000. A bath is valued at $7,000, and a patio at $2,000. Assuming all else is equal, what is the adjusted value of the comparable?

a. $402,000.
b. $407,000.
c. $395,000.
d. $405,000.

6.32 Which of the following statements properly describes the central methodology of the cost approach to appraisal?

a. Apply a depreciation factor to the reported actual cost of acquiring and improving the subject property.
b. Estimate the cost of building the improvements on the subject property.
c. Estimate the land value and add to this the actual cost of the improvements adjusted for competitive differences with similar properties.
d. Add the estimated land value and cost of improvements and subtract the accrued depreciation of the improvements.

6.33 One of the strengths of the cost approach is that it

a. takes into account the amount of money required to develop a similar property.
b. is very accurate for a property with new improvements that represent the highest and best use.
c. results in an actual price in dollars instead of an estimated value.
d. reveals the owner's return on money invested in the cost of development.

6.34 The principle underlying depreciation from physical deterioration is that

a. eventually, a property loses all of its value.
b. a property loses a portion of its value each year because of economic obsolescence.
c. a property loses the same increment of value each year over the economic life of the property.
d. the value lost to depreciation is incurable.

6.35 A property is being appraised by the cost approach. The appraiser estimates that the land is worth $150,000 and the replacement cost of the improvements is $475,000. Total depreciation from all causes is $50,000. What is the indicated value of the property?

a. $675,000.
b. $650,000.
c. $625,000.
d. $575,000.

6.36 Which of the following statements properly describes how to apply the income capitalization approach to appraisal?

a. Apply a rate of return to the price paid for an income property.
b. Divide the income a property generates by a rate of return.
c. Estimate the amount of income a property must generate to return the capital amount invested in it.
d. Estimate the rate of return a property owner receives from income generated by the property.

6.37 A strength of the income capitalization approach is that it

a. uses a rate of return that is required for all potential purchasers in a market.
b. yields an accurate projection of investment income.
c. uses a method that is also used by investors to determine how much they should pay for an investment property.
d. can be used with any type of property in any market.

6.38 A property is being appraised using the income capitalization approach. Annually, it has an estimated gross income of $60,000, vacancy and credit losses of $3,000, and operating expenses of $20,000. Using a capitalization rate of ten percent, what is the indicated value (to the nearest $1,000)?

a. $370,000.
b. $400,000.
c. $570,000.
d. $600,000.

6.39 An apartment building that sold for $450,000 had monthly gross rent receipts of $3,000. What is its monthly gross rent multiplier?

a. 12.5
b. .01.
c. .08.
d. 150.

6.40 A rental house has monthly gross income of $2,400. A suitable gross income multiplier derived from market data is 14.1. What estimated sale price (to the nearest $1,000) is indicated?

a. $338,000.
b. $204,000.
c. $406,000.
d. $346,000.

6.41 A certified appraiser is one who has received certification by

a. a licensed real estate school.
b. the Appraisal Institute.
c. the state in which the appraiser operates.
d. the Appraisal Review Board.

6.42 The act that required federally-related appraisals to be conducted by a certified appraiser is known as

a. The Financial Institutions Reform, Recovery and Enforcement Act (FIRREA).
b. The Uniform Standards of Professional Appraisal Practice Act (USPAPA).
c. The Appraisal Foundation Authorization and Reform Act (AFAR).
d. The Federal Institution for Regulation and Enforcement of Appraisal Act (FIREAA).

6.43 As a component of real estate value, the principle of substitution states that

a. if two similar properties are for sale, a buyer will purchase the cheaper of the two.
b. if one of two adjacent homes is more valuable, the price of the other home will tend to rise.
c. if too many properties are built in a market, the prices will tend to go down.
d. people will readily move to another home if it is of equal value.

6.44 Highest and best use of a property is that use which

a. is physically and financially feasible, legal, and the most productive.
b. is legal, feasible, and deemed the most appropriate by zoning authorities.
c. entails the largest building that zoning ordinances will allow developers to erect.
d. conforms to other properties in the area.

6.45 Lynne just bought a house. She paid $375,000, for it, even though it had been listed at $390,000. An adjoining property owner, Ken, had tried to buy the property for $370,000, but had been refused. He now offers Lynne $380,000 for the house. Lynne is interested, so she hires an appraiser. The appraiser returns an estimate of value of $400,000. Which of these numbers can be called the market value?

a. $375,000.
b. $380,000.
c. $390,000.
d. $400,000.

6.46 A notable weakness of the sales comparison approach to value is that

a. there may be no recent sale price data in the market.
b. the approach is not based on the principle of substitution.
c. the approach is only accurate with unique, special purpose properties.
d. sale prices cannot be compared, since all real estate is different.

6.47 In the market data approach, an appraiser

a. chooses nearby comparables, adjusts the subject for differences, and estimates the value.
b. gathers relevant price data, applies the data to the subject, and estimates the value.
c. selects comparable properties, adjusts the comparables, and estimates the value.
d. identifies the price previously paid, applies an appreciation rate, and estimates the value.

6.48 In the sales comparison approach, an adjustment is warranted if

a. the buyer obtains conventional financing for the property.
b. the seller offers below-market seller financing.
c. a comparable is located in another, albeit similar neighborhood.
d. one property has a hip roof and the other has a gabled roof.

6.49 To complete the sales comparison approach, the appraiser

a. averages the comparable values.
b. weights the comparables.
c. identifies the subject's value as that of the middle value of the comparables.
d. identifies the subject's value as that of the nearest comparable.

6.50 One weakness of the cost approach for appraising market value is that

a. builders may not pay market value for materials or labor.
b. market value is not always the same as what the property cost.
c. comparables used may not have similar quality of construction.
d. new properties have inestimable costs and rates of depreciation.

6.51 The cost of constructing a functional equivalent of a subject property is known as

a. reproduction cost.
b. replacement cost.
c. restitution cost.
d. reconstruction cost.

6.52 An office building lacks fiber optic cabling to accommodate the latest communications equipment. This is an example of

a. physical deterioration.
b. economic obsolescence.
c. incurable depreciation.
d. functional obsolescence.

6.53 A home is located in a neighborhood where homeowners on the block have failed to maintain their properties. This is an example of

a. curable external obsolescence.
b. incurable economic obsolescence.
c. functional obsolescence.
d. physical deterioration.

6.54 In appraisal, loss of value in a property from any cause is referred to as

a. deterioration.
b. obsolescence.
c. depreciation.
d. deflation.

6.55 In the cost approach, after estimating the value of the land and the cost of the improvements, the appraiser

a. estimates depreciation, subtracts depreciation from cost, and adds back the land value.
b. subtracts deterioration from cost, estimates land depreciation, and totals the two values.
c. estimates depreciation of land and improvements and subtracts the total from original cost.
d. estimates obsolescence and subtracts from the cost of land and improvements.

6.56 Which regulatory entity/code establishes standards for an appraiser's methods, reporting methods and disclosures?

a. Financial Institutions Reform, Recovery, and Enforcement Act (FIRREA)
b. Uniform Standards of Professional Appraisal Practice (USPAP)
c. National Association of Realtors®' Code of Ethics
d. Federal Appraisal Regulation and Licensing Board.

Test 7: Finance

7.1 What is a lien-theory state?

a. A state in which a mortgagee holds legal title to a secured property.
b. A state in which a mortgagee has equitable title to a secured property.
c. A state that allows a real estate owner's creditors to record liens against the owner's property.
d. A state in which a lien is considered as a conveyance.

7.2 What is the function of a note in a mortgage or trust deed financing arrangement?

a. It is the lender's security instrument in the collateral property.
b. It is evidence of ownership of the mortgage or trust deed.
c. It contains the borrower's promise to maintain the value of the property given as collateral for a loan.
d. It is evidence of the borrower's debt to the lender.

7.3 When homebuyer Henry pledges his newly purchased home as collateral for a mortgage loan, the evidence of the pledge is the

a. trust deed or mortgage.
b. promissory note.
c. loan commitment.
d. loan receipt.

7.4 The borrower in a mortgage loan transaction is known as the

a. mortgagee.
b. mortgagor.
c. lienor.
d. trustee.

7.5 If a borrower obtains an interest-only loan of $200,000 at an annual interest rate of 6%, what is the monthly interest payment?

a. $1,200.
b. $600.
c. $500.
d. $1,000.

7.6 If a borrower's monthly interest payment on an interest-only loan at an annual interest rate of 6% is $5,000, how much was the loan amount?

a. $720,000.
b. $1,000,000.
c. $1,200,000.
d. $500,000.

7.7 A borrower of a $250,000 interest-only loan makes annual interest payments of $18,750. What interest rate is the borrower paying?

a. 7.5%.
b. .75%.
c. 3.75%.
d. 8.5%.

7.8 Maria borrows $600,000 and pays two points for the loan. How much does she pay in points?

a. $1,200.
b. $12,000.
c. $7,200.
d. It depends on the interest rate.

7.9 Which of the following is true of an amortizing loan?

a. The amount of annual interest paid is the same for every year of the loan term.
b. Part of each periodic payment is applied to repayment of the loan balance in advance and part is applied to payment of interest in arrears.
c. Except for any points that may be paid, the interest on the loan balance is usually paid in advance.
d. The interest rate is reduced each year to maintain equal payments even though the outstanding loan balance is smaller.

7.10 For a loan that is not backed by the Federal Housing Administration or Veterans Administration, and for which the borrower is making a down payment of less than 20%, the lender is likely to require the borrower to obtain

a. a subrogation agreement.
b. private mortgage insurance.
c. a letter of credit.
d. a co-signer on the note.

7.11 What is a loan-to-value ratio?

a. The percentage of a lender's portfolio that is composed of mortgage loans.
b. The ratio of borrowed principal plus total interest to the appraised value of the collateral property.
c. The ratio of a lender's return on a mortgage loan to the value of the collateral property.
d. The fraction of the appraised value of the property offered as collateral which the lender is willing to lend.

7.12 The difference between what a borrower has to pay to purchase a property and the amount a lender will lend on the property is the

a. mortgage insurance coverage amount.
b. lender's profit margin.
c. buyer's down payment.
d. origination fee.

7.13 The Equal Credit Opportunity Act prohibits a lender from

a. refusing a loan because the borrower does not match the lender's target market.
b. including income from self-employment in the borrower's qualifying income.
c. requiring both spouses to sign the loan application form.
d. refusing a loan because a borrower has a defective credit report.

7.14 A loan applicant has an annual gross income of $72,000. How much will a lender allow the applicant to pay for monthly housing expense to qualify for a loan if the lender uses an income ratio of 28%?

a. $2,160.
b. $1,680.
c. $1,068.
d. $840.

7.15 AMC Bank discovers, in considering buyer Bob's application for a mortgage loan, that Bob has borrowed the down payment from an uncle and has to repay that loan. Bob should expect that AMC Bank will

a. refuse the application.
b. adjust the applicant's debt ratio calculation and lower the loan amount.
c. increase the loan amount to enable the borrower to pay off the loan to the relative.
d. require the borrower to make payments to an escrow account for repayment of the relative's loan.

7.16 The Federal Reserve's Regulation Z applies to which loans?

a. All loans.
b. All loans secured by real estate.
c. All loans secured by a residence.
d. All loans over $25,000.

7.17 If a particular loan falls under Regulation Z's right of rescission provision,

a. the lender has the right to change the terms of the loan within a certain period.
b. the lender has the right to accelerate repayment of the loan because of a change in the borrower's credit status.
c. the borrower has the right to pay off the loan ahead of schedule with no penalty.
d. the borrower has a limited right to cancel the transaction within a certain period.

7.18 Under the Equal Credit Opportunity Act, a lender, or a real estate agent who assists a seller in qualifying a potential buyer, may not

a. tell a rejected loan applicant the reasons for the rejection.
b. ask the buyer/borrower about his/her religion or national origin.
c. ask the buyer/borrower to explain unconventional sources of income.
d. use a credit report that has not been provided to the borrower.

7.19 A conventional mortgage loan is one that is

a. backed by the Federal National Mortgage Association.
b. insured under Section 203(b) of the Federal Housing Administration loan program.
c. guaranteed by the Government National Mortgage Association.
d. not FHA-insured or VA-guaranteed.

7.20 The assumability of an FHA-insured loan is

a. unrestricted.
b. limited by when the loan was originated.
c. limited to owner-occupied properties.
d. prohibited on all existing loans under current regulations.

7.21 A VA certificate of eligibility determines

a. how long an individual served in the military.
b. the maximum loan amount an approved lender can give to veterans.
c. how much of a loan the VA will guarantee.
d. whether a lender is approved to issue VA-guaranteed loans.

7.22 A borrower obtains a 30-year, fully amortizing mortgage loan of $450,000 at 8%. What is the principal balance at the end of the loan term?

a. $36,000.
b. $450,000.
c. $4,220.
d. Zero.

7.23 Which of the following describes a purchase money mortgage financing arrangement?

a. A bank gives a buyer a senior mortgage loan that fully covers the cost of purchasing the property.
b. The buyer gives the seller a mortgage and note as part of the purchase price of the property.
c. A land trust holds title to the property while the buyer makes periodic installment payments to the seller.
d. The seller uses the purchase money obtained from the buyer's mortgage loan to repay the seller's outstanding loan balance.

7.24 A homeowner borrows money from a lender and gives the lender a mortgage on the property as collateral for the loan. The homeowner retains title to the property. This is an example of

a. intermediation.
b. forfeiture.
c. hypothecation.
d. subordination.

7.25 Which of the following correctly describes the flow of money and documents in a mortgage loan transaction?

a. The borrower gives the lender a note and a mortgage in exchange for loan funds.
b. The lender gives the borrower a mortgage and receives a note in exchange for loan funds.
c. The borrower receives a note in exchange for a mortgage from the lender.
d. The lender gives the borrower a note, loan funds and a mortgage.

7.26 In a deed of trust transaction, which of the following occurs?

a. The beneficiary conveys title to a trustee in exchange for loan funds.
b. The trustee conveys title to a beneficiary in exchange for loan funds.
c. The trustor conveys title to a trustee in exchange for loan funds from the beneficiary.
d. The trustee conveys title to a trustor in exchange for loan funds from the beneficiary.

7.27 A lender lends money to a homeowner and takes legal title to the property as collateral during the payoff period. They are in a

a. title-theory state.
b. lien-theory state.
c. state allowing land trusts.
d. state where hypothecation is illegal.

7.28 A lender who charges a rate of interest in excess of legal limits is guilty of

a. redlining.
b. usury.
c. profit-taking.
d. nothing; there are no legal limits to interest rates.

7.29 A lender is charging 2.5 points on a $300,000 loan. The borrower must therefore pay the lender an advance amount of

a. $3,600.
b. $750.
c. $7,500.
d. $6,000.

7.30 The difference between a balloon loan and an amortized loan is

a. an amortized loan is paid off over the loan period.
b. a balloon loan always has a shorter loan term.
c. an amortized loan requires interest-payments.
d. a balloon loan must be retired in five years.

7.31 A distinctive feature of a promissory note is that

a. it is not assignable.
b. it must be accompanied by a mortgage.
c. it is a negotiable instrument.
d. it may not be prepaid.

7.32 When the terms of the mortgage loan are satisfied, the mortgagee

a. may retain any overage in the escrow account.
b. may inspect the property before returning legal title.
c. may be entitled to charge the borrower a small fee to close the loan.
d. may be required to execute a release of mortgage document.

7.33 In addition to income, credit, and employment data, a mortgage lender requires additional documentation, usually including

a. an appraisal report.
b. a criminal record report.
c. a subordination agreement.
d. a default recourse waiver.

7.34 The three overriding considerations of a lender's mortgage loan decision are

a. points, interest rate, and loan term.
b. the location of the mortgaged property, the borrower's cash, and the amount of the borrower's equity.
c. the ability to re-pay, the value of the collateral, and the profitability of the loan.
d. the amount of the loan, the borrower's income, and the down payment.

7.35 The reason lenders consider the loan-to-value ratio important in underwriting is that

a. they don't want to lend borrowers any more money than necessary.
b. they want to ensure there is more than enough collateral to cover the loan amount.
c. borrowers can only afford to borrow a portion of the entire purchase price.
d. the higher the loan-to-value ratio, the more profitable the loan.

7.36 The Equal Credit Opportunity Act (ECOA) requires lenders to

a. extend equal credit to all prospective borrowers.
b. consider the income of a spouse in evaluating a family's creditworthiness.
c. discount the income of a person involved in child-rearing or child-bearing.
d. specialize in lending activity by geographical area for improved customer service.

7.37 Lenders use an income ratio in qualifying to

a. insure a borrower has the earning power to make the loan payments.
b. compare a borrower's earnings to the borrower's short-term debt.
c. identify the highest possible interest rate that the borrower can afford.
d. quantify the borrower's assets to the fullest extent.

7.38 The debt ratio formula used to qualify borrowers is

a. total debt divided by debt payments.
b. gross income divided by assets.
c. gross income divided by debts.
d. debt payments divided by gross income.

7.39 At the closing of a mortgage loan

a. the borrower pays off the note and receives clear title.
b. the lender issues a firm loan commitment.
c. the parties complete all loan origination documents and the loan is funded.
d. the borrower's loan application is complete and the file closed.

7.40 Which laws or regulations require mortgage lenders to disclose financing costs and annual percentage rate to a borrower before funding a loan?

a. The Equal Credit Opportunity Act.
b. Truth-in-Lending laws and Regulation Z.
c. The Real Estate Settlement and Procedures Act.
d. Federal Fair Housing Laws.

7.41 Which laws or regulations prevent mortgage lenders from discriminating in extending credit to potential borrowers?

a. The Equal Credit Opportunity Act.
b. Truth-in-Lending laws.
c. The Real Estate Settlement and Procedures Act.
d. Federal Fair Housing Laws.

7.42 Which laws or regulations require mortgage lenders to provide an estimate of closing costs to a borrower and forbid them to pay kickbacks for referrals?

a. The Equal Credit Opportunity Act.
b. Truth-in-Lending laws.
c. the Real Estate Settlement and Procedures Act.
d. Federal Fair Housing Laws.

7.43 Which of the following are methods used by the Federal Reserve System to regulate the money supply?

a. Selling securities, printing money, and controlling lending underwriting requirements.
b. Buying securities, changing the discount rate, and controlling banking reserves.
c. Printing money, changing interest rates, and selling T-bills.
d. Controlling the prime rate, trading securities, and purchasing loans.

7.44 How does the secondary mortgage market aid borrowers seeking a mortgage loan?

a. It cycles funds back to primary lenders so they can make more loans.
b. It issues second mortgages and sells them in the home equity market.
c. It lends funds to banks so they can make more loans.
d. It pays off defaulted loans made by primary mortgage lenders.

7.45 The major organizations operating in the secondary mortgage market are

a. Fannie Mae, Freddie Mac, and Ginnie Mae.
b. Fannie Mae, GMAC, and MGIC.
c. Freddie Mac, FHA, and VA.
d. Fannie Mae, Freddie Mac, and the Federal Reserve.

7.46 What is the role of Fannie Mae in the secondary mortgage market?

a. It guarantees FHA-backed and VA-backed loans.
b. It insures FHA-backed and VA-backed loans.
c. It purchases FHA-backed and VA-backed loans.
d. It originates FHA-backed and VA-backed loans.

7.47 What is the role of the Federal Housing Authority in the mortgage lending market?

a. It guarantees loans made by approved lenders.
b. It insures loans made by approved lenders.
c. It purchases loans made by approved lenders.
d. It originates loans made by approved lenders.

7.48 What is the role of the Veteran's Administration in the mortgage lending market?

a. It guarantees loans made by approved lenders.
b. It insures loans made by approved lenders.
c. It purchases loans made by approved lenders.
d. It originates loans made by approved lenders.

7.49 In a graduated payment mortgage loan,

a. loan funds are disbursed to the borrower on a graduated basis.
b. the interest rate periodically increases in graduated phases.
c. the loan payments gradually increase.
d. the loan payments gradually increase and the loan term gradually decreases.

7.50 In a buydown,

a. the lender lowers the interest rate on a loan in exchange for a prepayment of principal.
b. the borrower pays additional interest at the onset in order to obtain a lower interest rate.
c. the lender requires the borrower to buy down the price of the property by increasing the down payment.
d. the borrower pays the lender additional funds to buy down the term of the loan.

7.51 Steve just purchased a house for $750,000 with a $700,000 mortgage loan and $50,000 cash downpayment. Which of the following will Steve's lender most likely require in order to approve this loan?

a. A personal guarantee
b. A buydown loan as a second lien
c. Private mortgage insurance
d. Additional points

7.52 Who is the primary customer for the Federal Agricultural Mortgage Corporation, or FAMC?

a. Military veterans from farming families
b. Primary medical market lenders
c. Economically liquid farmers
d. Agribusinesses

Test 8: Investments; Taxation; Professional Practices

8.1 When an investor has to pay a lender more to finance the investment than the investment property generates in income, the investor suffers from

a. negative amortization.
b. negative leverage.
c. a reverse mortgage.
d. a debt investment.

8.2 Cost recovery is allowed as a federal tax deduction on

a. principal residences that do not have a home office.
b. income properties.
c. land.
d. commercial properties owned by the federal government.

8.3 A homeowner paid $200,000 for a house three years ago. The house sells today for $239,000. How much has the property appreciated?

a. 8.4 %.
b. 6.5 %.
c. 19.5 %.
d. 16.3 %.

8.4 The primary tax benefit in owning a non-income property such as a residence is

a. depreciation of improvements.
b. appreciation of land.
c. a deduction for costs of operating the property.
d. a deduction for mortgage interest.

8.5 A house sold for $250,000. The seller paid a brokerage commission of six percent, legal fees of $600, and had other closing costs of $1,500. What are net proceeds from the sale?

a. $235,000.
b. $234,000.
c. $233,500.
d. $232,900.

8.6 A homeowner bought a house five years ago for $450,000. Since then, the homeowner has spent $9,000 to pave the driveway and has added a central heating/air conditioning system at a cost of $12,000. What is the homeowner's adjusted basis if the house is sold today?

a. $468,000.
b. $471,000.
c. $429,000.
d. $435,000.

8.7 A homeowner sold her house and realized a net proceeds amount of $420,000. Her adjusted basis in the home was $352,000. She immediately bought another house for $400,000. What was her capital gain?

a. $20,000.
b. $48,000.
c. $68,000.
d. None.

8.8 After five years of owner-occupancy, Simon Wilson sells his principal residence for a gain of $150,000, and the next month buys another principal residence that costs more than the adjusted sale price of the old home. Which of the following is true of the treatment of the tax on gain?

a. There is no taxable gain.
b. It must be paid in the year of the sale.
c. The homeowner may choose to pay it or defer it.
d. Tax is due on the difference between the cost of the new home and adjusted basis of the old one.

8.9 Ralph Roberts buys a small office building as an investment and participates actively in the management and operation of the building. This is an example of

a. syndication.
b. equity investment.
c. direct investment.
d. illiquidity.

8.10 Elmo Gilmore owns a small retail property that he inherited from his father. There are no mortgages or interest expenses connected with the property. Elmo takes an annual cost recovery expense of $5,000. The property has a monthly gross income of $1,500 and monthly operating expenses of $500. Elmo's taxable income from this property will be taxed at a rate of 30%. What is the tax liability for the year?

a. $2,100.
b. $3,600.
c. $3,900.
d. $7,000.

8.11 All investors desire their investments to increase in value. However,

a. the degree of return is inversely related to the degree of risk.
b. the more the investor stands to gain, the greater the risk that the investor may lose.
c. investments requiring intense management have lesser returns.
d. the more liquid an investment is, the greater the chances are that the investment will not appreciate.

8.12 Two of the financial rewards that investments offer are

a. income and tax benefits.
b. negative leverage and appreciation.
c. appreciation and taxation.
d. positive leverage and prestige.

8.13 Because a real estate investment can take a long time to sell, real estate investments are considered to be

a. management intensive.
b. insensitive to marketing.
c. vulnerable to seller's markets.
d. relatively illiquid.

8.14 Compared to a stock portfolio, a real estate investment would be considered

a. a riskier investment.
b. a more management-intensive investment.
c. a shorter-term investment.
d. a more leveraged investment.

8.15 Six investors purchase a shopping center. One investor manages the tenants and another handles the marketing and leasing. Two investors manage accounting and finance, and the remaining two run the management office. This is a possible example of

a. a general partnership.
b. a limited partnership.
c. a real estate investment trust.
d. an investment conduit.

8.16 The formula for determining taxable income produced by an income property is

a. gross income minus expenses plus land and building depreciation.
b. gross income minus expenses minus land and building depreciation.
c. gross income minus building depreciation plus land depreciation.
d. gross income minus expenses minus building depreciation.

8.17 In deriving taxable income on an investment property, it is generally legal to

a. deduct principal and interest payments from income.
b. deduct principal payments from income.
c. deduct interest payments from income.
d. deduct principal and interest payments from income and capital gain.

8.18 Jake does not use any part of his principal residence as a home office. Which of the following is true of the tax treatment of this property?

a. The owner may deduct the property's interest and principal from ordinary income.
b. The owner may depreciate the property and deduct depreciation expenses from ordinary income.
c. The owner can deduct any capital gain when the property is sold.
d. The owner may be able to avoid capital gain tax when the property is sold.

8.19 An investment property seller pays $14,000 in closing costs. These costs

a. may be deducted from personal income.
b. may be deducted from the property's income.
c. may be deducted from the sale price for gains tax purposes.
d. may be deducted from the adjusted basis for gains tax purposes.

8.20 The formula for calculating capital gain tax is the taxpayer's tax bracket multiplied by

a. the sum of the beginning basis plus gain.
b. the difference between amount realized and adjusted basis.
c. the sum of net sale proceeds and capital gain.
d. the difference between net sale proceeds and capital gain.

8.21 Which of the following entities can legally levy annual real property taxes?

a. The Internal Revenue Service.
b. A utility company.
c. A tax district.
d. A court of law.

8.22 Certain classes of property owner and types of property are exempted or immune from real property taxation in many areas. The protected categories usually include

a. recreational properties.
b. properties owned by a government agency.
c. properties that comply with the Americans with Disabilities Act.
d. properties occupied by single-parent families.

8.23 What is the purpose of an equalization factor in ad valorem taxation?

a. It modifies a local tax rate to bring it into conformity with statutory tax rates.
b. It changes the assessed value of an individual property to make it reflect the assessed values of other properties in the same neighborhood.
c. It adjusts assessments in a locality to make them more consistent with an average level for the state or other higher level jurisdiction.
d. It adjusts the amount of the homestead exemption in a certain area to make it proportionally equivalent to the average homestead exemption in other areas.

8.24 A school district's tax rate is 10 mills. The school district's required revenue from real estate taxes is $20,000,000. What is the tax base of the area?

a. $20,000,000.
b. $200,000,000.
c. $2,000,000,000.
d. $200,000,000,000.

8.25 A homeowner receives a tax bill that includes an amount for the library district, taxed at $1.00 per $1,000, and the fire protection district, taxed at $2.00 per $1,000. How much does the taxpayer have to pay for these two items if the property's taxable value is $441,000?

a. $4,701.
b. $471.
c. $4,230.
d. $1,323.

8.26 A town is replacing a sidewalk that serves five homes. The length of the sidewalk is 200 feet. Mary's property has 38 feet of front footage. If the cost of the project to be paid by a special assessment is $30,000, what will Mary's assessment be?

a. $6,000.
b. $5,700.
c. $789.
d. $1,579.

8.27 What is a tax deed?

a. A conveyance instrument for a property that is sold to enforce a tax lien.
b. A document recorded in title records showing that property taxes have been paid.
c. A notice to a homeowner that a tax lien has been entered against the property.
d. A document that gives a municipal authority the power to collect an individual tax bill.

8.28 If a property owner has the right to redeem his or her property after a tax sale, the owner has

a. a legal right of rescission.
b. an equitable right to acquire title.
c. a right of homestead exclusion.
d. a statutory right of redemption.

8.29 The formula for deriving a municipal jurisdiction's ad valorem tax base is

a. the jurisdiction's annual budget times the tax rate.
b. the total of all assessed values of properties minus exemptions.
c. the total amount of ad valorem taxes required by the budget.
d. the municipality's budget multiplied times the millage rate.

8.30 A homeowner's total tax bill is derived by

a. dividing the tax requirement by the tax base.
b. multiplying each district's tax rate times the market value of the property.
c. multiplying each district's tax rate times the taxable value of the property.
d. averaging the tax rate for each tax district, and multiplying the average tax rate times the assessed value.

8.31 The fair housing law that first protected people against discrimination in housing based on race was the

a. Civil Rights Act of 1866.
b. Civil Rights Act of 1968.
c. Executive Order 11063 of 1962.
d. Title VIII amendment to the Fair Housing Act.

8.32 The classes protected against discrimination by the Fair Housing Act of 1968 are

a. race only.
b. religion and gender only.
c. race, color, religion, and national origin.
d. age and gender only.

8.33 An agent is committing an act of discriminatory advertising by doing which of the following?

a. Telling prospective buyers about the positive and negative aspects of a certain neighborhood.
b. Telling a prospective seller that now would be a good time to put a property on the market.
c. Advertising a property as available to individuals of a particular race.
d. Telling a prospective buyer that the agent is too busy to show the buyer properties personally on a given day.

8.34 Which of the following is an example of blockbusting?

a. An agent shows a minority home buyer properties located in a neighborhood where there are no other minority homeowners.
b. An agent persuades a minority home buyer to avoid looking in a neighborhood where there are no minority homeowners.
c. An agent persuades a family to put their house on the market because ethnic minority families are beginning to move into the neighborhood.
d. An agent persuades a minority home buyer to buy a property located in an area where most of the homeowners belong to minority groups.

8.35 The practice of redlining is specifically prohibited by

a. The Home Mortgage Disclosure Act.
b. The Real Estate Settlement Procedures Act.
c. The Civil Rights Act of 1866.
d. The Americans with Disabilities Act.

8.36 Title VIII of the Civil Rights Act of 1968 applies to the sale of

a. all single-family residences.
b. all privately owned single-family residences.
c. privately owned single-family residences listed with a broker.
d. privately owned single-family residences for sale by owner.

8.37 A broker signs a listing agreement to sell a home for $400,000. An immigrant couple are interested in the house and ask the agent the price. The agent states the price as $420,000. According to the fair housing laws, such an action is

a. illegal, because the agent changed the terms of the sale to discourage this particular couple.
b. illegal, because the agent violated the listing agreement.
c. legal, because the quoted price increase did not exceed 10% of the listing price.
d. legal, because the increased price does not necessarily exclude the couple.

8.38 Which of the following actions is allowed under federal fair housing laws?

a. A broker, following the instructions of the seller, advertises the property as for sale to Christian families only.
b. A home seller, acting without a broker, places a "for sale-- mature, single men only" sign in front of the house.
c. The owner of four rental houses advertises one of the properties for rent to married couples, no children, no pets.
d. The owner of a duplex who resides in one of the units refuses to rent the other unit to a non-Christian.

8.39 Cecily Longstreet believes a real estate agent has kept her from seeing a certain property for rent because she is a woman. What actions should she take if she wants legal satisfaction for her complaint?

a. File charges of illegal discrimination with the police department that has jurisdiction over the local area.
b. File a complaint with HUD and/or file suit against the offending parties in a state or federal court within the prescribed time period.
c. Wait two years and then file a civil suit in federal court.
d. Sue HUD for damages under the Civil rights Act of 1866.

8.40 George Scott hires Shannon Lang to sell his house, with the condition that he will not be the first one in the neighborhood to sell to members of a certain ethnic group. What should Shannon do about this condition?

a. Inform Scott that the condition is illegal and that she cannot comply with it.
b. Note the condition on the listing agreement and have Scott initial it.
c. Pretend that she did not hear the condition and proceed to market the property to all groups.
d. Tell Scott that she will try to discourage members of that group from looking at the property, but that she cannot control cooperating brokers.

8.41 Under federal fair housing laws, the owner of a ten-unit apartment building may legally

a. advertise that the property is not available to anyone requiring wheelchair access.
b. refuse to rent to aliens.
c. require families without children to pay the same security deposit that families with children must pay.
d. require tenants to move out when they become 62 years old.

8.42 Sam Gough wants to rent out his home, but wants to exclude families with children because of his belief that they cause damage. Under what conditions would federal fair housing laws allow Gough to rent on these terms?

a. The owner has a consistent no-children policy in all his rental properties.
b. The owner can prove that costs to repair damage caused by previous tenants with children exceeded the tenants' security deposit.
c. It is a single-family house that is part of a federally-designated planned unit development.
d. It is a single-family house, and the owner owns only one other rental home in addition to his own residence.

8.43 Which of the following laws or rulings extended discrimination to include gender, handicapped status, and family status?

a. Executive Order 11063.
b. the Civil Rights Act of 1968.
c. the Fair Housing Amendments Act of 1988.
d. Jones v Mayer.

8.44 The Wallaces, a minority family, would like to buy a home in a certain price range. Agent Ambrose shows the family all available properties in a neighborhood of families with similar backgrounds. Ambrose does not mention a number of homes in the family's price range in other neighborhoods. This agent could be liable for

a. blockbusting.
b. providing unequal services.
c. steering.
d. nothing; his services were legal and acceptable.

8.45 An agent does not like a particular minority buyer, and is very short with the person, refusing to engage in lengthy conversation or show him any properties. A second minority party visits the office the next day. The agent is very forthcoming, and shows the person five prospective properties. This agent could be liable for

a. providing unequal services.
b. steering.
c. misrepresentation.
d. nothing; both parties were minorities, and therefore no discrimination occurred.

8.46 Following the client's recommendation, an agent conceals the availability of a property from an employed but pregnant and unmarried minority woman. This agent could be liable for

a. discriminatory misrepresentation by omission.
b. steering.
c. violating fiduciary duty.
d. nothing: an agent may show or not show any property at his or her discretion.

8.47. When must a Property Condition Disclosure Statement be used?

a. With a newly-constructed single family home
b. Immediately following the closing of any residential property
c. Prior to the sale of an occupied 1-4 unit dwelling
d. Prior to the closing of any commercial or residential re-sale

8.48. If a single-family resident has listed her property with a licensee, the Seller's Property Condition Disclosure form

a. can be substituted by the licensee's material facts disclosure form.
b. does not have to be completed prior to closing.
c. can be completed by either the seller or the licensee.
d. must still be completed according to local requirements.

8.49. Which of the following would be a non-material fact that would not have to be included in the Seller's Property Condition Disclosure form?

a. A house has a leaking roof.
b. A basement floods.
c. A previous occupant died in the house.
d. A previous occupant contaminated the house by manufacturing methamphetamine in the basement.

8.50 Jessica wishes to purchase seller Ryan's house. In putting together her offer documents, Jessica includes a handwritten note along with her full-price offer saying how much she loves the property and how she can imagine living at the home for the rest of her life. This personal note included with the offer is typically referred to as a

a. homestead pledge.
b. guaranteed resident assurance.
c. waiver of inspection.
d. love letter.

8.51 Real estate wholesaling is a method of profiting from a real estate transaction without actually buying any real estate. The wholesaler finds a willing seller, puts the property under contract, and finds a third-party buyer willing to buy at a higher price than what the wholesaler has agreed to pay the original seller. How are some states fighting the practice of real estate wholesaling?

a. By requiring the wholesaler to have a real estate license
b. By prohibiting the assignment of contracts within 10 days of closing.
c. By requiring any property to be fully occupied by any particular owner for 300 days
d. By banning wholesaling on transactions of $250,000 or more

Test 9: Closings; Risk Management; Property Management

9.1 The conditions of an escrow agreement cannot be met and the related transaction cannot be completed. In such a case, the escrow agent

a. levies a fine against the defaulting party.
b. assigns his or her fiduciary responsibilities to the seller's broker.
c. returns funds to the buyer.
d. cancels the sale contract and destroys the transaction documents.

9.2 To avoid violating the Real Estate Settlement Procedures Act, parties who are providing services to the buyer or seller in a transaction must

a. be paid before the closing date for any service they provide.
b. inform the closing agent of the cost of their services at least one week before the closing date.
c. receive payment only from the funds held in escrow, not directly from buyer or seller.
d. disclose in writing any business relationships they have with other parties involved in the transaction.

9.3 A certain item is to be prorated between a buyer and seller. If no outside party is concerned, which of the following statements is true?

a. The item must be prorated and recorded as a debit to one party and a credit to the other party for the same amount.
b. The item must be prorated and recorded as a debit to one party; the remainder is recorded as a credit to the other party.
c. The party who is owed money receives a credit for the entire item and a debit for the prorated amount.
d. The party who owes money receives a debit for the portion owed and a credit for the portion that is not owed.

9.4 An item is said to be paid in arrears if it is normally paid

a. on a monthly or yearly basis.
b. at some time after the expense is incurred.
c. only after it is billed.
d. whenever it is incurred.

9.5 A seller received a rental payment of $900 in advance. At closing, the seller has earned only $320 of this rent. What should appear on the closing statement?

a. A debit to the seller and credit to the buyer for $320.
b. A debit to the seller for $580 and a credit to the buyer for $320.
c. A debit to the seller for $320 and a credit to the buyer for $900.
d. A debit to the seller and credit to the buyer for $580.

9.6 A buyer will receive a water bill for an estimated $100 at the end of the month. At closing, the seller has used an estimated $43 in water. What should appear on the closing statement?

a. A debit to the seller and credit to the buyer for $57.
b. A debit to the seller and credit to the buyer for $43.
c. A debit to the buyer and credit to the seller for $57.
d. A debit to the buyer and credit to the seller for $43.

9.7 A sale transaction closes on April 1, the ninety-first day of the tax year. The day of closing belongs to the seller. Real estate taxes for the year, not yet billed, are expected to be $2,190. According to the 365-day method, what is the seller's share of the tax bill?

a. $1,644.00.
b. $546.00.
c. $959.30
d. $1,364.66.

9.8 A sale transaction closes on July 4 (184th day of the year). The day of closing belongs to the seller. On January 1, the seller paid a hazard insurance premium of $3,750 for the calendar year. According to the 12-month/30-day method, what is the seller's share of the insurance premium?

a. $1,833.33.
b. $1,875.00.
c. $1,890.50.
d. $1,916.67.

9.9 Waldo is buying Marianne's house. The closing date (day belongs to seller) of the sale transaction is September 1 (day 244 of the year). Current Year real estate taxes are $1,100 (will be billed to buyer next year). Use the 365-day method for prorating. What is Marianne's share of the real estate taxes?

a. $364.66.
b. $367.67.
c. $732.33.
d. $735.34.

9.10 Christie is buying John's house. The closing date (day belongs to seller) of the sale transaction is September 1 (day 244 of the year). Existing hazard insurance of $350 has been paid by John through December 31. Use the 365-day method for prorating. What is Christie's share of the existing hazard insurance already paid in full?

a. $116.03.
b. $117.99.
c. $232.01.
d. $233.97.

9.11 Julie is buying Florence's house. The closing date (day belongs to seller) of the sale transaction is September 1 (day 244 of the year). The buyer's loan amount is $787,500 (90%; 30 years @ 8%). The monthly payment on this loan is $5,778.40, with $5,250 going to interest in the first month. At closing, Julie must pre-pay interest for the period of Sept. 2-Sept. 30. Use the 365-day method for prorating. What is Julie's prepaid interest amount?

a. $5,075.00.
b. $5,250.00.
c. $5,431.00.
d. $5,585.80.

9.12 Melissa is buying Raymond's house. Melissa's loan amount is $887,500. She has agreed to pay 2 points at closing. How much will Melissa pay for points?

a. $1,575.
b. $1,775.
c. $17,750.
d. $8,875.

9.13 Tina is buying Terrell's house for $375,000. The broker's commission, to be paid by the seller, is 6%. How much will Terrell pay the broker?

a. $62,500.
b. $5,250.
c. $9,450.
d. $22,500.

9.14 A sale contract stipulates that a buyer is to pay the seller's transfer tax expenses. This practice is not customary in the area. In this case,

a. the buyer and seller must amend the contract before closing.
b. the contract is voidable, since the seller must pay the expense.
c. the buyer may pay or not pay the expense, at his or her option.
d. the buyer must pay the expense.

9.15 What a buyer has to pay at closing is equal to

a. the excess of the buyer's debits over the buyer's credits.
b. the excess of the buyer's credits over the buyer's debits.
c. the excess of the seller's debits over the seller's credits.
d. the excess of the seller's credits over the seller's debits.

9.16 The standard E & O policy covers damages resulting from

a. failure to disclose an environmental condition.
b. antitrust violations.
c. mishandling of earnest money deposits.
d. negligence, error or omission in carrying out professional services.

9.17 Which of the following is a common risk relating to the agency relationship?

a. Failing to inform and disclose properly.
b. Failing to take a personal interest in a transaction.
c. Acting as an exclusive agent without an oral agency agreement.
d. Forgetting to record the listing agreement.

9.18 Even after giving buyer and seller the required information about property condition disclosures, the licensee may still be subject to legal action for

a. failing to detect customer misrepresentations.
b. failing to disclose known adverse facts.
c. relying on publicly available market information.
d. advising the purchaser to exercise due diligence.

9.19 A licensee performing a comparative market analysis must be careful to

a. use the term "market value" whenever possible in the report.
b. show a low suggested selling price to avoid a complaint of misrepresenting the value.
c. include the results of a certified appraisal in the analysis.
d. avoid creating a false impression that the licensee is a certified appraiser.

9.20 One of the major risk areas in fulfilling a listing agreement is

a. finding a buyer who turns out to be unqualified.
b. exceeding the authority of the agreement.
c. showing the property without the presence of the owner.
d. cooperating with other licensees.

9.21 To reduce the risk of committing an error or omission in the contracting process, it is a good idea to

a. use a checklist of all items, contingencies, dates and responsibilities that must be met.
b. delegate some of your responsibilities to the licensee who represents the other party in the contract.
c. call the buyer and seller daily to check on progress.
d. cut the list of necessary tasks down to a few essentials and concentrate on tracking those.

9.22 Regarding contracts and forms,

a. once written and signed they cannot be changed except by a lawyer.
b. real estate licensees may alter forms but not contracts.
c. whoever originates them can make changes without the risk of unauthorized practice of law.
d. the principals may make changes as long as they sign or initial each change.

9.23 Fair housing laws are easily violated. An effective way for agents to minimize the risk of doing so is to

a. deal only with consumers who do not belong to a protected class.
b. obtain education in the content and intent of the laws.
c. make sure there is always a witness present at all meetings with consumers.
d. stay away from transactions involving public housing.

9.24 A licensee risks violating antitrust law by

a. being present at a conversation where the setting of commission rates is discussed.
b. being present at a discussion of antitrust laws.
c. charging a commission rate that happens to be the same as that charged by another firm.
d. cooperating with another firm to do market research.

9.25 How is an intentional misrepresentation penalized?

a. License discipline, fines, and possible incarceration.
b. License discipline and fines, but no incarceration.
c. License discipline only.
d. Fines only.

9.26 Of the following actions, the only one which avoids any risk of committing unintentional misrepresentation is

a. measuring and reporting property dimensions.
b. describing properties and amenities.
c. stating that a client should seek legal counsel.
d. making statements about the presence or absence of hazardous substances.

9.27 To reduce risks inherent in reporting transaction progress to a client, the licensee should

a. make reports orally only, never in writing.
b. leave progress reporting to the inspectors and other experts.
c. advise the client that it is company policy to make no progress reports until the contingency period is over.
d. avoid speculative statements in all reports

9.28 How does sharing the qualifying function with a lender protect a licensee?

a. It guarantees that a buyer will have a loan.
b. It reduces the chance of presenting an offer from an unqualified buyer.
c. It relieves the licensee of his or her due diligence responsibilities.
d. It allows the licensee to avoid asking embarrassing questions.

9.29 The area of agent activity where there is the greatest risk of failing to maintain client confidentiality is

a. trust fund handling.
b. office management.
c. the agency relationship.
d. the closing process.

9.30 The area of agent activity where there is the greatest risk of creating a false impression that the licensee is a certified appraiser is

a. performing a comparative market analysis.
b. writing property advertisements.
c. presenting written offers.
d. researching ownership documents.

9.31 One of the major risk areas in advertising a listed property is that an advertisement will

a. describe the property in excessively glowing terms.
b. fail to appear at the same time in all available media.
c. omit any mention of the owner's main selling points.
d. make a substantial misrepresentation.

9.32 Property managers have a ______ relationship with the property owner.

a. non-binding
b. partnership
c. fiduciary
d. subagency

9.33 One of the property manager's fundamental responsibilities is

a. obtaining construction loans for the principal.
b. financial reporting to the principal.
c. finding a buyer for the property.
d. maintaining good standing in a managers' professional association.

9.34 Effective gross income is defined as

a. the total of scheduled rents.
b. the total of all rents and revenues generated by a property.
c. potential gross income minus debt service and reserves.
d. revenue from all sources minus losses from uncollected rents, vacancies, and evictions.

9.35 The efficiency of marketing activities can be measured in terms of

a. cost per tenant prospect generated per lease.
b. number of ads produced per marketing dollar.
c. dollars expended per square foot of vacant space.
d. percentage of reserves expended on marketing.

9.36 If a property's vacancy rate is significantly lower than market rates, it may be a sign that the manager needs to

a. lower rental rates.
b. raise rental rates.
c. find better tenants.
d. improve management quality.

9.37 What are the three kinds of maintenance a manager has to carry out for a managed property?

a. Constructive, deconstructive, and reconstructive
b. Routine, preventive, and corrective
c. Scheduled, planned, and improvised
d. Emergency, elective, and optional

9.38 The Americans with Disabilities Act requires property managers to

a. ensure that disabled employees have the same level of access to facilities that all employees have.
b. hire the disabled whenever possible.
c. remove all existing barriers to the free movement of disabled persons within the property, regardless of the cost.
d. remodel the ground floor of the property in accordance with ADA standards if it was built before 1978.

9.39 Commercial fire and hazard insurance policies usually require coverage to equal at least 80 percent of the property's

a. replacement value.
b. reproduction value.
c. original cost.
d. depreciated basis.

9.40 Trust funds to be handled by a property manager are likely to include all of the following except

a. rents collected from tenants.
b. cash for the management firm's operating expenses.
c. security deposits.
d. capital contributions from the property owner.

9.41 What kind of agency is commonly created by a management agreement?

a. Universal
b. Specific
c. General
d. Vicarious

9.42 Which of the following describes a gross lease?

a. The tenant pays a base rent plus some or all of the operating expenses.
b. The tenant pays a fixed rent, and the landlord pays all operating expenses.
c. The tenant pays a base rent plus an amount based on income generated in the leased space.
d. The tenant pays a rent that increases at specified times over the lease term.

9.43 If an apartment contains a refrigerator that is not included in the lease,

a. the lessee is required to buy it from the landlord.
b. the landlord is required to remove it.
c. the lease is invalidated because of an incomplete property description.
d. the property manager does not have to maintain it.

9.44 A basic responsibility of a landlord is to

a. provide leased space at market rental rates.
b. deliver a habitable property.
c. keep the rental space freshly painted.
d. refrain from entering the leased space at any time during the lease term.

9.45 How does a constructive eviction occur?

a. A landlord obtains a court order to force the tenant to vacate the leased premises.
b. A court officer forcibly removes the tenant from the premises.
c. A tenant declares a landlord in default and vacates the leased premises.
d. A landlord declares a tenant in default and takes possession of the leased premises.

9.46 Among the essential elements of a management plan is consideration of

a. the competitive market for the property.
b. the property manager's career goals.
c. the property owner's net worth.
d. the management firm's income goals.

Test 10: Real Estate Math

10.1 A licensee sells 5/6 of an acre for \$28,000, and receives a 6% commission. If she splits with her broker 50-50, what did she receive per square foot?

a. \$.023 / SF
b. \$.046 / SF
c. \$.037/ SF
d. \$.002 / SF

10.2 Lots in the South Hyde subdivision are selling for approximately \$.50 / SF. The Grandersons want to build a 2,500 SF home on a 1.5 acre corner lot. The custom builder can build the home for \$135 / SF. What will the completed property cost the Grandersons?

a. \$359,170
b. \$370,170
c. \$32,670
d. \$374,070

10.3 Ivan owned a 1/4 acre lot. He wanted to construct a 120' x 80' tennis court on the lot. What approximate percentage of the lot will be left over, if any, when he has completed the construction?

a. 12%
b. 88%
c. 3%
d. 15%

10.4 A developer wants to develop a 16-acre subdivision. He figures that the streets and common area will take up about 30% of this overall area. If the minimum lot size is to be 12,000 SF, how many lots can the developer have on this property?

a. 42
b. 487
c. 40
d. 57

10.5 A homeowner wants to insulate the new recreation room in her basement. She has been told that 3" of insulation would do the job. The walls are all 9' high and respectively measure 13', 13', 18', and 18' in length. How many rolls will she need if each roll measures 3" x 2' x 50'?

a. 6
b. 56
c. 5
d. 9

10.6 Maria plans to mulch the flower area around her house. The house measures 40' x 30', and she figures she'll mulch an area 8' in width to form a big rectangle all around the perimeter. What is the square footage of the resulting mulched area?

a. 64 SF
b. 2,576 SF
c. 1,824 SF
d. 1,376 SF

10.7. Calculate how many acres are in the Southeastern ¼ of the Western ½ of the Eastern ½ of Section 9.

a. 20 acres
b. 40 acres
c. 60 acres
d. 5 acres

10.8. Homeowner Savannah owns the Southeastern ¼ of the Southwestern ¼ of the Northwestern ¼ of Section 4. How many acres is that property?

a. 4 acres
b. 40 acres
c. 10 acres
d. 8 acres

10.9 Yard of Pizza has a percentage lease on its 1,800 SF space in Lincoln Shops. The terms are $1.40 / SF / month rent plus 1.75% of the store's gross income. If monthly sales averaged $41,500 last year, how much annual rent did Yard of Pizza pay last year?

a. $38,955
b. $43,420
c. $30,240
d. $21,525

10.10 A home appreciated 2 2/3% one year, then 5 1/5% the next year, then 7 1/4% the third year. What was the average appreciation over the 3-year period expressed as a decimal?

a. 5.04%
b. 15.24%
c. 7.56%
d. 4.8%

10.11 A homeowner paid $185,000 for a house three years ago. The house sells today for $239,000. How much has the property appreciated?

a. 23%
b. 77%
c. 29%
d. 123%

10.12 Seller Frank receives an offer of $290,000 on a property he listed at $308,000. How much is the offer as a percent of the listing price?

a. 87%
b. 91%
c. 94%
d. 106%

10.13 A property is being appraised using the income capitalization approach. Annually, it has potential gross income of $30,000, vacancy and credit losses of $1,500, and operating expenses of $10,000. Using a capitalization rate of 9%, what is the indicated value (to the nearest $1,000)?

a. $206,000
b. $167,000
c. $222,000
d. $180,000

10.14 If gross income on a property is $75,000, net income is $30,000 and the cap rate is 8%, the value of the property using the income capitalization method is

a. $625,000
b. $375,000
c. $3,750,000
d. $937,500

10.15 The roof of a property cost $16,000. The economic life of the roof is 20 years. Assuming the straight-line method of depreciation, what is the depreciated value of the roof after 3 years?

a. $16,000
b. $13,600
c. $18,400
d. $12,000

10.16 Lee had to report his home office depreciation for the tax year. He has a 2,500 SF home and a 500 SF office area. Lee paid $280,000 for his home, and he figures the land portion carries about 25% of that value. If Lee depreciates on a 39-year basis, how much can he write off for his home office depreciation per year?

a. $1,077
b. $1,436
c. $5,384
d. $2,108

10.17 A property is being appraised by the cost approach. The appraiser estimates that the land is worth $80,000 and the replacement cost of the improvements is $350,000. Total depreciation from all causes is $54,000. What is the indicated value of the property?

a. $296,000
b. $456,000
c. $324,000
d. $376,000

10.18 An apartment owner paid $500,000 for her complex 5 years ago. An appraiser at that time valued the land @ $100,000, but land has appreciated 25% over this period. The investor has used a 40-year straight-line depreciation method to depreciate the property. What is its current value using the cost approach?

a. $437,500
b. $462,500
c. $475,000
d. $546,875

10.19 An apartment building that recently sold for $400,000 had monthly gross rent receipts of $3,200. What is its monthly gross rent multiplier?

a. 80
b. .01
c. 110
d. 125

10.20 A rental home has monthly gross income of $3,300. A suitable gross income multiplier derived from market data is 14.7. What estimated sale price (to the nearest $1,000) is indicated?

a. $297,000
b. $486,000
c. $582,000
d. $519,000

10.21 Amy obtains a 75% LTV loan on her new $400,000 home with an annual interest rate of 6%. What is the first month's interest payment?

a. $1,800
b. $500
c. $2,000
d. $1,500

10.22 Emily has an interest-only home equity loan at an annual interest rate of 5.3%. If her monthly payment is $1,580, how much is the loan's principal balance (to the nearest $1,000)?

a. $444,000
b. $358,000
c. $190,000
d. $292,000

10.23 The loan officer at Sixth Fourth Bank tells Amanda she can afford a monthly payment of $1,000 on her new home loan. Assuming this is an interest-only loan, and the principal balance is $249,000, what interest rate is Amanda getting?

a. 4.82%
b. 5.03%
c. 6.25%
d. 3.69%

10.24 The Keegans obtain a fixed-rate amortized 30-year loan for $280,000 @ 6.25% interest. If the monthly payments are $1,724, how much interest do the Keegans pay in the second month of the loan?

a. $1,748.33
b. $1,456.95
c. $1,458.33
d. $1,724.00

10.25 A lender offers the Greys two alternative loan packages for their $60,000 home equity application. One option is an interest-only loan for 5 years @ 6.5% interest with no points, and the second, a 6.25% interest-only loan for 5 years with 1 point to be paid at closing. Which loan will cost the Greys less total interest, and by how much?

a. The first option, by $150.
b. The second option, by 150.
c. The second option, by $750.
d. Both options charge the same amount of interest.

10.26 Jose recently obtained a 90% loan on his $410,000 home, and he had to pay $6,150 for points. How many points did he pay?

a. 1.4 points
b. 1.67 points
c. 2.48 points
d. 1.5 points

10.27 Mack is buying Roy's house for $500,000. Mack's loan amount is $325,000. He has agreed to pay 1.5 points at closing. How much will Mack pay for points?

a. $450
b. $4,500
c. $4,875
d. $7,500

10.28 A lender determines that a homebuyer can afford to borrow $390,000 on a mortgage loan. The lender requires an 80% loan-to-value ratio. How much can the borrower pay for a property and still qualify for this loan amount?

a. $414,000
b. $312,000
c. $487,500
d. $510,000

10.29 Home buyer Janet pays $1,600 / month for the interest-only loan on her new house. The loan's interest rate is 6.75%. If she obtained a 75% loan, what was the purchase price?

a. $313,333
b. $31,604
c. $379,259
d. $256,000

10.30 Loan applicant Taylor has an annual gross income of $76,000. How much will a lender allow Taylor to pay for monthly housing expense to qualify for a loan if the lender uses an income ratio of 30%?

a. $2,160
b. $1,900
c. $1,215
d. $4,433

10.31 An investor paid $80,000 for a lot and $600,000 to have an apartment building constructed on it. He has depreciated the property for the past 10 years on a 39-year straight-line schedule. If he sells the property this year and realizes $780,000, what is his capital gain?

a. $253,846
b. $274,000
c. $100,000
d. $179,000

10.32. A homeowner bought a house five years ago for $250,000. Since then, the homeowner has spent $2,000 to build a screened porch and has added a central air-conditioning system at a cost of $5,000. What is the homeowner's adjusted basis if the house is sold today?

a. $256,000
b. $257,000
c. $244,000
d. $245,000

10.33 A homeowner sold her house and had net proceeds of $265,000. Her adjusted basis in the home was $231,000. She immediately bought another house for $301,000. What was her capital gain?

a. $265,000
b. $36,000
c. $34,000
d. None

10.34 Debra bought a home for $360,000, paying $72,000 down and taking a mortgage loan of $288,000. The following year she had a new roof put on, at a cost of $15,000. What is Debra's adjusted basis in the house if she now sells the house for $450,000?

a. $87,000
b. $288,000
c. $303,000
d. $375,000

10.35 A certain investor wants an 11% return on investment from any real estate investment. A property priced at $360,000 has gross income of $60,000 and expenses of $22,000. Approximately how much too high or too low is the price of this property for the investor to obtain her desired return exactly?

a. $1,000 overpriced.
b. $8,000 underpriced.
c. $15,000 overpriced.
d. $16,000 underpriced.

10.36 An office building investor sees a listing of an office building which is priced at $2 million. He loves the property, but he knows he needs to make a return of at least 8% to satisfy his partners. If the building is 25,000 SF, rents for $10/SF per year, has 5% vacancy, and annual expenses of $70,000, should he buy it? What is his return?

a. No, since he will yield 2.00%.
b. Yes, since he will yield 8.375%.
c. Yes, since he will yield 8%.
d. Yes, since he will yield 9.125%.

10.37 Chad owns a small retail property that he inherited from his father. There are no mortgages or interest expenses connected with the property. Chad takes an annual cost recovery expense of $7,000. The property has a monthly gross income of $1,650 and monthly operating expenses of $600. Chad's taxable income from this property will be taxed at a rate of 30%. What is the tax liability for the year?

a. $1,680
b. $5,940
c. $2,100
d. $7,000

10.38 A property has a net income of $150,000, interest payments of $105,000, principal payments of $30,000, and annual cost recovery of $7,000. The property's tax rate is 28%. What is the property's annual tax on income?

a. $14,550
b. $40,040
c. $10,640
d. $2,240

10.39 An investor bought 4 oversized lots in order to subdivide. He paid $700,000 for the lots. After subdividing, the investor was able to sell each lot for $230,000. Excluding commissions and closing costs, what per cent profit did the investor realize?

a. 0%
b. 45%
c. 23.9%
d. 31.4%

10.40 A school district's tax rate is 10 mills. The school district's required revenue from taxes is $10,000,000. What is the tax base of the area?

a. $10,000,000
b. $100,000,000
c. $1,000,000,000
d. $100,000,000,000

10.41 A homeowner's residence has an assessed valuation of $280,000, and a market value of $340,000. The homestead exemption is $50,000. Tax rates for the property are 7 mills for schools; 3 mills for the city; 2 mills for the county; and 1 mill for the local community college. What is the homeowner's tax bill?

a. $2,990
b. $3,640
c. $2,300
d. $4,420

10.42 The village of Goodsprings has an annual budget requirement of $8,000,000 to be funded by property taxes. Assessed valuations are $400,000,000, and exemptions total $25,000,000. What must the tax rate be to finance the budget?

a. 2.00%
b. 2.13%
c. 1.32%
d. 21.33%

10.43 A property has sold for $508,000. The listing agreement calls for a commission of 7%, and the seller and listing broker have agreed in writing that the selling broker will receive half of this amount. How much will the listing agent receive if the agent is scheduled to get a 40% share from his broker?

a. $17,780
b. $14,224
c. $10,668
d. $7,112

10.44 Kevin, who works for selling broker Paul, sells a house listed by listing broker Adams. The house sells for $325,000. The co-brokerage split between Paul and Adams is 50-50. Kevin is on a 65% commission schedule with Paul. If the total commission rate is 6.5%, what is Kevin's commission?

a. $6,866
b. $5,282
c. $10,563
d. $13,731

10.45. A sale transaction closes on April 1, the ninety-first day of the tax year. The day of closing belongs to the seller. Real estate taxes for the year, not yet billed, are expected to be $3,150. According to the 365-day method, what should appear on the closing statement?

a. A debit to the buyer and credit to the seller for $2,364.62
b. A debit to the buyer and credit to the seller for $785.34
c. A credit to the buyer and debit to the seller for $785.34
d. A credit to the buyer and debit to the seller for $2,364.62

10.46 Alexis is buying Jack's house. The closing date (day belongs to seller) of the sale transaction is September 1 (day 244 of the year). Her loan has a monthly payment of $577.84, with $525 going to interest in the first month. At closing, Alexis must pre-pay interest for the period of Sept. 2-Sept. 30. Use the 365-day method for prorating. What is her prepaid interest amount?

a. $507.50
b. $525.00
c. $543.10
d. $558.58

10.47 A sale transaction on rental property closes on December 16. The landlord received the December rent of $1,380 on December 1. Assuming the closing day is the buyer's, and that the 365-day method is used for prorating, which of the following entries would appear on the settlement statement?

a. Debit seller $667.74.
b. Credit seller $1,380.00.
c. Debit buyer $712.26.
d. Credit buyer $712.26.

10.48 A home sells for $322,600 in Primm County. Here, transfer taxes are set at $1.00 per $500 of the sale price. Title insurance runs $450, and the attorney costs $550. The agent's commission is 7%, and the mortgage balance is $210,000. Annual real estate taxes are estimated to be $4,000, half of which will have to be charged to the seller. If the seller pays all of these expenses, what will she net at closing?

a. $86,873
b. $88,371
c. $81,372
d. $86,372

10.49 A farmer wants to net at least $5,000/acre on the sale of his 300-acre property. If he allows for 10% commissions and closing costs, and to allow for negotiating room, he wants to get 95% of the listing price as the selling price, what should his listing price be per acre?

a. $5,750
b. $5,882
c. $4,250
d. $5,848

10.50. The Wildes have purchased a $740,000 home. The land is worth 25%, and they insure the improvements @ 75% of their replacement value. If the Wildes suffer damage estimated at $500,000, and they have an 80% co-insurance clause, what will their recovery be from the policy?

a. Zero
b. $531,915
c. $500,000
d. $468,750

10.51 The Uptons carry a $280,000 property insurance policy which covers 75% of the replacement cost of their insurable property, valued at $380,000. They have an 80% co-insurance requirement in the policy. If the family incurs a $300,000 loss, what if any amount will the Uptons recover?

a. $319,999
b. $281,250
c. $280,000
d. $375,000

Section V: Montana-Specific Practice Tests

CONTENTS

Test 11: The Montana Regulatory Environment
- Board of Realty Regulation
- The Board's Powers
- Grounds for Suspension or Revocation
- Unprofessional Conduct
- Discipline and Sanctions
- Trust Account Compliance Citations
- Enforcement Against Unlicensed Practice

Test 12: Montana Real Estate Licensing
- Definitions Used in Board Rules
- Persons Requiring a Real Estate License
- Exemptions From Real Estate Licensure
- The Salesperson License
- The Broker License
- The Supervising Broker Endorsement
- Display of License and Pocket Card
- Continuing Real Estate Education
- Active and Inactive Status
- License Renewal and Reinstatement
- Reciprocity
- License Fees

Test 13: Montana Brokerage and Disclosure Regulation
- Advertising and Marketing
- Broker and Salesperson Relationship
- Unprofessional Conduct
- Compensation
- Disclosure
- Handling Documents and Trust Funds
- Listings and Buyer Brokerage Agreements
- Ethics and Illegal Inducements

Test 14: Montana Agency Regulation
- Agency: Authorized Relationships in Montana
- Agency Duties and Responsibilities
- Agency Disclosure Recap and Timing Summary

Test 15: Additional Montana Laws and Practices
- Errors and Omissions Insurance
- Landlord and Tenant Relationship
- Foreclosure and Redemption in Montana
- Place of Business and Officing Regulations
- Montana Fair Housing
- Land Description
- Common Interest Ownership and Condominiums
- The Statute of Frauds in Montana

Test 11: The Montana Regulatory Environment

11.1 The Montana Board of Realty Regulation consists of five members appointed by the Governor. How many of those members must be active Montana real estate licensees?

a. two
b. three
c. four
d. all five

11.2 A Montana broker is asked to serve as presiding officer of the Board of Realty Regulation while continuing to serve as an officer of a statewide real estate trade association. This arrangement is

a. permitted, because Board members are expected to be active in the industry.
b. permitted, if the broker discloses the association role to the Department.
c. prohibited, because Board members may not hold any outside employment.
d. prohibited, because the presiding officer may not be an officer or employee of a real estate association.

11.3 A Montana licensee cannot find a particular trust account requirement anywhere in Title 37, Chapter 51 of the Montana Code Annotated, yet the Board enforces it consistently. The requirement is most likely found in

a. the Board's administrative rules, which carry the same legal force as the statute.
b. the Board's internal policy manual, which is advisory only.
c. federal regulations that preempt Montana law.
d. the NAR Code of Ethics, which the Board enforces directly.

11.4 The Board of Realty Regulation exercises authority over Montana real estate education in all of the following ways EXCEPT

a. approving prelicense courses.
b. approving continuing education courses.
c. rejecting a course that fails to meet its topic or quality requirements.
d. writing and scoring the national portion of the licensing examination.

11.5 A sworn written complaint alleging misrepresentation is filed against a Montana salesperson. Before the Board may suspend or revoke the license, it must

a. obtain a criminal conviction against the licensee.
b. determine guilt by majority vote following a hearing.
c. refer the matter to the attorney general for prosecution.
d. obtain the consent of the licensee's supervising broker.

11.6 A Montana salesperson advertises a home listed with a competing brokerage. The salesperson has neither a listing agreement on the property nor the consent of the owner or the listing agent. Under Section 37-51-321, MCA, this conduct is

a. acceptable, because the property is already on the market.
b. acceptable, so long as the salesperson names the listing brokerage in the advertisement.
c. grounds for suspension or revocation, because no signed listing agreement was valid on the date of the advertisement.
d. grounds for suspension or revocation only if the owner files a complaint.

11.7 A Montana broker recommends a home inspector to a buyer client. The inspector is the broker's brother-in-law, and the broker says nothing about the relationship. Under ARM 24.210.641, the broker has

a. committed unprofessional conduct by failing to disclose the family relationship.
b. committed unprofessional conduct only if the inspection later proves inadequate.
c. acted properly, because the recommendation was made in good faith.
d. acted properly, because family relationships need not be disclosed.

11.8 Which of the following is unprofessional conduct under the Board's rules?

a. Recommending that a client consult an attorney about a title question
b. Acting as a buyer agent without a written buyer broker agreement
c. Declining to give a client legal advice about a contract provision
d. Refusing to alter a document without the client's written authority

11.9 In choosing a sanction against a Montana licensee, the Board weighs the seriousness of the violation, the licensee's prior disciplinary history, and

a. the licensee's years of experience in the industry.
b. the amount of harm, or risk of harm, caused to Montana consumers.
c. the size of the brokerage that employs the licensee.
d. whether the licensee belongs to a REALTOR association.

11.10 A Department audit of a Montana broker's trust account produces a citation. The broker neither pays the fine nor files a written dispute within the response period. The result is that

a. the citation is automatically dismissed.
b. the fine is doubled and the matter is closed.
c. the matter is referred to the county attorney for criminal prosecution.
d. the failure to respond is itself unprofessional conduct and triggers additional Board discipline.

11.11 Following the issuance of a trust account citation, a Montana licensee has how long to pay the fine or file a written dispute?

a. 5 business days
b. 10 business days
c. 30 calendar days
d. 60 calendar days

11.12 An unlicensed individual who lives in Idaho advertises Montana ranch property to Montana residents and negotiates a sale entirely by telephone and email, never setting foot in Montana. Under Montana license law, this person

a. has not violated Montana law, because the activity took place outside the state.
b. has not violated Montana law, because a single transaction is exempt.
c. has violated Montana law, because dealing with Montana real estate and soliciting Montana residents is practicing within the state.
d. has violated Montana law only if a commission was actually collected.

Test 12: Montana Real Estate Licensing

12.1 A Montana licensee emails detailed information about a specific listing to one prospective buyer who asked for it. Under the Board's rules, this communication

a. is not advertising, because information sent to one specific prospect on request is excluded.
b. is not advertising, because email is not a covered medium.
c. is advertising and must carry licensee identification.
d. is advertising only if the listing belongs to another brokerage.

12.2 A Montana corporation intends to operate a real estate brokerage. Under Montana law,

a. the corporation itself is licensed, and its officers need no individual licenses.
b. the corporation is licensed and each officer performing licensed acts is endorsed on the corporate license.
c. the corporation must register with the Board, but licensing is optional for its officers.
d. no entity license exists, and every person in the entity who performs licensed acts must hold an individual license.

12.3 Which of the following persons must hold a Montana real estate license?

a. An attorney performing legal duties for a client who is selling real property
b. A court-appointed executor selling property of an estate
c. A person leasing land on behalf of an owner for mineral prospecting
d. A person who, for a fee, negotiates leases of apartments owned by others

12.4 An applicant passes the Montana salesperson licensing examination in March. The applicant has still not applied for a license by March of the following year. The result is that

a. the examination results expire and the examination must be retaken.
b. the applicant may apply late upon payment of a penalty fee.
c. the results remain valid for a total of 24 months.
d. the applicant must complete an additional 30 hours of prelicense education.

12.5 A Montana salesperson holding an advanced degree in real estate has been licensed for 14 months and applies for a broker license. The application will be

a. approved, because the advanced degree substitutes for the experience requirement.
b. approved, provided the salesperson completes the 60-hour broker prelicense course.
c. denied, because the salesperson has not been a licensed Montana salesperson for at least 2 years.
d. denied, because a broker license requires 5 years of licensed experience.

12.6 A Montana broker holding an active broker license wants to begin supervising two newly licensed salespersons. Before doing so, the broker must

a. notify the Board of the names of the salespersons to be supervised.
b. obtain a supervising broker endorsement under Section 37-51-302, MCA.
c. complete 2 additional years of licensed experience.
d. post a surety bond with the Department.

12.7 A Montana supervising broker will be away and arranges for another broker to supervise one salesperson temporarily. The written agreement must be filed with the Board

a. at least 3 business days before the temporary supervision begins.
b. within 3 business days after the temporary supervision begins.
c. at least 10 days before the temporary supervision begins.
d. within 30 days after the temporary supervision ends.

12.8 Where must the original license of a Montana salesperson be kept?

a. On the salesperson's person while conducting real estate business
b. At the salesperson's home office
c. With the supervising broker, displayed at the designated address
d. On file with the clerk and recorder of the county where the salesperson works

12.9 A Montana licensee completes 18 hours of approved continuing education during one licensing year. At renewal, the licensee

a. may carry the extra 6 hours forward to the next licensing year.
b. receives credit for 12 hours, and the extra 6 hours do not carry forward.
c. must obtain individual Board approval for the extra hours.
d. is credited with 18 hours toward a 24-hour two-year requirement.

12.10 To receive credit for an approved continuing education course, a Montana licensee must attend

a. at least 75% of the total course hours.
b. at least 90% of every hour of the course.
c. 100% of the course, with no exceptions.
d. at least 90% of the first hour and 100% of each hour after that.

12.11 A Montana licensee who has been on inactive status for three licensing years applies to return to active status. The licensee must complete

a. no continuing education, because inactive licensees are exempt.
b. the continuing education that would have been required during the inactive period, capped at 24 hours.
c. 36 hours of continuing education, one full year's requirement for each year inactive.
d. the 70-hour prelicense course a second time.

12.12 A Montana salesperson leaves one brokerage on October 15 and has not affiliated with another when the October 31 renewal deadline arrives. The salesperson

a. may renew normally, because the license remains in force.
b. may renew, provided the former supervising broker signs the renewal application.
c. cannot renew while in cancellation status, and must first go inactive or affiliate with a new supervising broker.
d. cannot renew, and the license is permanently terminated.

12.13 Montana's authority to enter a reciprocity agreement with another state depends on

a. the other state granting the same privileges to Montana licensees.
b. approval by the Montana Legislature for each individual state.
c. the applicant holding a broker rather than a salesperson license.
d. the applicant having practiced in the other state for at least 5 years.

12.14 A Montana city proposes an annual business license fee that real estate brokers would have to pay in order to practice within city limits. Under Montana license law, the proposal is

a. permitted, because cities may regulate local business activity.
b. permitted, if the fee applies equally to all professions.
c. not permitted, unless the Board first approves the fee schedule.
d. not permitted, because no city or county may charge a separate license fee or tax as a condition of practicing real estate in Montana.

Test 13: Montana Brokerage and Disclosure Regulation

13.1 A property on a Montana licensee's website closed three weeks ago but is still displayed as available. Under ARM 24.210.430, the licensee has failed the requirement that internet advertising be

a. current, because a listing must be updated or removed within 7 days of a material change.
b. accurate, because the property was correctly described when it was first posted.
c. identified, because the licensee's name appears on the page.
d. approved, because the Board reviews website content before publication.

13.2 A Montana salesperson sends a marketing email to a list of past clients. Licensee identification must appear

a. only in the signature block on the brokerage website.
b. at the beginning or the end of the email message.
c. nowhere, because email is exempt from the internet advertising rules.
d. only if the email promotes a property listed with another brokerage.

13.3 With the owner's consent and the listing agent's cooperation, a Montana broker condenses MLS data about another brokerage's listing for an advertisement. Besides identifying the listing brokerage, the advertisement must

a. reproduce the MLS data in full and without alteration.
b. include the listing agent's license number.
c. state that the material was abstracted from another source and that buyers should request further information.
d. be approved in writing by the MLS before publication.

13.4 A Montana brokerage operating under a national franchise runs a newspaper advertisement showing only the franchise logo. The advertisement is

a. acceptable, because the franchise logo identifies the brokerage.
b. acceptable, because newspaper advertising falls outside the internet rules.
c. deficient, because the advertisement must display the brokerage's license number.
d. deficient, because the brokerage must work its own name or trade name into franchise advertising.

13.5 A Montana licensee posts photographs of a vacant listing in which the furniture has been added digitally. To comply with Montana advertising standards, the licensee must

a. remove the photographs, because virtual staging is prohibited.
b. label the photographs as virtually staged.
c. obtain Board approval before posting them.
d. identify the company that produced the images.

13.6 A Montana salesperson resigns while a commission dispute with the supervising broker is still unresolved. The broker refuses to return the salesperson's license to the Board until the dispute is settled. The broker has

a. acted properly, because the license stays with the broker until accounts are settled.
b. acted properly, provided the broker notifies the Board of the dispute.
c. acted improperly, because the license must be returned immediately and a dispute is not grounds for delay.
d. acted improperly, but only once the salesperson has found a new supervising broker.

13.7 A Montana salesperson has been licensed for four years but closed only 6 transaction sides during the past calendar year. The supervising broker must provide

a. reasonable supervision, because the salesperson has more than 2 years of experience.
b. no supervision beyond an annual file review.
c. reasonable supervision, unless the salesperson asks for more.
d. high-level supervision, because the salesperson closed fewer than 10 transaction sides.

13.8 A Montana salesperson negotiates and signs a listing agreement with a seller on Monday. The supervising broker reviews, signs, and dates it on Thursday. The listing agreement became valid

a. Thursday, when the supervising broker reviewed, signed, and dated it.
b. Monday, when the seller signed it.
c. Monday, because the salesperson acted within the scope of the broker's authority.
d. only once it was entered into the MLS.

13.9 A Montana broker relocates the brokerage office. Under Section 37-51-308, MCA, the broker must notify the Department

a. within 30 days after the move.
b. at the next annual renewal.
c. before the move or within 10 days after it.
d. at least 3 business days before the move.

13.10 A Montana salesperson owns a rental house and decides to sell it personally, without involving the supervising broker. Before entering the transaction, the salesperson must

a. obtain the supervising broker's written consent.
b. transfer the listing to the brokerage.
c. place any earnest money in the broker's trust account.
d. disclose to the other party that this is the salesperson's personal transaction and does not involve the broker or firm.

13.11 A Montana broker wants to share a commission with a broker licensed in Wyoming who referred a buyer but performed no services in Montana. The payment is

a. permitted, provided the Wyoming broker performed no services in Montana for the fee.
b. permitted only if the Wyoming broker first obtains a Montana license.
c. prohibited, because commissions may be shared only between Montana licensees.
d. prohibited, because referral fees between brokers are unprofessional conduct.

13.12 A buyer asks a Montana licensee to draft a custom financing contingency and to explain how a Montana court would interpret it. The licensee should

a. draft the provision, because licensees routinely complete contract forms.
b. decline to draft the provision or interpret the law, and recommend that the buyer consult an attorney.
c. draft the provision but decline to explain it.
d. explain the law but decline to draft the provision.

13.13 A Montana licensee takes a listing from a person who claims to own the property. The licensee makes no inquiry of any kind into ownership, and the person turns out to hold no interest in the property. The licensee has

a. no exposure, because a title search is not required.
b. no exposure, because the seller made the misrepresentation.
c. exposure only if the property is later sold.
d. exposure, because making no inquiry at all into ownership can support discipline.

13.14 Since August 17, 2024, an offer of compensation to a buyer broker may

a. not be communicated through an MLS, in any field or in the remarks.
b. appear in the MLS remarks field but not in a dedicated compensation field.
c. appear in the MLS for residential listings only.
d. appear in the MLS if the seller consents in writing.

13.15 A Montana buyer asks a licensee to show a home in person. Under the practice changes effective in 2024, a written buyer broker agreement must be signed

a. within 3 days after the showing.
b. before the buyer tours the home, whether in person or by live virtual tour.
c. before an offer is written.
d. only if the buyer expects the seller to pay the buyer broker.

13.16 A buyer broker agreement provides that the brokerage will be paid 'whatever the seller is offering'. This provision is

a. acceptable, because the amount can be determined at closing.
b. acceptable, provided the buyer initials the clause.
c. not acceptable, because compensation must be a specific, objectively ascertainable amount or rate.
d. not acceptable, because a buyer broker may not be paid by a seller.

13.17 A Montana buyer defaults and forfeits the earnest money. The broker and the seller wish to divide it between them. The division is permitted

a. only if a written agreement between the broker and the seller provides for it.
b. automatically, on an equal basis.
c. only with the defaulting buyer's written consent.
d. only after the Board approves the division.

13.18 A Montana seller instructs the listing agent not to mention a recurring basement flooding problem. The listing agent

a. must follow the instruction, because the seller is the client.
b. must disclose the condition, because the duty to disclose adverse material facts belongs to the licensee independently of the seller.
c. may stay silent unless a buyer asks directly.
d. must withdraw from the listing but may not disclose the condition.

13.19 Which of the following must a Montana seller disclose when the seller has the information?

a. A completed statewide property condition disclosure form
b. A written statement of the property's assessed value
c. The results of a radon test the seller has received
d. A certification that the property is free of environmental hazards

13.20 A Montana licensee who has signed no written agreement with anyone begins helping a buyer locate property. The required initial relationship disclosure must be given

a. when the buyer makes an offer.
b. when the licensee first shows a property.
c. at closing.
d. when the licensee first begins to locate property for the buyer.

13.21 A Montana licensee representing a seller receives an offer from a buyer the licensee also represents. Written consent to dual agency must be obtained

a. within 24 hours after the offer is presented.
b. before or at the moment the dual agency arises, never afterward.
c. at closing, when both parties sign the settlement statement.
d. only if either party asks for it.

13.22 A Montana buyer asks a licensee whether any registered offenders live near a property. The licensee is obligated to

a. search the registry and report the results to the buyer.
b. decline to discuss the subject, because it is not a material fact.
c. tell the buyer that the information may be maintained and by whom, and disclose any actual knowledge the licensee has about the property.
d. refer the buyer to the listing agent.

13.23 A Montana salesperson receives an earnest money check from a buyer on Friday. Absent a contrary agreement of the parties, the funds must reach the broker's trust account

a. the same business day.
b. within 24 hours.
c. within 5 business days.
d. within 3 business days of receipt.

13.24 A Montana broker keeps a small balance of personal funds in the brokerage trust account to cover bank service charges. This practice is

a. permitted up to $1,000, provided the broker keeps a chronological ledger of those deposits and disbursements.
b. permitted in any amount, because the funds belong to the broker.
c. prohibited, because any personal funds in a trust account constitute commingling.
d. permitted only with the written consent of every client whose funds are in the account.

13.25 A Montana broker's commission becomes due at closing. The broker must withdraw it from the trust account

a. immediately upon closing.
b. within 3 business days.
c. within 10 business days of becoming due.
d. at any time before the annual audit.

13.26 Which of the following is permitted for a Montana broker's trust account?

a. A certificate of deposit maturing in 90 days
b. An overnight sweep account at a Montana bank
c. A repurchase agreement secured by government obligations
d. An insured checking account at a financial institution located in Montana

13.27 Montana requires a broker to retain trust account records and real estate documents for

a. 8 years from the later of the date of receipt or the date the transaction was completed.
b. 3 years from the date of closing.
c. 5 years from the date of receipt.
d. 8 years from the date the license is surrendered.

13.28 A Montana licensee shows properties to a buyer and negotiates an accepted offer, all without any written buyer broker agreement. The licensee has

a. acted properly, because a written agreement is required only on the seller side.
b. committed unprofessional conduct under ARM 24.210.641.
c. acted properly, because the buyer never objected.
d. committed a criminal offense punishable by fine.

13.29 A Montana licensee learns that a seller is under a written exclusive listing agreement with another brokerage and contacts the seller directly to solicit the listing. This conduct is

a. acceptable, because sellers may change brokerages at any time.
b. acceptable, if the current listing expires within 30 days.
c. acceptable, if the licensee notifies the other brokerage afterward.
d. unprofessional conduct, unless the seller has consented to direct communication and that consent is documented.

13.30 A Montana listing agreement provides that it continues 'until the property sells'. This provision is

a. improper, because a listing agreement must state a specific duration.
b. proper, because the parties are free to set their own terms.
c. proper, provided the seller may cancel on 30 days notice.
d. improper, because a listing may not exceed 6 months.

13.31 A Montana brokerage offers a drawing for a television set. Anyone may enter free of charge, with no purchase, appointment, or agreement required. The promotion is

a. unprofessional conduct, because all contests are prohibited.
b. permissible, because participation is free and no further commitment is required.
c. permissible only if the prize is worth less than the average commission.
d. unprofessional conduct, unless the Board approves the drawing in advance.

13.32 A Montana licensee accepts a payment from a title company for each closing the licensee steers to it. This arrangement

a. is acceptable if the licensee discloses it to the client.
b. is acceptable, because referral relationships are lawful in Montana.
c. violates RESPA and can also support a Montana discipline finding.
d. is acceptable if the amount is reasonable in relation to services performed.

Test 14: Montana Agency Regulation

14.1 A Montana licensee argues that a common law agency principle should govern a client relationship because the statute does not address it. The argument fails because

a. Section 37-51-313, MCA, replaces the common law of agency, and only the five authorized statutory relationships apply.
b. common law applies only to commercial transactions in Montana.
c. the Board has adopted the common law of agency by rule.
d. Montana courts abolished the law of agency entirely.

14.2 A Montana licensee begins working with a buyer, has signed no written agreement, and has disclosed no other relationship. The licensee's relationship to the buyer is presumed to be

a. buyer agent.
b. statutory broker.
c. dual agent.
d. subagent of the seller.

14.3 A Montana listing agent offers subagency to a cooperating broker. The cooperating broker says nothing in response and proceeds to show the property. The cooperating broker is

a. a subagent, because subagency was offered.
b. a buyer agent by operation of law.
c. a statutory broker, because subagency takes an explicit acceptance.
d. a dual agent, because the broker is working with both sides.

14.4 Two salespersons in one Montana brokerage end up on opposite sides of the same transaction. The supervising broker names one an in-house seller agent designate and the other an in-house buyer agent designate. Each designate is

a. a dual agent, because the brokerage represents both parties.
b. a statutory broker as to the party not designated.
c. a subagent of the supervising broker.
d. the agent of only the designated party, and not a dual agent.

14.5 A Montana broker lists a property and then decides to buy it personally. The broker proposes to act as a dual agent with the seller's written consent. This is

a. prohibited, because a licensee who is a principal in the transaction cannot be a dual agent.
b. permitted, because written consent cures the conflict.
c. permitted, if the supervising broker approves the arrangement.
d. permitted, if the broker reduces the commission.

14.6 A Montana seller agency relationship terminates when the listing expires unsold. After termination, the former agent continues to owe the seller

a. all of the duties owed during the agency.
b. the duty to account for money and property, and the duty of confidentiality.
c. no further duties of any kind.
d. only the duty to obey lawful instructions.

14.7 A Montana seller agent knows the septic system failed an inspection last year. An unrepresented buyer tours the property and asks nothing about it. The seller agent must

a. say nothing, because the buyer is not the agent's client.
b. disclose the condition only if the buyer asks about the septic system.
c. disclose the adverse material fact to the buyer.
d. inspect the septic system and report the results to the buyer.

14.8 A Montana seller agent wants to list a second property that will compete directly with an existing client's listing. The agent may do so

a. only after the first listing expires.
b. without any disclosure, because listings are not exclusive to a market area.
c. only if the two properties are in different counties.
d. after written disclosure to the seller and with the seller's written consent.

14.9 A Montana statutory broker assists a buyer and a seller in the same transaction. The statutory broker's obligations include

a. disclosing to the buyer adverse material facts about the property, disclosing to the seller adverse material facts about the buyer's ability to perform, and exercising reasonable care, skill, and diligence.
b. acting solely in the best interests of the buyer.
c. inspecting the property and verifying the seller's statements.
d. safeguarding the confidences of both parties as a dual agent would.

14.10 A Montana dual agent learns from the seller, in confidence, that the roof leaks badly in heavy rain. The dual agent must

a. keep the information confidential, because the seller gave it in confidence.
b. disclose the condition, because the duty to disclose adverse material facts overrides confidentiality.
c. withdraw from the transaction without disclosing anything.
d. disclose it only if the buyer's inspector fails to find it.

14.11 Without written consent, a Montana dual agent may NOT disclose all of the following EXCEPT

a. that the buyer is willing to pay more than the offered purchase price.
b. that the seller is willing to accept less than the asking price.
c. a known structural defect in the foundation.
d. the factors motivating either party to buy or sell.

14.12 A Montana property manager signs a management contract with an owner and begins leasing units. Regarding relationship disclosure, the property manager must

a. deliver the Section 37-51-314 initial disclosure to every tenant.
b. deliver the Section 37-51-314 subsequent disclosure whenever a lease is negotiated.
c. make no disclosure, because property management falls outside the agency statute.
d. disclose the contractual relationship to owners and tenants, with no separate Section 37-51-314 disclosure required.

14.13 A Montana licensee is accused of concealing a boundary dispute and responds that nobody mentioned it and no inquiry was made. Under Section 37-51-313(13), MCA, this response

a. does not protect the licensee, because every licensee must endeavor to ascertain all pertinent facts about a property.
b. protects the licensee, because a licensee is not an inspector.
c. protects the licensee, because only the seller must disclose defects.
d. does not protect the licensee, because a survey is required on every transaction.

14.14 Which of the following is NOT an adverse material fact a Montana licensee must disclose?

a. A failing roof
b. That a prior occupant died by suicide in the home
c. A positive radon test result
d. An unrecorded easement across the property

14.15 Three years after a Montana listing ended, the former seller agent now represents a buyer interested in that same property. The agent still recalls the seller's confidential bottom-line price. The agent

a. may use the information, because the agency relationship ended.
b. may use the information, because the agent now owes duties to the buyer.
c. may not use the information, because confidentiality survives termination of the agency.
d. may use the information if the buyer insists on it.

14.16 A Montana subagent who is an independent contractor makes a misrepresentation to a buyer. The broker had no knowledge of it and it did not originate with the broker. Under Section 37-51-315, MCA, the broker is

a. liable, because a broker is always responsible for a subagent's statements.
b. liable, because the broker supervises the subagent.
c. liable only if the buyer suffers a financial loss.
d. not liable, because the broker lacked actual knowledge, the subagent is not an employee, and the statement did not originate with the broker.

14.17 A Montana seller agent must deliver the initial relationship disclosure to the seller

a. at the time the listing agreement is executed.
b. when the property is entered into the MLS.
c. when the first offer is presented.
d. at closing.

14.18 A Montana licensee's subsequent disclosure must be delivered

a. within 3 days after an offer is accepted.
b. before or at the time negotiations commence with the other side.
c. only if the other party is unrepresented.
d. at the first showing of the property.

14.19 The initial relationship disclosure form used in Montana must set out the statutory dual agency advisory

a. in a footnote at the bottom of the page.
b. only when dual agency is anticipated.
c. reproduced in all capital letters.
d. only on the buyer's copy.

14.20 A Montana subsequent disclosure must include

a. a description of every relationship authorized by Montana law.
b. the licensee's license number and expiration date.
c. a copy of the listing or buyer broker agreement.
d. identification of the type of relationship, the signature of the seller or buyer, the licensee's signature, and the date.

14.21 A Montana licensee working as a statutory broker for a buyer later signs a written buyer broker agreement with that same buyer. At that point the licensee must

a. give the buyer a new initial disclosure reflecting the buyer agency relationship.
b. do nothing further, because a disclosure was already given.
c. give only a subsequent disclosure to the seller.
d. obtain the seller's written consent to the change.

14.22 A Montana brokerage wants to reduce paperwork by placing the required relationship disclosure inside its listing agreement form. This is

a. not permitted, because the disclosure must be a separate document.
b. permitted, because the disclosure need not be a separate document.
c. permitted only with prior Board approval of the combined form.
d. not permitted, because a listing agreement may not contain a disclosure.

Test 15: Additional Montana Laws and Practices

15.1 A Montana licensee's errors and omissions coverage lapses for two days while the licensee changes carriers. The license remains active throughout. Under Section 37-51-325, MCA, the licensee

a. is out of compliance, because coverage must be continuous during the entire period of active licensure.
b. is in compliance, because a lapse of less than 30 days is excused.
c. is in compliance, because replacement coverage was obtained.
d. must place the license on inactive status retroactively.

15.2 A Montana salesperson enrolled in the Board's group errors and omissions policy transfers to a new supervising broker. The salesperson's coverage

a. terminates and must be replaced within 30 days.
b. continues, because coverage under the group policy is specific to the individual licensee.
c. transfers only if the new broker also participates in the group policy.
d. must be converted to an individual policy.

15.3 A Montana property manager handles rentals of mobile home lots in a park. These tenancies are governed by

a. Title 70, Chapter 24, MCA, the Residential Landlord and Tenant Act.
b. Title 70, Chapter 25, MCA, the security deposit statute.
c. Title 70, Chapter 33, MCA, the separate mobile home lot rental act.
d. no statute, because lot rentals are purely contractual.

15.4 A Montana tenant vacates and the landlord intends to deduct cleaning costs from the security deposit. The landlord must deliver the balance together with a written itemized list of deductions within

a. 10 days after the tenant vacates.
b. 14 days after the tenant vacates.
c. 21 days after the tenant vacates.
d. 30 days after the tenant terminates the tenancy and vacates.

15.5 A Montana tenant fails to pay rent when due and the landlord serves a written 3-day notice to pay or vacate. The tenant pays the full amount owed on the third day. The landlord

a. may not evict, because payment in full within the 3 days continues the tenancy.
b. may evict, because the notice period had already begun.
c. may evict only if the tenant has paid late before.
d. must serve a second 3-day notice before filing.

15.6 Which of the following is exempt from the Montana Residential Landlord and Tenant Act?

a. A single-family home rented for one year
b. A room in a hotel occupied by a transient guest
c. A condominium unit rented to a tenant
d. A two-bedroom apartment in a fourplex

15.7 A Montana lender is financing the purchase of a 55-acre parcel. The security instrument

a. may be a trust indenture, because the loan is for residential use.
b. may be a trust indenture, if the borrower waives the right of redemption.
c. must be treated as a mortgage, because a trust indenture is limited to parcels of 40 acres or less.
d. must be a trust indenture, because Montana requires nonjudicial foreclosure.

15.8 A Montana trust indenture is foreclosed nonjudicially and the sale brings less than the balance owed. The lender

a. may obtain a deficiency judgment for the shortfall.
b. may obtain a deficiency judgment if the borrower holds other assets.
c. may pursue the borrower personally after a 1-year waiting period.
d. may not obtain a deficiency judgment, and the unpaid balance is discharged.

15.9 A purchaser buys at a Montana trustee's sale under the Small Tract Financing Act. The purchaser is entitled to possession

a. on the 10th day following the sale.
b. immediately at the close of the auction.
c. after the 1-year redemption period expires.
d. after the sheriff issues a certificate of sale.

15.10 A Montana broker runs a brokerage entirely online and uses a post office box as the address of record. Under Section 37-51-308, MCA, this arrangement is

a. acceptable, because the broker maintains a mailing address.
b. not acceptable, because the designated address must be a physical location.
c. acceptable, if the broker stores all records electronically.
d. acceptable, if the broker is the only licensee in the firm.

15.11 A Montana broker closes the brokerage office and retires two years after a transaction closes. The obligation to retain the records of that transaction

a. ends when the office closes.
b. ends when the license is surrendered.
c. continues for the full 8 years, regardless of the closing or the retirement.
d. transfers automatically to the Board.

15.12 The Montana Human Rights Act protects three classes beyond those covered by the federal Fair Housing Act. They are

a. source of income, veteran status, and student status.
b. age, gender identity, and marital status.
c. creed, occupation, and marital status.
d. age, creed, and marital status.

15.13 An owner-occupied Montana duplex qualifies for an exemption from the age and familial status prohibitions. The owner places an advertisement stating 'no children'. The advertisement is

a. unlawful, because no exemption excuses discriminatory advertising.
b. lawful, because the property is exempt.
c. lawful, because the owner occupies one of the two units.
d. lawful, if the advertisement runs only in a local newspaper.

15.14 A Montana township contains

a. 16 sections of one square mile each.
b. 36 sections of one square mile each.
c. 36 sections of 320 acres each.
d. 640 sections of one acre each.

15.15 How many acres are contained in the northeast quarter of the southwest quarter of a Montana section?

a. 10 acres
b. 20 acres
c. 40 acres
d. 160 acres

15.16 Before a Montana condominium declaration may be recorded, it must be approved by

a. the Board of Realty Regulation.
b. the county planning board.
c. the Montana Association of REALTORS.
d. the Department of Revenue.

15.17 A Montana developer who still owns a majority of the units in a condominium project gives a prospective buyer the Unit Ownership Act, the bylaws, and the administrative regulations. The buy-sell agreement the buyer signs the same day

a. is not effective until 72 hours after the buyer received the documents, and the buyer may withdraw without penalty during that period.
b. is effective immediately upon signature.
c. is void, because a majority owner may not sell directly to a buyer.
d. becomes effective after a 3-day period beginning when the seller countersigns.

15.18 A Montana condominium unit is sold at foreclosure of the first trust indenture. Unpaid common expense assessments that came due before the sale are

a. the personal obligation of the foreclosure purchaser.
b. a common expense of all the unit owners, including the purchaser.
c. extinguished entirely, with no one responsible for them.
d. collectible only from the association's reserve fund.

15.19 A Montana seller orally promises a broker a commission for finding a buyer. The broker produces a ready, willing, and able buyer and the sale closes. If the seller refuses to pay, the broker

a. may sue and recover, because the broker performed.
b. may sue and recover, because the seller accepted the benefit of the work.
c. cannot recover, because an agreement employing a broker to sell real estate must be in writing.
d. may recover only the reasonable value of the services rendered.

15.20 Which of the following agreements may be oral and still be enforceable in Montana?

a. A listing agreement
b. A contract for the sale of a vacant lot
c. A two-year commercial lease
d. A residential lease for a term of one year

Section VI: Montana License Examination Sample Test

Sample Test: Montana Practice Exam

S 1. A farmer temporarily installs produce coolers in a leased farm stand in order to prevent spoilage. The coolers would be considered which of the following?

a. Trade fixtures that are real property.
b. Trade fixtures that are personal property.
c. Temporary real property.
d. Emblements.

S 2. Property can be converted from real to personal property and from personal property to real property by means of which processes, respectively?

a. Assemblage and plottage.
b. Application and dissolution.
c. Severance and affixing.
d. Planting and harvesting.

S 3. The highest form of ownership interest one can acquire in real estate is the

a. legal life estate.
b. conventional life estate.
c. defeasible fee simple estate.
d. absolute fee simple estate.

S 4. The distinguishing feature of a defeasible fee simple estate is that

a. it can be passed on to heirs.
b. it has no restrictions on use.
c. the estate may revert to a grantor or heirs if the prescribed use changes.
d. it is of unlimited duration.

S 5. Maria acquires a property from her uncle Alfonso. When Maria dies, the estate will pass to Alfonso's other niece, Serena. The type of estate that Maria has in the property is a

a. conventional life estate.
b. legal life estate.
c. fee simple defeasible estate.
d. tenancy by the entireties.

S 6. One difference between a cooperative estate and a condominium estate is that

a. a condominium owner owns a unit of air space whereas the co-op owner owns a proprietary lease.
b. a condominium sale adversely affects other unit owners.
c. the coop owner owns stock and a freehold real estate interest whereas the condominium owner simply a proprietary lease.
d. the condominium owner owns the common elements and the airspace whereas the coop owner only owns the apartment.

S 7. Who are the essential parties involved in an estate in trust?

a. Owner, trustor and lawyer.
b. Owner, trustor and trustee.
c. Trustee, title company, and beneficiary.
d. Trustor, trustee and beneficiary.

S 8. A condominium owner enjoys a

a. share in an association that owns one's apartment.
b. tenancy in common interest in airspace and common areas of the property.
c. fee simple ownership of the airspace in a unit and an undivided share of the entire property's common areas.
d. fee simple ownership of a pro rata share of the entire property.

S 9. With various types of junior liens, the order of payment priority is generally established according to

a. the date of recordation.
b. what form of tax is in question.
c. the order of disbursement.
d. whether the lien was subordinated.

S 10. What is a lien-theory state in contrast to a title-theory state?

a. A state in which liens are given priority over other encumbrances.
b. A state in which a mortgagor retains title to the property when a mortgage lien is created.
c. A state in which the holder of a mortgage lien receives title to the mortgaged property until the debt is satisfied.
d. A state in which liens must be recorded to be enforceable.

S 11. A property owner has an easement appurtenant on her property. One day the property is sold to another party who is opposed to the easement. Following the closing, this particular form of easement

a. terminates.
b. transfers with the property.
c. transfers with the owner to a new property.
d. becomes a license on the property.

S 12. What fundamental legal purpose is fulfilled by title records?

a. Keeping the county apprised of tax payments.
b. Preventing identity theft.
c. Giving constructive notice of one's rights and interests in the property.
d. Assembling all relevant documents in a single place.

S 13. What is "chain of title?"

a. The list of all parties who have ever owned real estate.
b. The bundle of rights linked to the recorded title to a parcel.
c. A chronology of successive owners of record of a parcel of real estate.
d. Involuntary conveyance of title by statutory rules of descent.

S 14. Which of the following provides the strongest evidence of marketable title?

a. A general warranty deed.
b. A title certificate.
c. Title insurance.
d. An attorney's opinion.

S 15. A store owner enters into a lease that charges rent per square foot, a common area fee, and a portion of the store owner's gross income from the property. This kind of lease is a

a. triple charge, or triple net lease.
b. proprietor's lease.
c. percentage lease.
d. retailer's gross lease.

S 16. An owner leases a property to a business in exchange for rent. The tenant is required to pay all operating expenses as well. This is an example of a

a. proprietary lease.
b. percentage lease.
c. gross lease.
d. net lease.

S 17. A lease automatically terminates under which of the following circumstances?

a. The tenant fails to pay rent.
b. The leased property is foreclosed.
c. The tenant goes out of business.
d. The landlord cancels the lease.

S 18. A county or municipal authority usually grants a certificate of occupancy for new construction only after

a. all contractors' work has been inspected.
b. all work has been completed for at least sixty days.
c. the construction conforms to building codes.
d. the tax assessor has valued the improvement.

S 19. A property owner is precluded by deed restriction from developing a thirty foot boat dock. The limitation prompts the owner to sell to another party. The new owner

a. is free to build the dock since the next door neighbor built a similar dock two weeks later.
b. takes title subject to the same restriction.
c. can build the dock with special permission from the zoning board.
d. may build, since the restriction is extinguished by the sale.

S 20. Emily sells Rycole a property containing a deed condition. The condition stipulates that the forested portion of the property must never be razed for development. Three months later, Rycole proceeds to harvest the trees and turn the area into an executive golf course. What recourse, if any, does Emily have under the deed condition?

a. She has the right to re-possess the property because the grantee has violated the condition.
b. The condition has ceased to apply because she allowed the violation to continue for a certain period of time.
c. She can claim the proceeds from the harvested trees.
d. She can force Rycole to sell the property to a new owner who agrees to comply with the condition.

S 21. What is the essential purpose of legal descriptions of real property?

a. To create a consistent, unchanging standard for uniquely locating a property.
b. To enable courts and attorneys to calculate property size accurately.
c. To comply with common law for real property.
d. To eliminate cumbersome metes and bounds descriptions.

S 22. Which of the following characterizes metes and bounds descriptions?

a. They use meridians and base lines.
b. They identify an enclosed area, beginning and ending at the same point.
c. They use lot and block numbers.
d. They incorporate elevation into the descriptions.

S 23. A buyer agrees to all terms of a seller's offer except the length of time for a contingency to procure financing. The buyer extends the financing period in the offer by one week, signs the form, and mails it back to the seller. At this point, the seller's offer

a. is void.
b. becomes an executory contract.
c. becomes a counteroffer.
d. has been accepted, since the modification was a contingency.

S 24. Real estate contracts that are not personal service contracts

a. may be assigned.
b. are not assignable.
c. must be in writing.
d. are exempt from the statute of frauds.

S 25. Which of the following contracts must be in writing to be enforceable?

a. A parol contract.
b. A six-month lease.
c. A two-year lease.
d. An executory contract.

S 26. Agent Bob, who works for Broker Bill, obtains an owner listing to lease a building. Bill's other agent, Sue, locates a tenant for Bob's listing. Broker Bill in this instance is

a. an implied agent.
b. a dual agent.
c. a single agent.
d. a subagent.

S 27. A transaction broker should disclose his or her agency relationship to prospective buyers and sellers

a. upon first substantive communication.
b. upon completion of the listing agreement.
c. immediately following completion of any offer.
d. immediately prior to closing.

S 28. A transaction facilitator in a residential transaction represents

a. the seller.
b. the buyer.
c. both seller and buyer.
d. neither seller nor buyer.

S 29. A principal instructs an agent to inform minority buyers that the property for lease was just leased an hour ago and is no longer available. The agent refuses to comply. In this case,

a. the agent should exercise caution until the listing expires, then decline to renew it.
b. the principal has proposed an illegal act, which should not be obeyed.
c. the agent is liable for breaching the listing terms.
d. the agent may sue the principal for discrimination and misrepresentation.

S 30. The amount of a real estate broker's commission is established by

a. agreement among competing brokers.
b. negotiation with clients.
c. the local Board of Realtors®.
d. state real estate license law.

S 31. A client revokes an exclusive right-to-sell listing two months prior to expiration. The reason stated: the client is too busy to meet with the agent. In this case,

a. the client is criminally liable for negligence.
b. the client may be liable for a commission and marketing expenses.
c. the agent can sue the client for specific performance, even if no customer had been located.
d. the agent must accept the revocation without the possibility of damage recovery.

S 32. A protection period clause in an exclusive listing provides that

a. the owner is protected from all liabilities arising from the agent's actions performed within the agent's scope of duties.
b. the agent has a claim to a commission if the owner sells or leases to a party within a certain time following the listing's expiration.
c. agents are entitled to extend a listing agreement's term if a transaction is imminent.
d. an owner is not liable for a commission if a prospective customer delays in completing an acceptable offer.

S 33. Real estate advertising must conform to regulatory standards and requirements. One requirement is

a. a broker may only place blind ads in social media outlets.
b. a broker must have all advertising approved by the local real estate board.
c. the advertising must not be deceptive.
d. sales agents may only advertise in their own name.

S 34. The three principal brokerage firms in a market agree to pay sales agents 15% more than any other competitor currently in practice. This is an example of

a. collusion.
b. price fixing.
c. allocation of markets.
d. steering.

S 35. Two leading agencies jointly agree to raise commissions charged to residential sellers to 7.5% of the sales price. Which of the following is true?

a. This is a perfectly legitimate business practice.
b. The brokers have illegally fixed prices.
c. The brokers have allocated markets.
d. The brokers have engaged in legal collusion.

S 36. A sale contract contains an open-ended financing contingency: if the buyer cannot obtain financing within a reasonable time, the deal is off. Six months later, the buyer still cannot secure financing. Which of the following is true?

a. The seller may cancel the contract, since it can be ruled invalid.
b. The buyer can continue indefinitely to seek financing, and the seller's property must remain off the market, since "reasonable" is not defined.
c. The escrow agent is entitled to the buyer's deposit.
d. The seller can force a lender to commit to a loan under fair financing laws.

S 37. In the event of a buyer's default, a provision for liquidated damages in a sale contract enables a seller to

a. sue the buyer for specific performance.
b. force the buyer to quitclaim equitable title.
c. sue the buyer for the broker's marketing expenses.
d. claim the deposit as compensated damages for the buyer's failure to perform.

S 38. Which of the following is true of an option-to-buy agreement?

a. The potential buyer, the optionee, is obligated to buy the property once the option agreement is completed.
b. The optionor must perform if the optionee takes the option, but the optionee is under no obligation to do so.
c. The contract can be executed at no cost to the optionee.
d. It is a bilateral agreement.

S 39. If a manufacturer that is the major employer in a small city moves its operations to another city, it is reasonable to expect

a. a fall in housing demand, but no other changes in the real estate market.
b. a decline in demand for all types of real estate in the real estate market.
c. an immediate fall in the demand for industrial real estate, but no other changes in the real estate market.
d. an immediate decline in the prices for industrial and office real estate, but no impact on the residential market.

S 40. If a commercial real estate market is undersupplied, it is likely that

a. rental prices in that market will fall.
b. rental prices in that market will rise.
c. rental prices will remain stable until equilibrium is reached.
d. construction will increase to the point of equilibrium.

S 41. The amount of available property that becomes occupied over a period of time is called

a. vacancy.
b. absorption.
c. equilibrium.
d. occupation.

S 42 The roof of a property cost $20,000. The economic life of the roof is 20 years. Assuming the straight-line method of depreciation, what is the depreciated value of the roof after 3 years?

a. $20,000.
b. $17,000.
c. $14,000.
d. $3,000.

S 43. The income capitalization approach to appraising value is most applicable for which of the following property types?

a. Single family homes.
b. Apartment buildings.
c. Undeveloped land.
d. Churches.

S 44. In the income capitalization approach, an appraiser

a. estimates gross income and multiplies times the gross income multiplier.
b. estimates effective income, subtracts tax, and applies a capitalization rate.
c. estimates net income and applies a capitalization rate to it.
d. estimates potential income and applies a capitalization rate to it.

S 45. Net operating income is equal to

a. potential income minus expenses minus debt service.
b. effective gross income minus potential income.
c. potential gross income minus vacancy and credit loss minus expenses.
d. effective gross income minus vacancy and credit loss.

S 46. If net income on a property is $40,000 and the cap rate is 10%, the value of the property using the income capitalization method is

a. $100,000.
b. $400,000.
c. $1,000,000.
d. $4,000,000.

S 47. The key feature of an adjustable mortgage loan is that

a. the interest rate may vary.
b. the monthly payment increases over the life of the loan.
c. the principal balance does not amortize.
d. the loan term can be shortened or lengthened.

S 48. Why is a wraparound mortgage loan potentially interesting to a home seller as an investment?

a. It is a senior loan that can be easily subordinated for additional debt.
b. A wraparound lender can profit when the interest rate of the wraparound exceeds that of the underlying mortgage.
c. The underlying loan is retired early.
d. The second mortgage borrower may make payments directly to the first mortgage lender.

S 49. A builder is required to secure a loan with mortgages on three properties. This is an example of

a. a participation mortgage loan.
b. a blanket mortgage loan.
c. a permanent mortgage loan.
d. a bridge loan.

S 50. Which of the following is true of a loan with negative amortization?

a. The interest rate on the loan increases as the principal balance decreases.
b. Payments are not sufficient to retire the loan.
c. The loan balance is diminishing, or going negative.
d. Additional interest is being added to the monthly payment.

S 51. The loan-to-value ratio is used as an underwriting mechanism because

a. the LTV determines the profitability of the loan.
b. the loan amount needs to be less than the property's value.
c. borrowers tend to inflate the true value of the property.
d. a full-price loan overfinances the borrower.

S 52. In the past, borrowers were often surprised by unexpected or undisclosed borrowing fees and expenses at closing. This phenomenon has been largely corrected through disclosure requirements mandated by which of the following laws?

a. Equal Credit Opportunity Act
b. Truth-in-Lending laws
c. National Disclosure Procedures Act
d. Federal Fair Housing Laws

S 53. Which of the following is an important function of the secondary mortgage market?

a. Participants borrow funds from banks so the banks can make more loans.
b. Participants issue tax certificates and sell them to primary lenders.
c. Participants purchase pools of defaulted loans from lenders to keep them solvent.
d. Participants sell mortgage-backed securities in order to buy pools of loans.

S 54. Cash flow is a measure of how much pre-tax or after-tax cash an investment property generates. To derive cash flow it is therefore necessary to exclude

a. cost recovery expense.
b. interest expense.
c. loan principal payments.
d. net operating income.

S 55. The method for deriving an investor's return on investment, or ROI, is by

a. dividing net operating income by cash flow.
b. multiplying the required yield times after-tax cash flow.
c. dividing net income by the price paid for the property.
d. multiplying cash flow times the price paid for the property.

S 56. Which of the following items would affect a homeowner's adjusted basis?

a. Installing a higher capacity air conditioning and purifying system.
b. Replacing a washing machine.
c. Stripping and staining hardwood floors.
d. Replacing a broken picture window.

S 57. Which of the following is true with respect to real property taxation by the federal government?

a. It imposes ad valorem property taxes and capital gain tax.
b. It may not impose property taxes or tax liens.
c. There are no federal ad valorem taxes on real property.
d. It imposes ad valorem tax, but not capital gain tax.

S 58. Ad valorem taxes are based on

a. the replacement value of property.
b. the assessed value of property.
c. the millage value of property.
d. the broker's estimate of value.

S 59. A retirement facility prohibits ownership of any unit by persons under 55 years of age. The association claims it has made the prohibition properly. Which of the following is true?

a. They are violating the Civil Rights Act of 1866.
b. They are violating the Fair Housing Amendments Act of 1988.
c. They are guilty of age discrimination.
d. The prohibition may be legal if performed correctly.

S 60. An agent receives a full-price offer from a minority party. The agent presents the offer to the seller and discloses the buyer's minority status. The seller at that point instructs the agent to inform the buyer that the property has just gone under contract. The agent duly complies, telling the offeror that the home has just been temporarily removed from the market and is unavailable – but may be available soon if the contract falls through. Which party or parties, if any, have violated fair housing laws?

a. The agent only.
b. The owner only.
c. The agent and the owner.
d. Neither agent nor owner.

S 61. Which of the following are examples of closing items not prorated between buyer and seller?

a. Taxes.
b. Inspection fees.
c. Utilities.
d. Condominium assessments.

S 62. Which of the following activities is not allowed under the Real Estate Settlements and Procedures Act?

a. A broker having any business relationship with an insurance company that is involved in the broker's transaction.
b. A broker pre-qualifying a buyer for a mortgage loan.
c. A lender requiring a deposit from a borrower for a tax and insurance escrow account.
d. A lender paying a fee to a broker for referring a borrower to the lender.

S 63. Which of the following communication records must (as opposed to should) be kept?

a. Notes on every conversation.
b. Copies of required communications to principals.
c. Notes from company training sessions.
d. Business cards of licensees one meets at open houses.

S 64. To minimize the risk of violating fair housing laws, a licensee should

a. refuse to use terms that refer to or describe any of the classes of persons protected by the laws.
b. avoid working in neighborhoods that are predominantly occupied by a single ethnic group.
c. make discriminatory or derogatory remarks in conversation only, never in writing.
d. give better service to members of a protected class than is standard for other clients or customers.

S 65. What are "tenant improvements?"

a. Modifications to a rental suite to conform to a tenant's usage specifications
b. Marketing programs that yield a higher quality of tenant
c. Increased revenue resulting from a rise in rental rates
d. Increased occupancy resulting from a population increase in the market area

S 66. For the proper handling of client and owner monies, a property manager is generally required to

a. deposit all funds every month in the management firm's central operating account.
b. employ a notary to witness and record every deposit or payment received.
c. maintain a special trust account in a qualified financial depository.
d. disburse all funds to their legal owners on a weekly basis.

S 67. Jennifer advised her clients they needed to paint their living room before showing the property. The walls of these rooms were all 8' high. The wall lengths were 14', 18', 16', and 18'. If a gallon of paint covers 200 SF, how many whole gallons would the homesellers have to buy?

a. 1
b. 2
c. 3
d. 6

S 68. An investor just purchased a rectangular 2-acre retail lot for $250 a frontage foot. If she paid $100,000 total, what was the depth of the lot?

a. 400'
b. 250
c. 871'
d. 218'

S 69. Andra can afford to spend $5,000 in closing costs to refinance her home. The lender quotes closing costs of $800 plus 2 points. The house appraised out at $240,000, and she can get an 80% loan. Can Annika afford to refinance?

a. No, she is short by $64.
b. No, she is short by $1,600.
c. Yes, with $360 left over.
d. Yes, she in fact breaks even.

S 70. A lender offers an investor a maximum 70% LTV loan on the appraised value of a property. If the investor pays $230,000 for the property, and this is 15% more than the appraised value, how much will the investor have to pay as a down payment?

a. $93,150
b. $79,350
c. $90,000
d. $69,000

S 71. A house is being appraised using the sales comparison approach. The house has three bedrooms, two bathrooms, and a patio. The appraiser selects a comparable house that has three bedrooms, 2.5 bathrooms, and no patio. The comparable house just sold for $100,000. A half-bath is valued at $5,000, and a patio at $1,000. Assuming all else is equal, what is the adjusted value of the comparable?

a. $100,000
b. $104,000
c. $96,000
d. $106,000

S 72. A family purchased a $90,000 lot to build a custom home. At the date of closing, the lot was assessed at $84,550 and the tax rate was $1.91 / $100 assessed valuation. When they completed the home, the assessment increased by $235,000 to include the new construction. If the monthly tax escrow is based on the assessed value, what will the monthly tax escrow be?

a. $517
b. $6096
c. $508
d. $367

S 73. The James family purchased a home for $180,000 five years ago and obtained an 80% LTV loan. Now the property has appreciated 25%. In addition, the loan has been paid down $11,000. What is the James's current equity in the home?

a. $47,000
b. $81,000
c. $45,000
d. $92,000

S 74. George and Mary have owned a rental house for 10 years. They bought it for $240,000 and estimated the land value @ 25%. If the property is depreciated on a 39-year schedule, and appreciation totals 50% over the period, what is their gain if they sell the property today?

a. $159,230
b. $166,150
c. $181,538
d. $120,000

S 75. Adelpha's home is valued at $250,000. She has insurance coverage of $160,000 with an 80% co-insurance clause. If Adelpha has a damage claim amounting to $100,000, how much will she receive from her policy?

a. $32,000
b. $60,000
c. $80,000
d. $100,000

S 76. Montana's Board of Realty Regulation includes one member who represents the public. That member

a. may not hold a Montana real estate license.
b. must be a licensed appraiser.
c. serves without Senate confirmation.
d. votes only on rulemaking matters.

S 77. The Department may escalate a trust account citation to the Board's complaint screening panel when the violations are significant. Significant means

a. any violation involving client funds.
b. a violation the licensee disputes in writing.
c. a violation found during a scheduled audit rather than through a complaint.
d. too many violations in one audit, repeat violations across audits, or a single severe violation.

S 78. A Montana salesperson's pocket card identifies

a. the salesperson's prelicense education provider.
b. the salesperson's errors and omissions carrier.
c. the supervising broker and the designated address.
d. the date the salesperson's license was first issued.

S 79. Besides the experience requirement and the broker prelicense course, a Montana broker applicant must demonstrate

a. 30 activity points earned within the prior 36 months.
b. 20 closed transactions in the prior 12 months.
c. membership in a REALTOR association.
d. 5 years of continuous licensure.

S 80. A Montana brokerage runs a banner advertisement on a local news website. Licensee identification

a. is not required on banner advertisements.
b. must appear only on the brokerage's own website.
c. must be read aloud in any accompanying audio.
d. must be displayed in the banner, or the banner must link to a page that displays it.

S 81. A complaint is filed with the Board against a Montana salesperson. The supervising broker

a. also receives the complaint and must respond to it.
b. is notified only if the salesperson is found guilty.
c. has no role unless the broker personally participated.
d. may respond on the salesperson's behalf instead of the salesperson.

S 82. A Montana broker may not disburse funds from the trust account until

a. the transaction has closed.
b. the corresponding deposit has been verified.
c. the buyer and seller have both signed a release.
d. 3 business days have passed since the deposit.

S 83. How long must a Montana broker retain documentation of compensation arrangements?

a. 3 years
b. 5 years
c. 6 years
d. 8 years

S 84. A Montana licensee refers a client to a title company in which the licensee holds a financial interest. The licensee must disclose that interest

a. at closing.
b. within 3 days after the referral.
c. before engaging or recommending the title company.
d. only if the client asks about it.

S 85. Montana requires disclosure of methamphetamine contamination

a. when the property is offered for sale or lease.
b. only when the buyer requests testing.
c. only for properties built before 1978.
d. only if law enforcement has issued a citation.

S 86. Interest earned on a Montana broker's trust account may be paid to the broker

a. in all cases, because the broker maintains the account.
b. never, because the funds belong to clients.
c. only if the account is non-interest bearing.
d. only if a written agreement identifies it as compensation for services performed.

S 87. A Montana buyer broker agreement should state who is expected to pay the compensation and

a. the maximum price the buyer will offer.
b. how any shortfall in the expected compensation will be handled.
c. the buyer's credit score and lender.
d. the specific properties the buyer intends to tour.

S 88. Which of the following must a Montana broker maintain for the trust account?

a. A separate chronological ledger for each transaction, with a running balance
b. A quarterly reconciliation performed by an outside accountant
c. A surety bond equal to the highest monthly balance
d. Duplicate paper copies of every record, in addition to electronic copies

S 89. High-level supervision of a Montana salesperson adds which of the following to reasonable supervision?

a. Weekly written performance evaluations
b. A separate trust account for that salesperson's transactions
c. Contract preparation review and pre-closing document review
d. Board approval of each transaction before closing

S 90. A Montana brokerage offers a gift card to anyone who attends a listing presentation. The promotion is

a. permissible, because attendance is voluntary.
b. permissible, if the gift card is of nominal value.
c. permissible, if disclosed in the listing agreement.
d. unprofessional conduct, because the prize is conditioned on a commitment.

S 91. When a Montana salesperson leaves a brokerage, the listings the salesperson obtained

a. remain with the broker, who must immediately notify all principals.
b. transfer with the salesperson to the new brokerage.
c. terminate automatically.
d. are divided by agreement between the two brokers.

S 92. A Montana buyer agent wants to represent two buyers interested in the same property. This is permitted

a. only if the buyers are related.
b. after written disclosure to each buyer and with each buyer's written consent.
c. only if the agent withdraws from one relationship before an offer is written.
d. under no circumstances.

S 93. A Montana statutory broker working with a buyer begins negotiations with the listing agent. The statutory broker must deliver a subsequent disclosure to

a. the buyer only.
b. no one, because a statutory broker represents no one.
c. the Board, within 10 days.
d. the seller or the seller's agent.

S 94. When a Montana supervising broker appoints in-house designates for the buyer and the seller in one transaction, the brokerage must

a. maintain information barriers so one principal's protected information does not reach the other.
b. obtain the Board's approval of the arrangement.
c. treat the supervising broker as a dual agent.
d. reduce the total commission by half.

S 95. A Montana buyer agency agreement reaches its stated expiration date without a purchase. The agency relationship

a. continues until the buyer signs with another brokerage.
b. continues for a 30-day holdover period in every case.
c. ends, though the duties of accounting and confidentiality survive.
d. ends, and all duties including confidentiality end with it.

S 96. Property management is one of Montana's five authorized relationships. It arises from

a. a subagency offer accepted by the manager.
b. the statutory broker presumption.
c. an oral understanding with the owner.
d. a contract between the property manager and the owner.

S 97. At the start of a Montana residential tenancy, the landlord must disclose

a. the name and address of the person authorized to manage the property.
b. the landlord's purchase price for the property.
c. the assessed value of the unit.
d. the names of the other tenants in the building.

S 98. After a judicial foreclosure of a Montana mortgage, the borrower's right of redemption runs

a. 10 days from the sale.
b. 60 days from the sale.
c. 1 year from the date of the sale.
d. until the purchaser records the sheriff's deed.

S 99. The undivided interest in the common elements belonging to a Montana condominium unit

a. may be sold separately from the unit.
b. may be partitioned on the demand of any unit owner.
c. is recalculated annually by the association.
d. passes with the unit even if the deed does not mention it.

S 100. A person who believes a Montana housing discrimination violation has occurred may file a complaint with the Montana Human Rights Bureau within

a. 90 days of the discriminatory act.
b. 180 days of the discriminatory act.
c. 1 year of the discriminatory act.
d. 2 years of the discriminatory act.

Section VII: Answer Key

NATIONAL TEST 1: Rights; Interests and Estates; Ownership

1.1 (a) Wells, driveways, and signs on a parcel of land.
The legal concept of real estate encompasses land and all man-made structures that are "permanently" attached to the land. The phrase "permanently attached" refers primarily to one's intention in attaching the item. Obviously, very few if any man-made structures can be permanently attached to the land in the literal sense. But if a person constructs a house with the intention of creating a permanent dwelling, the house is considered real estate. By contrast, if a camper affixes a tent to the land with the intention of moving it to another camp in a week, the tent would not be considered real estate.

1.2 (c) A chicken coop permanently attached to land.
Improvements to real estate include such things as fences, streets, buildings, wells, sewers, sidewalks and piers. Modifications to land or a developer's preparations of a parcel of land can include such activities as grading or clearing, neither of which are considered to be "improvements" in this sense of the word.

1.3 (b) The center of the earth and infinite space above the earth.
The legal concept of land encompasses the surface area of the earth; everything beneath the surface of the earth extending downward to its center; all natural things permanently attached to the earth; and the air above the surface of the earth extending outward to infinity. Land, therefore, includes minerals beneath the earth's surface, water on or below the earth's surface, and the air above the surface.

1.4 (a) enjoyed by the owner of a property.
This group of rights includes the right to Possess, Use, Transfer, Encumber, and Exclude others from using the property. (Remember: "PUTEE") Transfer rights include the right to sell, rent, donate, assign, or bequeath. The owner may also encumber the item by mortgaging it as collateral for debt.

1.5 (b) Any item of property that is not definable as real property.
Personal property is any owned item which is not real estate, and the rights associated with owning the personal property item. Items of personal property are also called chattels or personalty.

1.6 (b) pledge the property as collateral for debt.
The right to encumber the property essentially means the right to mortgage the property as collateral for debt. There may be restrictions to this right, such as a spouse's right to limit the degree to which a homestead may be mortgaged.

1.7 (a) transfer of a portion of the bundle of rights.
An ordinary lease is a common example of the transfer of a portion of one's bundle of rights. The owner relinquishes the right to possess portions of the surface, perhaps a building, in return for rent. The tenant enjoys the rights to possess and use the building over the term of the lease, after which these rights revert to the landlord. During the lease term, the tenant has no rights to the property's subsurface or airspace other than what the building occupies. Further, the tenant does not enjoy any of the other rights in the bundle of rights: he or she cannot encumber the property or transfer it. To a limited degree, the tenant may exclude persons other than the legal owner from the property.

1.8 (d) Yes. The drones infringe on his air rights.
Air rights apply to the space above the surface boundaries of the parcel, as delineated by imaginary vertical lines extended to infinity. Since the advent of aviation, property owners' air rights have been curtailed to allow aircraft to fly over one's property provided the overflights do not interfere with the owner's use and enjoyment of the property. The issue of violation of air rights for the benefit of air transportation is an ongoing battle between aircraft owners, airlines, airports, and nearby property owners.

1.9 (c) Navigable lakes, seas, and oceans.
Littoral rights concern properties abutting bodies of water that are not moving, such as lakes and seas. Owners of properties abutting a navigable, non-moving body of water enjoy the littoral right of use, but do not own the water nor the land beneath the water. The legal premise underlying the definition of littoral

rights is that a lake or sea is a navigable body of water, therefore, public property owned by the state. By contrast, a body of water entirely contained within the boundaries of an owner's property is not navigable. In such a case, the owner would own the water as well as unrestricted rights of usage.

1.10 (a) the high water mark of the body of water at the shoreline.
Ownership extends to the high-water mark of the body of water. The low water mark would imply that the owner owned the water itself at times of high water levels!

1.11 (d) They transfer with the property when the property is sold.
Littoral rights attach to the property. When the property is sold, the littoral rights transfer with the property to the new owner.

1.12 (c) Streams and rivers.
Riparian rights concern properties abutting moving water such as streams and rivers. If a property abuts a stream or river, the owner's riparian rights are determined by whether the water is navigable or not navigable. If the property abuts a non-navigable stream, the owner enjoys unrestricted use of the water and owns the land beneath the stream to the stream's midpoint. If the waterway in question is navigable, the waterway is considered to be a public easement. In such a case, the owner's property extends to the water's edge as opposed to the midpoint of the waterway.

1.13 (b) An item of personal property that has been converted to real property.
A personal property item that has been converted to real property by attachment to real estate is called a fixture. Typical examples are chandeliers, toilets, water pumps, septic tanks, and window shutters. The owner of real property inherently owns all fixtures belonging to the real property. When the owner sells the real property, the buyer acquires rights to all fixtures.

1.14 (a) the owner originally intended to remove it after a period of time.
One's original intention can override the test of movability in determining whether an item is a fixture or not. If someone attached an item to real property, yet intended to remove it after a period of time, the article may be deemed personal property. If a person intended an article to be a fixture, even though the item is easily removable, the article may be deemed a fixture. For example, an apartment renter installs an alarm system, fully intending to remove the system upon lease expiration. Here, the alarm system would be considered personal property.

1.15 (c) Fifty percent of the estate consisting of the indivisible whole of the real property.
An undivided interest is an owner's fractional interest in an entire (undivided) estate, but not in a physical portion of the real property itself. An owner who has an undivided equal interest with another cannot exercise exclusive rights over a portion of the real estate, which is an indivisible whole.

1.16 (a) an estate in land.
Interests are principally distinguished by whether they include possession. If the interest-holder enjoys the right of possession, the party is considered to have an estate in land, or, familiarly an estate. Freehold and leasehold estates in land are further distinguished by whether the duration of the owner's rights can be determined.

1.17 (a) a public interest.
Public entities may own or lease real estate, in which case they enjoy an estate in land. However, government entities also have non-possessory interests in real estate which act to control land use for the public good within the entity's jurisdiction. The prime example of public interest is police power, or the right of the local or county government to zone. Another example of public interest is the right to acquire ownership through the power of eminent domain.

1.18 (c) a freehold estate.
In a freehold estate, the duration of the owner's rights cannot be determined: the rights may endure for a lifetime, for less than a lifetime, or for generations beyond the owner's lifetime. By contrast, leasehold estates have expirations.

1.19 (d) that the estate is limited by a lease term.
A leasehold estate is distinguished by its specific duration, as represented by the lease term. Further, leasehold tenants only enjoy limited property rights: use; temporary possession, and limited exclusion.

1.20 (d) Fee simple defeasible.
The defeasible fee estate is perpetual, provided the usage conforms to stated conditions. Essential characteristics are that the property must be used for a certain purpose or under certain conditions, and, if the use changes or if prohibited conditions are present, the estate reverts to the previous grantor of the estate.

1.21 (c) An ordinary life estate.
A life estate is limited in duration to the life of the owner or other named person. Upon the death of the owner (ordinary life estate) or other named individual (pur autre vie life estate), the estate passes to the original owner (a reversionary interest) or another named party (a remainder interest). Thus with the life estate, the owner enjoys full ownership rights during the estate period, and holders of the future interest own either a reversionary or a remainder interest.

1.22 (b) a legal life estate.
Homestead, dower, and curtesy are legal life estates. A legal life estate is created by state law as opposed to being created by a property owner's agreement. The focus of a legal life estate is defining and protecting the property rights of surviving family members upon the death of the husband or wife.

1.23 (b) The boat, house, and motorcycle.
Separate property consists of: property owned by either spouse at the time of the marriage; property acquired by either spouse through inheritance or gift during the marriage; property acquired with separate-property funds; and income from separate property. Community property consists of all other property earned or acquired by either party during the marriage. A spouse owns separate property free and clear of claims by the other spouse. He or she can transfer it without the other spouse's signature. Upon the death of the separate property owner, the property passes to heirs by will or laws of descent. Community property cannot be transferred or encumbered without the signatures of both spouses. Upon the death of either spouse, half of the deceased's community property passes to the surviving spouse, and the other half passes to the decedent's heirs.

1.24 (d) The right to possess and use the premises.
Leasehold tenants are entitled to possess and use the leased premises during the lease term in the manner prescribed in the lease. They also have restricted rights to exclusion.

1.25 (a) the tenant makes, and landlord accepts, regular rent payments.
In an estate from period-to-period, also called a periodic tenancy, the tenancy period automatically renews as long as the tenant pays rent in a timely manner and the landlord accepts it. At the end of a tenancy period, if the landlord accepts another regular payment of rent, the leasehold is considered to be renewed for another period. A conveyance of leased property does not cancel a leasehold interest.

1.26 (c) terminates on the death of lessor or lessee.
The estate at will, also called a tenancy at will, has no definite expiration date and hence no "renewal" cycle. The landlord and tenant agree that the tenancy will have no specified termination date, provided rent is paid on time and other lease conditions are met. For example, a son leases a house to his father and mother "forever," or until they want to move. The estate at will is terminated by proper notice, or by the death of either party.

1.27 (a) an estate at sufferance.
In an estate at sufferance, a tenant occupies the premises without consent of the landlord or other legal agreement with the landlord. Usually such an estate involves a tenant who fails to vacate at the expiration of the lease, continuing occupancy without any right to do so. For example, a tenant violates the provisions of a lease and is evicted. The tenant protests and refuses to leave despite the eviction order.

1.28 (b) Estate from period to period.
In an estate from period-to-period, also called a periodic tenancy, the tenancy period automatically renews for an indefinite period of time, subject to timely payment of rent. At the end of a tenancy period, if the landlord accepts another regular payment of rent, the leasehold is considered to be renewed for another period.

1.29 (a) tenancy in severalty.
If a single party owns the fee or life estate, the ownership is a tenancy in severalty. Synonyms are sole ownership, ownership in severalty, and estate in severalty.

1.30 (c) tenancy in common.
The tenancy in common, also known as the estate in common, is the most common form of co-ownership when the owners are not married (though tenants in common can be married). The defining characteristics are: two or more owners; identical rights; interests individually owned; electable ownership shares; no survivorship; and no unity of time. With "identical rights", co-tenants share an indivisible interest in the estate, i.e., all have equal rights to possess and use the property subject to the rights of the other co-tenants.

1.31 (a) Parties must acquire respective interests at the same time.
To create a joint tenancy, all owners must acquire the property at the same time, use the same deed, acquire equal interests, and share in equal rights of possession. These are referred to as the four unities.

1.32 (b) cannot will their interest to a party outside the tenancy. The survivorship feature of joint tenancy presents an advantage to tenancy in common, in that interests pass without probate proceedings. On the other hand, joint tenants relinquish any ability to will their interest to parties outside of the tenancy.

1.33 (c) Legal life estate.
A legal life estate is created by state law as opposed to being created by a property owner's agreement. The focus of a legal life estate is defining and protecting the property rights of surviving family members upon the death of the husband or wife.

1.34 (a) A homestead interest cannot be conveyed by one spouse.
A homestead is one's principal residence. Homestead laws protect family members against losing their homes to general creditors attempting to collect on debts. Homestead laws generally provide that: the homestead interest cannot be conveyed by one spouse; both spouses must sign the deed conveying homestead property.

1.35 (a) sell or transfer his interest without the consent of the other tenants in common.
All tenants in common have distinct and separable ownership of their respective interests. Co-tenants may sell, encumber, or transfer their interests without obstruction or consent from the other owners. A co-tenant may not, however, encumber the entire property.

1.36 (c) Income derived from community property
If an income-producing property has been defined as community property, the revenue accruing from the investment is likewise community property.

1.37 (c) The beneficiary
A land trust allows the trustor to convey the fee estate to the trustee and to name himself or herself the beneficiary. The land trust applies only to real property, not to personal property. The agreement, or deed in trust, grants the beneficiary the rights to possess and use the property, and to exercise control over the actions of the trustee.

1.38 (c) The Buick and the second property
Community property laws define property rights of legal spouses before, during, and after their marriage, as well as after the death of either spouse. Community property law distinguishes real and personal property into categories of separate and community property. Separate property belongs to one spouse; community property belongs to both spouses equally. Separate property is that property which is acquired prior to the marriage, by gift or inheritance during the marriage, property acquired by separate-property funds, or income from separate property.

1.39 (a) A cooperative may hold an owner liable for the unpaid operating expenses of other tenants.
Since the corporation owns an undivided interest in the cooperative property, debts and financial obligations apply to the property as a whole, not to individual units as in a condominium.

1.40 (b) The owners enjoy an indivisible interest.
The tenancy in common, also known as the estate in common, is the most common form of co-ownership when the owners are not married (though tenants in common can be married). The defining characteristics

are: two or more owners; identical rights; interests individually owned; electable ownership shares; no survivorship; and no unity of time. With "identical rights," co-tenants share an indivisible interest in the estate, i.e., all have equal rights to possess and use the property subject to the rights of the other co-tenants.

1.41 (a) sell her interest to a third party without the consent of Robert
All tenants in common have distinct and separable ownership of their respective interests. Co-tenants may sell, encumber, or transfer their interests without obstruction or consent from the other owners. A co-tenant may not, however, encumber the entire property.

1.42 (d) It passes by probate to the deceased tenant's heirs.
A deceased co-tenant's estate passes by probate to the decedent's heirs and devisees rather than to the other tenants in common. Any number of heirs can share in the ownership of the willed tenancy.

1.43 (c) The tenants have an equal and indivisible ownership interest.
In a joint tenancy, two or more people collectively own a property as if they were a single person. Rights and interests are indivisible and equal: each has a shared interest in the whole property which cannot be divided up. Joint tenants may only convey their interests to outside parties as tenant-in-common interests. One cannot convey a joint tenant interest.

1.44 (a) there is a single title to the property.
Whereas tenants in common hold separate title to their individual interests, joint tenants together hold a single title to the property. This is referred to as unity of ownership.

1.45 (a) the new owner becomes a tenant in common with the other owners, who continue to hold a joint tenancy with each other and a tenancy in common with the new owner.
A joint tenant may transfer his or her interest in the property to an outside party, but only as a tenancy in common interest. Whoever acquires the interest co-owns the property as a tenant in common with the other joint tenants. The remaining joint tenants continue to own an undivided interest in the property, less the new co-tenant's share.

1.46 (d) It passes to the surviving joint tenants.
In most states, joint tenants enjoy rights of survivorship: if a joint tenant dies, all interests and rights pass to the surviving joint tenants free from any claims of creditors or heirs. When only one joint tenant survives, the survivor's interest becomes an estate in severalty, and the joint tenancy is terminated.

1.47 (c) If they are married.
Tenancy by the entireties is a form of ownership reserved exclusively for husband and wife. It features survivorship, equal interests, and limited exposure to foreclosure. In some states it now applies to same-sex couples.

1.48 (c) The trustee.
In an estate in trust, a fee owner-- the grantor or trustor-- transfers legal title to a fiduciary-- the trustee-- who holds and manages the estate for the benefit of another party, the beneficiary. The trust may be created by a deed, will, or trust agreement.

1.49 (a) sell or mortgage the unit without impediment from individual owners of neighboring units.
Condominium units can be individually sold, mortgaged, or otherwise encumbered without interference from other unit owners. An owner may not sell interests in the apartment separately from the interest in the common elements. Unit owners exclusively possess their apartment space, but must share common areas with other owners.

1.50 (b) the unit's pro rata share of the property value as defined in the declaration.
The unit's pro rata share of the property's ownership as defined in the declaration determines the amount of a unit owner's assessment. For example, if a unit represents a 2% share of the property value, that unit owner's assessment will be 2% of the property's common area expenses.

1.51 (a) shares in a corporation or association and a proprietary lease in a physical unit.
In a cooperative, or co-op, one owns shares in a non-profit corporation or cooperative association, which in turn acquires and owns an apartment building as its principal asset. Along with this stock, the shareholder acquires a proprietary lease to occupy one of the apartment units.

1.52 (d) the corporate entity of the cooperative association.
The corporate entity of the cooperative association is the only party in the cooperative with a real property interest. The association's interest is an undivided interest in the entire property. There is no ownership interest in individual units, as with a condominium.

1.53 (a) undivided interests in the property as tenants in common.
In a freehold time-share, or interval ownership estate, tenants in common own undivided interests in the property. Expense prorations and rules governing interval usage are established by separate agreement when the estate is acquired.

1.54 (c) As soon as it is affixed to the ground.
Mobile home units and manufactured homes are personal property until they are secured to the foundation of the lot in whatever form. Prior to affixing these items are personal property.

1.55 (b) The estate becomes a holdover tenancy, a periodic leasehold estate.
If a tenant with a leasehold estate for years remains in possession of the leased premises after lease expiration, a holdover lease is created. In the absence of a new lease agreement stating otherwise, the holdover tenancy becomes a periodic tenancy.

NATIONAL TEST 2: Encumbrances; Liens; Title Transfer and Recording; Leases

2.1 (c) A third party's interest in a real property that limits the interests of the freehold property owner.
An encumbrance is an interest in and right to real property that limits the legal owner's freehold interest. In effect, an encumbrance is another's right to use or take possession of a legal owner's property, or to prevent the legal owner from enjoying the full bundle of rights in the estate.

2.2 (a) They involve the property that contains the easement and a non-owning party. An easement is an interest in real property that gives the holder the right to use portions of the legal owner's real property in a defined way. One cannot own an easement over one's own property. Easement rights may apply to a property's surface, subsurface, or airspace, but the affected area must be defined. An easement may be affirmative, allowing a use, such as a right-of-way, or negative, prohibiting a use, such as an airspace easement that prohibits one property owner from obstructing another's ocean view.

2.3 (d) An easement appurtenant.
An easement appurtenant gives a property owner a right of usage to portions of an adjoining property owned by another party. The property enjoying the usage right is called the dominant tenement, or dominant estate. The property containing the physical easement itself is the servient tenement, since it must serve the easement use.

2.4 (c) easement by necessity.
An easement by necessity is an easement appurtenant granted by a court of law to a property owner because of a circumstance of necessity, most commonly the need for access to a property. Since property cannot be legally landlocked, or without legal access to a public thoroughfare, a court will grant an owner of a landlocked property an easement by necessity over an adjoining property that has access to a thoroughfare.

2.5 (b) an unauthorized physical intrusion of one property into another.
An encroachment is the unauthorized, physical intrusion of one owner's real property into that of another. Examples of encroachments are: a tree limb extending into the neighbor's property, violating his or her airspace; a driveway extending beyond the lot line onto the neighbor's land; and a fence built beyond the property line.

2.6 (c) a trespasser has been using an owner's property for a certain period with the owner's knowledge but without permission.
If someone uses another's property as an easement without permission for a statutory period of time and under certain conditions, a court order may give the user the easement right by prescription, regardless of

the owner's desires. For a prescriptive easement order to be granted, the following circumstances must be true: the use has been occurring without permission or license; the owner knows or is presumed to have known of the use; and the use has been generally uninterrupted over the statutory prescriptive period.

2.7 (d) how a property may be used and what improvements may be built on it.
A deed restriction is a limitation imposed on a buyer's use of a property by stipulation in the deed of conveyance or recorded subdivision plat. A deed restriction may apply to a single property or to an entire subdivision. A developer may place restrictions on all properties within a recorded subdivision plat. Subsequent re-sales of properties within the subdivision are thereby subject to the plat's covenants and conditions.

2.8 (c) the creditor's claim against the property as collateral security for the loan.
A lien is a creditor's claim against personal or real property as security for a debt of the property owner. If the owner defaults, the lien gives the creditor the right to force the sale of the property to satisfy the debt. For example, a homeowner borrows $5,000 to pay for a new roof. The lender funds the loan in exchange for the borrower's promissory note to repay the loan. At the same time, the lender places a lien on the property for $5,000 as security for the debt. If the borrower defaults, the lien allows the lender to force the sale of the house to satisfy the debt.

2.9 (d) An equitable interest.
A lienor generally has an equitable interest in the property, but not legal ownership. The exception is a mortgage lien on a property in a title-theory state. In these states, the mortgage transaction conveys legal title to the lender, who holds it until the mortgage obligations are satisfied. During the mortgage loan period, the borrower has equitable title to the property.

2.10 (a) Payment of the debt that is the subject of the lien and recording of the satisfaction.
A lien terminates on payment of the debt and recording of documents. Payment of the debt and recording of the appropriate satisfaction documents ordinarily terminate a lien. If a default occurs, a suit for judgment or foreclosure enforces the lien. These actions force the sale of the property.

2.11 (d) involuntary general lien.
A general lien is one placed against any and all real and personal property owned by a particular debtor. An example is an inheritance tax lien placed against all property owned by the heir. A specific lien attaches to a single item of real or personal property and does not affect other property owned by the debtor. In addition, judgment liens are junior, involuntary liens.

2.12 (a) Real estate tax lien.
The category of superior, or senior, liens ranks above the category of inferior, or junior, liens, meaning that superior liens receive first payment from the proceeds of a foreclosure. The superior category includes liens for real estate tax, special assessments, and inheritance tax. Other liens, including income tax liens, mortgage liens and judgment liens, are inferior.

2.13 (d) subordinate the lien.
A lienor can change the priority of a junior lien by voluntarily agreeing to subordinate, or lower, the lien's position in the hierarchy. This change is often necessary when working with a mortgage lender who will not originate a mortgage loan unless it is senior to all other junior liens on the property. The lender may require the borrower to obtain agreements from other lien holders to subordinate their liens to the new mortgage.

2.14 (c) A proceeding to enforce a lien by forcing the sale or transfer of a secured property.
All liens can be enforced by the sale or other transfer of title of the secured property, whether by court action, operation of law, or through powers granted in the original loan agreement. The enforcement proceedings are referred to as foreclosure. Note that lienors already possess equitable title, so they do not need to undertake a legal proceeding to establish this.

2.15 (b) file a foreclosure suit.
Judicial foreclosure occurs in states that use a two-party mortgage document (borrower and lender) that does not contain a "power of sale" provision. Lacking this provision, a lender must file a foreclosure suit and undertake a court proceeding to enforce the lien.

2.16 (a) strict foreclosure. Strict foreclosure is a court proceeding that gives the lender title directly, by court order, instead of giving cash proceeds from a public sale. On default, the lender gives the borrower official notice. After a prescribed period, the lender files suit in court, whereupon the court establishes a period within which the defaulting party must repay the amounts owed. If the defaulter does not repay the funds, the court orders transfer of full, legal title to the lender.

2.17 (d) A license, which terminates upon the owner's death.
A license is a personal right that a property owner grants to another to use the property for a specific purpose (to reach the kindergarten school bus). Unlike a personal easement in gross, which terminates only on the death of the grantee (Betty Luanne, in this instance), a license is revocable at any moment, is not transferable and does not attach to the land. It ceases on the death of either party, or on the sale of the property.

2.18 (d) Dominant tenement.
An easement appurtenant gives a property owner a right of usage to portions of an adjoining property owned by another party. The property enjoying the usage right is called the dominant tenement, or dominant estate. The property containing the physical easement itself is the servient tenement, since it must serve the easement use.

2.19 (b) a deed restriction.
A private party who wants to control the quality and standards of a property can establish a deed restriction. Deed restrictions take precedence over zoning ordinances if they are more restrictive.

2.20 (a) It involves a monetary claim against the value of a property.
A lien is a creditor's claim against personal or real property as security for a debt of the property owner. If the owner defaults, the lien gives the creditor the right to force the sale of the property to satisfy the debt. Liens do not necessarily alter the property value. Liens can be involuntary as well as voluntary. Finally, liens attach to the property, but so do other encumbrances.

2.21 (d) It is knowledge received or imparted through direct experience.
The term "notice" is synonymous with "knowledge." A person who has received actual notice has actual knowledge of something. Receiving actual notice means learning of something through direct experience or communication. Thus, a document in itself cannot be actual notice. It is the seeing of the document that makes it actual notice.

2.22 (b) It is knowledge one could have or should have obtained. Constructive notice, or legal notice, is knowledge of a fact that a person could have or should have obtained. The foremost method of imparting constructive notice is by recordation of ownership documents in public records, specifically, title records. Since public records are open to everyone, the law generally presumes that when evidence of ownership is recorded, the public at large has received constructive notice of ownership.

2.23 (a) grant, deed, and will.
Voluntary transfer, or voluntary alienation, is an unforced transfer of title by sale or gift from an owner to another party. If the transferor is a government entity and the recipient is a private party, the conveyance is a public grant. If the transferor is a private party, the conveyance is a private grant. A living owner makes a private grant by means of a deed of conveyance, or deed. A private grant that occurs when the owner dies is a transfer by will.

2.24 (c) It gives constructive notice of ownership.
Recording is not necessary to make a deed valid. However, it is in the grantee's best interests to do so. Recording the deed gives the public constructive notice of the grantee's ownership.

2.25 (b) granting clause.
The granting, or premises, clause is the only required clause. It contains the conveyance intentions; names the parties; describes the property; and indicates a nominal consideration.

2.26 (a) general warranty deed.
The general warranty deed, or warranty deed for short, contains the fullest possible assurances of good title and protection for the grantee. The deed is technically a bargain and sale deed in which the grantor promises to defend against any and all claims to the title. The overall general warranty covenant is: "I own

and will defend."

2.27 (d) To have an encumbrance removed if the lienholder cannot prove its validity.
Where there is a possibility that prior errors in deeds or other recorded documents might cloud (encumber) the title, the relevant parties execute a quitclaim deed to convey "any and all" interest to the grantee. If a party responsible for encumbering title refuses to quitclaim the interest, the owner may file a quiet title suit. This requires the lienor to prove the validity of an interest. If the defendant is unable to do so, the court removes the cloud by decree.

2.28 (a) A transfer tax based on the price of the property being conveyed.
State law usually requires payment of a documentary stamp tax on a conveyance of real property. The tax is based on the actual price of the property conveyed, thus enabling taxing authorities to ascertain current market value for ad valorem tax purposes. Payment of the tax is evidenced on the deed.

2.29 (b) probate.
A court proceeding called probate generally settles a decedent's estate, whether the person has died testate (having left a valid will) or intestate (having failed to do so).

2.30 (a) It will escheat to the state or county.
If an intestate decedent has no heirs, the estate escheats, or reverts, to the state or county after all claims and debts have been validated and settled.

2.31 (d) Eminent domain.
Various government and public entities can transfer private property to the public sphere by the power of eminent domain. The transfer is involuntary, even though the owner receives compensation. For example, a city government wants to widen a highway to accommodate growth. The government uses eminent domain to condemn and purchase all properties abutting the thoroughfare in order to complete the construction project.

2.32 (a) openly possessing and claiming the property without the owner's consent.
To claim legal title, the adverse possessor must be able to show a claim of right or color of title as reason for the possession; have notorious possession, which is possession without concealment; maintain a consistent claim of hostile possession, which is a claim to ownership and possession regardless of the owner's claims or consent; occupy the property continuously for a statutory period of time; in some states, pay taxes.

2.33 (c) The buyer.
Title records protect the buyer by revealing whether a property has marketable title, one free of undesirable encumbrances. The buyer is legally responsible for knowing the condition of title, since it is a matter of public record.

2.34 (a) a clouded title.
Chain of title refers to the succession of property owners of record dating back to the original grant of title from the state to a private party. If there is a missing link in the chronology of owners, or if there was a defective conveyance, the chain is said to be broken, resulting in a clouded title to the property.

2.35 (b) standard owner's title insurance policy.
An owner's policy may have standard coverage or extended coverage. Standard coverage protects against title defects such as incompetent grantors, invalid deeds, fraudulent transaction documents, and defects in the chain of title. Extended coverage protects against liabilities that may not be of public record, including fraud, unrecorded ownership claims, unintentional recording errors, and unrecorded liens.

2.36 (a) voluntary alienation.
Voluntary alienation is an unforced transfer of title by sale or gift from an owner to another party.

2.37 (d) A quitclaim deed.
A quitclaim deed transfers real and potential interests in a property, whether an interest is known to exist or not. The grantor makes no claim to any interest in the property being conveyed and offers no warrants to protect the grantee. Where there is a possibility that prior errors in deeds or other recorded documents might cloud (encumber) the title, the relevant parties execute a quitclaim deed to convey "any and all"

interest to the grantee.

2.38 (a) pass to the heirs by the laws of descent and distribution.
In this circumstance, the estate, including real property, will pass to lawful heirs according to the state's laws of descent and succession or distribution. These laws apportion the estate without regard to the wishes of the heirs or the intentions of the decedent. Escheat, by which the state takes the property, applies only if there are no legal heirs.

2.39 (d) declined because possession was secretive.
One of the preconditions for a claim of ownership based on adverse possession is notorious possession, or possession without concealment. Even if the length of possession in this case meets the statutory requirement, the drifter's secretiveness would invalidate the claim.

2.40 (b) free of undisclosed defects and encumbrances.
Marketable title is, by definition, one that is free and clear of undesirable and unknown encumbrances, claims, clouds, or other defects. Attorney's abstracts and title certificates do not guarantee that a title is marketable.

2.41 (c) Estate at will.
Three of the four principal types of leasehold estate are: the estate for years, which has a specific lease term; the estate from period-to-period, where the lease term of a specific period automatically renews; and the estate at will, which has no specified lease term. The fourth principal type, the estate at sufferance, is a tenancy without consent that therefore also has no specific term.

2.42 (b) for specified reasonable purposes.
A tenant has the sole right to occupy and use the premises without interference from outside parties, including the landlord. The landlord may enter the premises for specified purposes such as inspections, but the interference must be reasonable and limited. In addition, the landlord can do nothing outside of the lease's express provisions that would impair the tenant's enjoyment of income deriving from use of the premises.

2.43 (a) compliance with the rules and regulations of the building.
The lease defines the tenant's obligations, which principally are to pay the rent on time; maintain the property's condition; and comply with the rules and regulations of the building.

2.44 (b) providing required building support and services.
The lease defines the landlord's obligations, which principally are to provide the necessary building support and services, and maintain the condition of the property. It is the tenant's responsibility to obtain insurance and to determine the fairness of the rent.

2.45 (d) the tenant's estate is still obligated under the lease.
A valid lease creates obligations that survive the death of the landlord or tenant, with certain exceptions. A tenant's estate remains liable for payment of rent if the tenant dies; the landlord's estate remains bound to provide occupancy despite the landlord's death.

2.46 (a) The remaining tenant is responsible for the full rent obligation.
Multiple tenants who sign a single lease are jointly and severally responsible for fulfilling lease obligations. Thus, if one renter abandons an apartment, the other renters remain liable for rent.

2.47 (c) sublease.
Subletting (subleasing) is the transfer by a tenant, the sublessor, of a portion of the leasehold interest to another party, the sublessee, through the execution of a sublease. The sublease spells out all of the rights and obligations of the sublessor and sublessee, including the payment of rent to the sublessor. The sublessor remains primarily liable for the original lease with the landlord. The subtenant is liable only to the sublessor.

2.48 (d) net lease.
A net lease requires a tenant to pay for utilities, internal repairs, and a proportionate share of taxes, insurance, and operating expenses in addition to rent. In effect, the landlord "passes through" actual property expenses to the tenant rather than charging a higher rent level. Net leases vary as to exactly what

expenses the tenant is responsible for. The purest form of net lease requires tenants to cover all expenses, including major repairs and property taxes.

2.49 (a) gross lease.
A gross lease, or full service lease, requires the landlord to pay the property's operating expenses, including utilities, repairs, and maintenance, while the tenant pays only rent. Rent levels under a gross lease are higher than under a net lease, since the landlord recoups expense outlays in the form of added rent.

2.50 (b) An owner-developer wants to retain ownership of the land portion of the improved real property.
Ground leases are primarily used when an owner wishes to lease raw land to an agricultural or mining interest; when unimproved property is to be developed and the owner wants to retain ownership of the land; when the developer or future users of the property do not want to own the land; or when the owner of an improved property wishes to sell an interest in the improvements while retaining ownership of the underlying land.

2.51 (a) either party giving proper notice.
In the absence of an explicit term with a beginning and ending date, a court will generally construe the lease to be a tenancy at will, cancelable upon proper notice.

2.52 (b) a tenancy from period-to-period.
URLTA sets standards for improving oral, vague, or unbalanced lease agreements. In the case of an unclear lease expiration date, the lease is generally deemed to be a periodic tenancy.

2.53 (a) a hotel.
State laws based on URLTA generally do not apply to transient occupancies, such as hotel and motel rentals, proprietary leases in cooperatives, or to occupancy in a residence that is under a contract for deed.

2.54 (c) a temporary possessory interest.
A lease is both an instrument of conveyance and a contract between principal parties to uphold certain covenants and obligations. As a conveyance, a lease conveys an interest, called the leasehold estate, but does not convey legal title to the property. For this reason, a leasehold is also called a less-than-freehold estate.

2.55 (d) A leased fee estate.
In conveying the leasehold estate, the landlord acquires a leased fee estate, which entails the rights to: receive rent; re-possess the property following the lease term; and monitor the tenant's obligations to maintain the premises.

2.56 (c) occupy the property.
The legal essence of a valid lease is that it conveys an exclusive right to use and occupy a property for a limited period of time in exchange for rent and the return of the property after the lease term is over.

2.57 (a) The buyer acquires title subject to the lease, which remains in effect.
The landlord may sell, assign, or mortgage the leased fee interest. However, transferring and encumbering the leased property do not extinguish the obligations and covenants of a lease. Buyers and creditors, therefore, must take their respective interests subject to the terms of the lease.

2.58 (c) When either party gives proper notice.
In the absence of an explicit term with a beginning and ending date, a court will generally construe the lease to be a tenancy at will, cancelable upon proper notice.

2.59 (c) a five-year lease must be in writing to be enforceable.
Generally, a lease for a period exceeding one year cannot be oral but must be in writing to be enforceable because of the statute of frauds.

2.60 (b) The original tenant retains primary responsibility for performance of the original lease contract.
In a sublease-- a transfer of a portion of the leasehold-- the sublessor (original tenant) remains primarily liable for the original lease with the landlord. The subtenant is liable only to the sublessor.

2.61 (d) deficiency judgment.
Whenever there are insufficient funds to retire a defaulted and foreclosed mortgage loan, a deficiency judgment may be ordered – if allowed by law – to make up the difference. To comply with the judgment, the borrower must raise additional funds from other sources to make up the difference between the outstanding loan balance and the proceeds from the foreclosure sale.

2.62 (b) The possession must have been unconcealed, for the necessary length of time, and without permission
Adverse possession is only possible if the possession is open, continuous for the statutory period, and the possessor claims ownership.

2.63 (a) Recording instruments establishes the title's marketability.
When deeds, tax stamps, and liens are recorded, the public is given notice of the property's indebtedness and encumbrances. In turn, any future buyer can visualize what must be done to clear title and convey marketable title.

2.64 (c) A broker's lien
Many states allow a broker in specified circumstances to file a broker's lien against a property following the closing of a transaction. Here, the party who is obligated to pay the broker a commission refuses to pay. The broker's lien, once filed, attaches to the real estate interest owned by the obligated party.

2.65 (a) The lender must approve of the modified loan and selling terms.
The conventional transaction principles are the buyer and the seller. In a short sale, the loan must typically be modified so that the parties can feasibly proceed with the sale. Any time the loan must be modified, the lender assumes a primary role in the negotiations, and must in turn approve of the loan modifications made.

NATIONAL TEST 3: Land Use Regulation & Control; Legal Descriptions; Contract Law

3.1 (d) Zoning ordinances are a primary means of keeping land use in harmony with the master plan.
The master plan fuses state and regional land use laws with local land use objectives that correspond to the municipality's social and economic conditions. The completed plan becomes the overall guideline for creating and enforcing zones, building codes, and development requirements.

3.2 (c) specify usage for every parcel within the zoning authority's jurisdiction.
The intent of zoning ordinances is to specify land usage for every parcel within the jurisdiction. In some areas, state laws permit zoning ordinances to apply to areas immediately beyond the legal boundaries of the city or county.

3.3 (b) To separate land uses so that they do not interfere with each other.
One of the primary applications of zoning power is the separation of residential properties from commercial and industrial uses. Proper design of land use in this manner preserves the aesthetics and value of neighborhoods and promotes the success of commercial enterprises through intelligently located zones. Six common types of zone are: residential; commercial; industrial; agricultural; public; and planned unit development (PUD).

3.4 (c) The public interest
The principal forms of exceptions to a conforming use is legal nonconforming use (grandfathered in); variance based on hardship; and special exception based on the public interest.

3.5 (d) The area of a commercial or industrial facility in relation to the size of the site.
Commercial zoning regulates intensity of usage by limiting the area of store or office per site area. Intensity regulation is further achieved by minimum parking requirements, setbacks, and building height restrictions.

3.6 (c) It requires that multiple tracts of land be developed according to a single design.
Planned unit development zoning restricts use to development of whole tracts that are designed to use space efficiently and maximize open space. A PUD zone may be for residential, commercial, or industrial uses,

or combinations thereof.

3.7 (a) A homeowner in a residential zone converts her residence to a private school.
A legal nonconforming use can be illustrated as follows. A motel is situated in a residential area that no longer allows commercial activity. The zoning board rules that the motel may continue to operate until it is sold, destroyed or used for any other commercial purpose. An illegal nonconforming use is one that conflicts with ordinances that were in place before the use commenced. For instance, if the motel in the previous example is sold, and the new owner continues to operate the property as a motel, the motel is now an illegal, nonconforming use.

3.8 (b) A variance is granted by the zoning board if the owner has a justifiable reason.
A nonconforming use is one that clearly differs from current zoning and is subject to change upon conveyance. A zoning variance allows a use that differs from the applicable ordinance for a variety of justifiable reasons.

3.9 (c) certificate of occupancy.
Building inspectors inspect a new development or improvement for code compliance. If the work complies, the municipality or county issues a certificate of occupancy which officially clears the property for occupation and use.

3.10 (c) It conveys legal title to the acquiring entity.
Eminent domain allows a government entity to purchase a fee, leasehold, or easement interest in privately owned real property for the public good, regardless of the owner's desire to sell or otherwise transfer any interest. In exchange for the interest, the government pays the owner a "just" compensation. To acquire a property, the public entity initiates a condemnation suit. Transfer of title extinguishes all existing leases, liens, and other encumbrances on the property.

3.11 (d) parties responsible for improper disposal of hazardous waste could be charged for the cleanup costs.
Under CERCLA and the Superfund Amendment of 1986, current landowners as well as previous owners of a property may be held liable for environmental violations, even if "innocent" of a violation. Sellers often carry the greatest exposure, and real estate licensees may be held liable for improper disclosure.

3.12 (a) Individual property rights and the public's interest.
The optimum management of real property usage must take into account both the interests of the individual and the interests of the surrounding community. While maintaining the value of an individual estate is important, the owner of an estate must realize that unregulated use and development can jeopardize the value not only of the owner's estate but of neighboring properties.

3.13 (c) police power.
At the local level, county and city governments control land use through the authority known as police power. The most common expressions of police power are county and municipal zoning.

3.14 (d) The owner must sell the property in exchange for market-value compensation.
Eminent domain allows a government entity to purchase a fee, leasehold, or easement interest in privately owned real property for the public good, regardless of the owner's desire to sell or otherwise transfer any interest. In exchange for the interest, the government pays the owner a "just" compensation.

3.15 (a) reasonably promote community health, safety and welfare.
Local planners do not have unlimited authority to do whatever they want. Their zoning ordinances must be clear in import, apply to all parties equally, and promote health, safety, and welfare of the community in a reasonable manner.

3.16 (d) To ensure that improvements comply with codes.
Local governments enforce zoning ordinances by issuing building permits to those who want to improve, repair, or refurbish a property. To receive a permit, the project must comply with all relevant ordinances and codes.

3.17 (b) To regulate the density of dwellings in the residential zone.
Residential zoning regulates density, by limiting the number and size of dwelling units and lots in an area.

3.18 (a) a special exception.
A special exception grant authorizes a use that is not consistent with the zoning ordinance in a literal sense, yet is clearly beneficial or essential to the public welfare and does not materially impair other uses in the zone.

3.19 (c) a legal nonconforming use.
An illegal nonconforming use is one that conflicts with ordinances that were in place before the use commenced. For instance, if a motel that was allowed as a legal nonconforming use is sold, and the new owner continues to operate the property as a motel, the motel is now an illegal, nonconforming use.

3.20 (b) a plat of subdivision.
In addition to complying with zoning ordinances, a developer of multiple properties in a subdivision must meet requirements for subdivisions, including submission of a plat of subdivision.

3.21 (a) accurately identifies the boundaries of the property as distinct from all other properties.
A legal description of real property is one which accurately locates and identifies the boundaries of the subject parcel to a degree acceptable by courts of law in the state where the property is located. The general criterion for a legal description is that it alone provides sufficient data for a surveyor to locate the parcel. A legal description identifies the property as unique and distinct from all other properties.

3.22 (c) reference points, angles, and distances.
A metes and bounds description identifies the boundaries of a parcel of real estate using reference points, distances, and angles. The description always identifies an enclosed area by starting at an origination point, called point of beginning, or POB, and returning to the POB at the end of the description.

3.23 (b) two consecutive common meridians.
The "vertical" area between consecutive meridians is called a range. A range is identified by its relationship to the principal meridian. All ranges are six miles wide.

3.24 (c) two consecutive parallels.
The "horizontal" area between two parallels is called a tier, or a township strip. A tier is identified by its relationship to the base parallel. All tiers are six miles wide.

3.25 (b) Six miles by six miles, or 6 miles square.
A township is the area enclosed by the intersection of two consecutive meridians and two consecutive parallels. Since the parallels and meridians are six miles apart, a township is a square with six miles on each side. Its area is therefore 36 square miles. Remember to differentiate square miles from miles square: 4 square miles is a measure of area (2 miles x 2 miles); 4 miles square is a representation of the sides of a square (4 miles by 4 miles).

3.26 (d) 1/64.
The size in acres of a subsection of a township is a fraction of 640 acres, since there are 640 acres in a section. Thus ten acres is 10/640, or 1/64th of a section.

3.27 (d) properties in a subdivision.
The recorded plat method, also called the lot and block system, is used to describe properties in residential, commercial, and industrial subdivisions. Under this system, tracts of land are subdivided into lots. The entire group of lots comprises the subdivision. In a large subdivision, lots may be grouped together into blocks for ease of reference.

3.28 (c) Metes and bounds.
A metes and bounds description identifies the point of beginning and describes the distance and direction from that point to the first monument, and thence to subsequent monuments and back to the beginning to define the property's enclosed perimeter.

3.29 (d) Thirty-six.
The rectangular survey system divides a township into thirty-six sections.

3.30 (a) 640.
Each side of a section is one mile in length. Thus the area of a section is one square mile, or 640 acres.

3.31 (c) something of value traded in exchange for something of value.
A contract must contain a two-way exchange of valuable consideration as compensation for performance by the other party. The contract is not valid or enforceable if just one party provides consideration. Valuable consideration may be something of tangible value, such as money, or something the party promises to do. It may also be something intangible that a party must give up.

3.32 (a) contain a legal description of the property.
In addition to satisfying the requirements of a valid contract in general, a contract that conveys an interest in real estate must be in writing, contain a legal description of the property, and be signed by one or more of the parties.

3.33 (d) A reasonable time, or until the expiration date on the offer.
If an offer contains an expiration date and the phrase "time is of the essence," the offer expires at exactly the time specified. In the absence of a stated time period, the offeree has a "reasonable" time to accept an offer.

3.34 (b) The buyer's death terminated the offer.
Any of the following actions or circumstances can terminate an offer: acceptance; rejection; revocation; lapse of time; counteroffer; or death or insanity of either party.

3.35 (c) A contract for the sale of undeveloped land.
A real estate contract that is not a personal contract for services can be assigned to another party unless the terms of the agreement specifically prohibit assignment. Listing agreements, for example, are not assignable, since they are personal service agreements between agent and principal. Sales contracts, however, are assignable, because they involve the purchase of real property rather than a personal service.

3.36 (b) the parties act is if there is a contract.
An implied contract is an unstated or unintentional agreement that may be deemed to exist when the actions of any of the parties suggest the existence of an agreement.

3.37 (b) A sale contract before closing.
An executory contract is one in which performance is yet to be completed. A sales contract prior to closing is executory: while the parties have agreed to buy and sell, the buyer has yet to pay the seller and the seller has yet to deed the property to the buyer.

3.38 (a) both parties promise to do something in exchange for the other party's performance.
A bilateral contract is one in which both parties promise to perform their respective parts of an agreement in exchange for performance by the other party. An example of a bilateral contract is an exclusive listing: the broker promises to exercise due diligence in the efforts to sell a property, and the seller promises to compensate the broker when and if the property sells.

3.39 (c) The broker may have a claim for marketing expenses expended during the listing term.
The damaged party may elect the following legal remedies: rescission; forfeiture; suit for damages; or suit for specific performance. However, the broker must show that the seller has breached the contract.

3.40 (d) the failure of a party to perform according to the terms of the contract.
A breach of contract is a failure to perform according to the terms of the agreement.

3.41 (b) The act of declaring that a contract is no longer in effect for a given party.
Parties to a contract may rescind a contract by mutual consent, or a damaged party may rescind the contract unilaterally. This act of rescission cancels the contract and returns the parties to their pre-contract condition, including the refunding of any monies already transferred.

3.42 (a) reflect a mutual understanding or agreement.
Mutual consent, also known as offer and acceptance and meeting of the minds, requires that a contract involve a clear and definite offer and an intentional, unqualified acceptance of the offer.

3.43 (c) unenforceable.
A valid contract that is in writing is enforceable within a statutory time period. A valid contract that is made orally is also generally enforceable within a statutory period, with the exception that some contracts are enforceable only if they are in writing. These laws apply in particular to the transfer of interests in real estate. A void or voidable contract was not a truly valid contract.

3.44 (b) is possibly valid and enforceable.
Incompetent parties, or parties of "unsound mind," may not enter into enforceable contracts. However, during the period of one's incompetency, a court may appoint a guardian who may act on the incompetent party's behalf with court approval.

3.45 (c) a counteroffer.
By changing any of the terms of an offer, the offeree creates a counteroffer, and the original offer is void. At this point, the offeree becomes the offeror, and the new offeree gains the right of acceptance. If accepted, the counteroffer becomes a valid contract provided all other requirements are met.

3.46 (d) valuable consideration.
Valuable consideration can be something of tangible value, such as money, or something a party promises to do or not do. For example, a home builder may promise to build a house for a party as consideration for receiving money from the home buyer.

3.47 (c) is void.
The content, promise, or intent of a contract must be lawful. A contract that proposes an illegal act is void.

3.48 (a) must act within a statutory period.
The statute of limitations restricts the time period for which an injured party in a contract has the right to rescind or disaffirm the contract. A party to a voidable contract must act within the statutory period.

3.49 (b) require certain conveyance-related contracts to be in writing.
The statute of frauds requires that certain contracts must be in writing to be enforceable. Real estate contracts that convey an interest in real property fall in this category, with the exception that a lease of one year's duration or less may be oral.

3.50 (b) The buyer has no obligations to the seller whatsoever.
The mutual consent required for a valid contract is reached through the process of offer and acceptance. If the offeree accepts all terms without amendment, the offer becomes a contract. The exact point at which the offer becomes a contract is when the offeree gives the offeror notice of the acceptance. If an offer contains an expiration date and the phrase "time is of the essence," the offer expires at exactly the time specified.

3.51 (c) may not be discriminatory.
HOA's must use caution in developing restrictions for a new subdivision's land use regulations. In particular no restriction may be discriminatory -- such as an improper resident age requirement -- nor can the restriction violate fair trade laws.

NATIONAL TEST 4: Agency; Listing Agreements

4.1 (b) the laws of agency, or in some states, by statute.
In every state, a body of law, generally called the law of agency, defines and regulates the legal roles of this relationship. While the relationship is subject to contract law, agency law dictates how the relationship will achieve its purposes, regardless of what the listing contract states.

4.2 (c) The relationship is independent of any compensation arrangement.
It is important to understand that the agency relationship does not require compensation or any form of consideration. Nor does compensation define an agency relationship: a party other than the principal may compensate the agent.

4.3 (c) The defaulting party may have a financial consequence.
Involuntary termination of the relationship may create legal and financial liability for a party who defaults

or cancels. For example, a client may renounce an agreement but then be held liable for the agent's expenses or commission.

4.4 (b) present all offers to the principal regardless of their amount.
A conventional listing agreement does not authorize an agent to obligate the client to contracts, and it does not allow the agent to conceal offers to buy, sell, or lease coming from a customer or another agent. Further, since a client relies on a broker's representations, a broker must exercise care not to offer advice outside of his or her field of expertise.

4.5 (c) confidentiality.
The confidentiality standard is one of the duties that extends beyond the termination of the listing: at no time in the future may the agent disclose confidential information.

4.6 (d) comparable to that of other practitioners in the area.
The agent is hired to do a job, and is therefore expected to do it with diligence and reasonable competence. Competence is generally defined as a "standard of practice" equal to the level of real estate marketing skills and knowledge of other practitioners in the area.

4.7 (c) disclose the information to the seller.
An agent has the duty to inform the client of all material facts, reports, and rumors that might affect the client's interests in the property transaction. This includes: the agent's opinion of the property's condition; information about the buyer's motivations and financial qualifications; discussions between agent and buyer regarding the possibility of the agent's representing the buyer in another transaction.

4.8 (a) the Andersons.
Since Gerry executed an agency agreement with the Andersons, they become the client and the Lincolns the customer, regardless of who pays the commission.

4.9 (c) a broker who has an agency relationship with a client.
In a subagency, a broker or licensed salesperson works as the agent of a broker who is the agent of a client. Subagents might include a cooperating licensed broker, that broker's licensed salespeople, and the listing broker's licensed salespeople, all of whom agree to work for the listing broker on behalf of the client.

4.10 (b) One agent represents both sides in a transaction.
Dual agency means representing both principal parties to a transaction. The agent represents both buyer and seller or tenant and owner.

4.11 (c) disclosing material facts that affect the value of the property to both parties.
In the role of facilitator, the broker's only fiduciary duties and standards of conduct are those of accounting; skill, care, and diligence; honesty and fair dealing; and disclosure to both parties of all material facts in residential sale transactions affecting the property's value. Some states do not allow for this form of relationship in a real estate transaction.

4.12 (a) The agent is showing the client's property to a prospective buyer.
Agency disclosure must occur upon "substantive contact" between the listing agent and a customer. Examples of substantive contact include: showing the prospect a property; eliciting confidential information from a prospect regarding needs, motivation, or financial qualification; and executing a contractual offer to sell or lease.

4.13 (d) good faith, trust and confidence.
The essence of the agency relationship is trust, confidence, and mutual good faith. The principal trusts the agent to exercise the utmost skill and care in fulfilling the authorized activity, and to promote the principal's best interests. The agent undertakes to strive in good faith to achieve the desired objective, and to fulfill the fiduciary duties.

4.14 (b) general.
In a general agency, the principal delegates to the agent ongoing tasks and duties within a particular business or enterprise. Such delegation may include the authority to enter into contracts.

4.15 (b) special.
Under a special agency agreement, the principal delegates authority to conduct a specific activity, after which the agency relationship terminates. In most cases, the special agent may not bind the principal to a contract. Real estate brokerage is commonly based on a special agency.

4.16 (c) a party creates an agency relationship outside of an express agreement.
An agency relationship can arise by implication, intentionally or unintentionally. Implication means that the parties act as if there were an agreement. For example, if an agent promises a buyer to do everything possible to find a property at the lowest possible price, and the buyer accepts the proposition, there may be an implied agency relationship even though there is no specific agreement.

4.17 (a) Condemnation of the property
An agency relationship may terminate contrary to the wishes of the parties by reason of: death or incapacity of either party; abandonment by the agent; condemnation or destruction of the property; renunciation; breach; bankruptcy; or revocation of the agent's license.

4.18 (a) The agent has violated the duty of confidentiality.
An agent may not disclose any information that would harm the client's interests or bargaining position, or anything else the client wishes to keep secret. The confidentiality standard is one of the duties that extends beyond the termination of the listing: at no time in the future may the agent disclose confidential information.

4.19 (b) the agent has not violated fiduciary duty.
Since it is illegal to refuse to show buyers the property based on where the buyers live, the agent has not violated fiduciary duty. The duty of obedience only applies to legal activities.

4.20 (d) inform the seller.
An agent has the duty to inform the client of all material facts, reports, and rumors that might affect the client's interests in the property transaction.

4.21 (a) prior to completing a listing agreement.
An agent who intends to represent a seller or owner must disclose the import of the proposed agency relationship in writing before the listing agreement is executed.

4.22 (c) Whenever substantive communication is made beyond casual conversation.
A listing agent must disclose in writing to a buyer or tenant that the agent represents the owner in the transaction. This disclosure must occur before or at the first "substantive contact" with the customer prospect. In some states, buyer representatives must disclose the agency relationship to sellers or their agents upon initial contact.

4.23 (b) upon initial contact.
A buyer agent must disclose the agency relationship to the seller or seller's agent on first contact. Substantive contact is assumed to occur immediately in this circumstance.

4.24 (a) may not represent one party's interests to the detriment of the other.
A dual agent's first duty is to disclose the agency relationship to both principal parties or to withdraw from one side of the duality. After disclosing, the agent must obtain the written consent of both parties. If both parties accept the dual agency, the agent owes all the fiduciary duties to both parties except full disclosure, undivided loyalty, and exclusive representation of one principal's interests.

4.25 (d) practicing law without a license.
An agent should not act or speak outside the agent's area of expertise. A customer may rely on anything an agent says, and the agent will be held accountable. For example, an agent represents that a property will appreciate. The buyer interprets this as expert investment advice and buys the property. If the property does not appreciate, the buyer may hold the agent liable.

4.26 (a) Fiduciary and contractual obligations with the client.
A listing agreement establishes an agency relationship between agent and client that commits the agent to the full complement of fiduciary duties to the client in fulfilling the agreement.

4.27 (d) market, sell and show the property.
Special agency limits the scope of the broker's authority to specific activities, generally those which generate customers and catalyze the transaction. A special agency agreement usually does not authorize a broker to obligate the client to a contract as a principal party. Normally, principals do not delegate the authority to negotiate price to an agent in a residential transaction.

4.28 (b) An implied agency may have been created, with obligations to perform for both seller and agent.
Clients and agents may also create an implied agency listing based on substantive actions rather than on an express agreement. For example, if a seller allows a broker to undertake certain activities toward effecting a transaction without a specific authorization, but with full knowledge and consent, an implied agency may have been created.

4.29 (a) The agent cannot assign the listing agreement.
Since a listing agreement is a personal service contract, it is not assignable. In particular, a broker cannot assign a listing to another broker.

4.30 (b) exclusive right to sell.
The exclusive right to sell listing, or "exclusive," gives the agent the most control over the property and the greatest likelihood of being compensated for his or her marketing efforts.

4.31 (c) A listing that is entered in a multiple listing service.
Though not a distinct type of listing agreement, multiple listing is a significant feature of brokerage practice. Multiple listing is an authorization to enter a listing in a multiple listing service.

4.32 (b) The customer must be legally competent to undertake the transaction.
Effecting a completed transaction means finding a customer who is not only ready, willing, and able, but one who makes an acceptable offer. A ready, willing, and able customer is one who is: amenable to the terms of the transaction (ready and willing), and is financially capable of paying the price and legally capable of completing the transaction (able).

4.33 (a) obtain and distribute compensation.
In the normal course of business, a listing broker delegates marketing responsibilities to salespeople. A salesperson may not, however, seek compensation directly from a client. Only the broker can obtain and disburse the compensation.

4.34 (c) Perry, since he found the customer.
The two principal determinants of procuring cause are being first to find the customer, and being the one who induces the customer to complete the transaction.

4.35 (d) It may be terminated against the agent's will.
A listing may terminate on grounds of: performance; infeasibility; mutual agreement; revocation; abandonment; breach; lapse of time; invalidity of the contract; incapacitation of either party; destruction of the property; or, in this case; involuntary title transfer.

4.36 (b) Sue the broker for money damages.
If the broker cancels the listing or otherwise defaults, the client may sue the broker for money damages.

4.37 (b) exclusive agency agreement.
An exclusive agency listing authorizes a single broker to sell the property and earn a commission, but leaves the owner the right to sell the property without the broker's assistance, in which case no commission is owed.

4.38 (c) open listing.
An open listing is a non-exclusive authorization to sell or lease a property. The owner may offer such agreements to any number of brokers in the marketplace. With an open listing, the broker who is the first to perform under the terms of the listing is the sole party entitled to a commission.

4.39 (d) net listing.
A net listing is one in which an owner sets a minimum acceptable amount to be received from the transaction and allows the broker to have any amount received in excess as a commission, assuming the broker has earned a commission according to the other terms of the agreement.

4.40 (a) the client.
Generally, buyer and tenant representation agreements are subject to the same laws and regulations as those applying to owner listings. The only difference is the client and his or her transaction expectations.

4.41 (a) To list the owner's property in a multiple listing service.
A multiple listing is not a distinct listing contract but rather a provision in an exclusive listing authorizing the broker to place the listing into a multiple listing service. A multiple listing service is a database of available properties.

4.42 (d) The broker assigns who is to represent the buyer and seller.
The designated agency agreement allows a broker to select a salesperson and associate brokers to act as the client's agent. A designated agency agreement must contain the name of all associate brokers who are authorized to act as supervisory brokers.

NATIONAL TEST 5: Brokerage Business; Sale Contracts

5.1 (d) Non-profit corporation.
A non-profit corporation is a corporate entity which is not legally entitled to generate profit. A non-profit organization may not broker real estate.

5.2 (c) are properly licensed.
A joint venture is a partnership formed to complete a specific business endeavor, such as a real estate development. Individuals, general and limited partnerships, and corporations may participate. A joint venture may broker real estate, provided the co-venturers are duly licensed.

5.3 (b) a single employing broker who has an active broker's license.
Only a broker with an active broker's license can hire and employ a licensed salesperson. A licensed salesperson may work only for the employing broker and may not work for or receive direct compensation from any other broker.

5.4 (c) Offer a property for lease on behalf of the employing broker.
A sales agent is only authorized to represent a broker and carry out such duties as the broker may legitimately delegate. Thus a sales agent does not directly represent the client in a transaction but is rather the agent of the broker and subagent of the client.

5.5 (d) The employing broker.
Agents can only receive compensation from their employing brokers. Co-op commissions, referral fees, and other compensations always flow through the broker to the sales agent.

5.6 (d) $4,940.
First calculate the total commission, then the co-brokerage splits, then the agent-broker split. Thus: $380,000 x 6.5% = $24,700 total commission. ($24,700 x 50%) = $12,350 total listing broker share. ($12,350 x 40% = $4,940 agent's share.

5.7 (c) $4,278.
The total commission is ($245,000 x 3%) = $7,350. The agent gets (65% x $7,350) - $500, which equals $4,278.

5.8 (c) complete the signing of the listing.
Once the seller signs the listing, the next critical task is to get it signed by the appropriate licensee, thereby making the listing a contract. Some states allow a salesperson to do this and in other states, the listing must be given to the broker for signing. This result will set in motion the process of marketing the property. The agency disclosures must take place prior to the execution of the agreement.

5.9 (b) Present the offer to the seller at the earliest possible moment.
When a buyer or tenant makes an offer, the agent must present it to the seller or landlord at the earliest possible moment. If the terms of the offer are unacceptable, the agent may assist the seller in developing a counteroffer.

5.10 (c) The broker has illegally converted security funds for business use.
Conversion is the act of misappropriating escrow funds for the broker's business or personal use. Conversion carries serious consequences, including license revocation.

5.11 (d) Never.
All advertising must reveal the identity of the broker; licensed brokers and agents may not use blind ads that conceal their identities.

5.12 (a) fair trade and anti-trust laws.
Brokerage companies, like other businesses, are subject to anti-trust laws designed to prevent monopolies and unfair trade practices. In real estate brokerage, the primary manifestations of unfair trade practice are collusion, price fixing and market allocation. In this instance the brokers are price fixing.

5.13 (b) Outside brokers assist a listing agent in procuring a buyer.
A transaction involving a cooperating subagent is called co-brokerage. In a co-brokered transaction, the listing broker may split the commission with the "co-broker," typically on a 50-50 basis.

5.14 (d) Only members of the National Association of Realtors®.
The term Realtor® is a protected trade name of the National Association of Realtors®. Only members of this organization may use the term to refer to themselves.

5.15 (a) represent their employing broker in procuring clients and customers.
Agents may only act on behalf of their broker. They may not assume responsibilities for other listings since listings are not transferable.

5.16 (a) The IC is responsible for his or her own taxes; the broker does not withhold.
Generally, a broker has limited control over the actions of a contractor. Specifically: a broker can require performance results, but is limited in demanding how a contractor performs the work; and the broker does not take responsibility for a contractor's income and social security taxes.

5.17 (b) competitive conditions.
Commission structures are negotiated between the agent and employing broker as a function of competitive market conditions. The amount of commission being paid is negotiated between the brokerage firm and the client.

5.18 (c) avoid disclosing what price the owner will accept.
An agent must be extremely careful at this point to abide by fiduciary obligations to the client, whoever that party may be. Discussions of price are particularly delicate: whether the client is buyer or seller, the agent's duty is to uphold the client's best interests. Thus it is not acceptable to suggest to a customer what price the client will or will not accept.

5.19 (d) mixing escrow funds with the broker's operating funds.
Commingling, a prohibited activity, is the act of mixing the broker's personal or business funds with escrow funds.

5.20 (a) There is insufficient evidence of anything other than a normal business practice.
Charging identical commission rates in itself is legitimate. Price-fixing occurs when competitors have in fact colluded together to set prices.

5.21 (c) all the obligations and promises are performed and the transaction is closed.
An executory contract is one for which the signatories have yet to perform their respective obligations and promises. Upon closing, the sale contract is fully performed and no longer exists as a binding agreement.

5.22 (a) Use a standard contract promulgated by a state agency or a real estate board.
It is advisable, and legally required in most states, for a broker to use a standard contract form promulgated by state agencies or real estate boards, as such forms contain generally accepted language. This relieves the broker of the dangers of creating new contract language, which can be construed as a practice of law for which the broker is not licensed.

5.23 (b) be written.
A contract for the sale of real estate is enforceable only if it is in writing. A buyer or seller cannot sue to force the other to comply with an oral contract for sale, even if the contract is valid.

5.24 (a) The contract has been legitimately cancelled and is null and void.
To be valid, a contract must meet the criteria of: competent parties, voluntary act of good faith, mutual consent, legal purpose, and valuable consideration. The buyer broke the mutual consent requirement by opting out before being told of the seller's acceptance. Thus, there is no valid contract.

5.25 (c) An offer and acceptance.
A contract of sale is created by full and unequivocal acceptance of an offer. Offer and acceptance satisfy the mutual consent requirement for a valid contract. The offeree must accept the offer without making any changes whatsoever.

5.26 (d) Equitable title.
A sale contract gives the buyer an interest in the property that is called equitable title, or ownership in equity. If the seller defaults and the buyer can show good faith performance, the buyer can sue for specific performance, that is, to compel the seller to transfer legal title upon payment of the contract price.

5.27 (b) a condition that, if unmet, renders the contract unenforceable.
A contingency is a condition that must be met before the contract is enforceable. If one party cannot meet a contingency condition by a specified deadline, the other party may cancel the contract.

5.28 (c) The buyer may be able to have the contract canceled.
The termite inspection clause is a contingency clause. If one party cannot meet a contingency condition by a specified deadline, the other party may cancel the contract. Did the clause state that the inspector had to be properly licensed? If so, the buyer has a good case for cancellation.

5.29 (a) Until the seller communicates acceptance of the offer.
An offeror may revoke an offer for any reason prior to communication of acceptance by the offeree.

5.30 (b) Fred has entered into contracts with both Jack and Sally to sell the same property.
Jack's acceptance of Fred's offer creates a valid contract, just as Fred's acceptance of Sally's offer creates a valid contract. Fred should have revoked his offer to Jack before accepting Sally's offer.

5.31 (d) agency relationships and property condition.
It is common for the seller to disclose the property condition requiring the buyer to acknowledge receipt of the disclosure. The broker discloses the applicable agency relationships in the transaction and names the party who must pay the brokerage commission.

5.32 (b) valuable consideration and a right to buy.
An option-to-buy is an enforceable contract in which a potential seller, the optionor, grants a potential buyer, the optionee, the right to purchase a property before a stated time for a stated price and terms. In exchange for the right of option, the optionee pays the optionor valuable consideration.

5.33 (a) Schmidt must sell to Carboy for $10,000.
Mary's option-to-buy contract is enforceable, assuming she paid a consideration for it.

5.34 (d) It is always assignable unless the contract prohibits assignment.
A real estate contract that is not a personal service contract can be assigned to another party unless the terms of the agreement specifically prohibit assignment. An option-to-buy is therefore assignable in the absence of such a prohibiting clause.

5.35 (c) At the end of the contract period, the vendor conveys legal title, provided the vendee has fulfilled all obligations.
A contract for deed is a bilateral agreement between a seller, the vendor, and a buyer, the vendee, in which the vendor defers receipt of some or all of the purchase price of a property over a specified period of time. At the end of the period, the buyer completes payment to the vendor of the full purchase price and the vendor deeds legal title to the vendee.

5.36 (b) the parties have completed a verbal, executory contract.
As a sale contract created by an offer and acceptance, the parties have an executory contract: the parties have yet to perform their respective obligations and promises. However, as a contract for the sale of real estate, this verbal contract is not enforceable. An enforceable real estate sale contract must be in writing.

5.37 (c) The assignor has completed a legal action.
Either party to a sale transaction can assign the sale contract to another party, subject to the provisions and conditions contained in the agreement.

5.38 (d) any conveyance may trigger an acceleration of any loans secured by the property.
The mortgage agreement may or may not state that the seller's loan will be accelerated by the lender and called due on sale. The due-on-sale clause in the sale contract merely stipulates that the buyer and seller recognize the possibility that loans that survive the closing may be called due.

5.39 (d) The option is expired, and the tenant has no rightful claim to money paid for the option.
The option automatically expires at the end of the option period. The landlord has no obligation, either to sell the property or to return the consideration, after the expiration date.

5.40 (c) the seller retains legal title while the buyer makes partial payments until the contract is fully executed.
In a contract for deed, the seller, or vendor, defers receipt of some or all of the purchase price of a property over a specified period of time. During the period, the vendor retains legal title and the vendee acquires equitable title. At the end of the period, the buyer pays the vendor the full purchase price and the vendor deeds legal title to the vendee.

5.41 (d) Telephone Consumer Protection Act
The TCPA was enacted to rein in invasive telemarketing practices by requiring certain identification procedures, compliance with do-not-call requests, and a Do-Not-Call list registry.

5.42 (a) the CAN-SPAM Act.
The CAN-SPAM Act bans unwanted commercial messages sent to wireless devices, requires prior authorization to transmit certain messages, and requires an opt-out provision where the receiver can shut off the advertiser from sending future messages.

5.43 (b) Keeping enough operating funds in a trust account to cover bank fees.
Brokers may maintain an amount of operating funds in the trust account in order to pay monthly banking fees.

5.44 (a) fair trade practices.
The activity is called group boycotting and is a violation of fair trade laws. It is an illegal activity for a number of competitors in a given market to "gang up" on a competitor in that market so as to limit the boycotted party's access to customers and patrons.

NATIONAL TEST 6: Economics; Appraisal

6.1 (b) demand for the item is increasing in relation to supply of the item.
In a market economy, the primary interactions between supply, demand and price are: if supply increases relative to demand, price decreases; if supply decreases relative to demand, price increases; if demand increases relative to supply, price increases; and if demand decreases relative to supply, price decreases.

6.2 (d) Supply and demand are equal, and price and value are equal.
A market tends toward a state of equilibrium in which supply equals demand, and price, cost, and value are

identical. According to this principle, market demand moves to meet supply, and supply moves to meet demand. If there is an extreme shortage of an item for which there is normally a strong demand, suppliers will rush to increase production to close the gap. If inventories of an item are very high, suppliers will stop production until the oversupply has been depleted.

6.3 (c) the uniqueness of every parcel.
In comparison with other economic products and services, real estate has certain unique traits. Traits of real estate include: inherent product value; uniqueness of every property; demand must come to the supply; illiquidity; slow to respond to changes; and a decentralized local market.

6.4 (d) Prices rise.
If demand is increasing and a moratorium slows supply, demand will begin to outpace supply, forcing prices to rise as the product becomes scarcer in relation to demand.

6.5 (b) an increase in demand for all types of real estate.
New businesses will arise to support the new company. They will hire new employees, some from out of town. The new employees will need housing. Hence the demand for residential real estate, as well as for commercial and industrial, will intensify, and it will also stimulate new construction.

6.6 (d) The number of available units that become occupied over a period of time.
Absorption is the amount of available property that becomes occupied over a period of time.

6.7 (a) rising prices.
Within the business cycle of real estate, declining vacancy indicates a combination of increasing demand which "fills up" supply which in turn decreases. As space becomes scarcer, rents for available space increase.

6.8 (b) desire, utility, scarcity, and purchasing power.
The value of something is based on the answers to four questions: how much do I desire it; how useful is it; how scarce is it; and am I able to pay for it.

6.9 (b) will increase.
If there is no longer a supply to meet the increasing demand of a growing population, prices for existing supply will rise.

6.10 (d) the market tending toward equilibrium.
A market tends toward a state of equilibrium in which supply equals demand, and price, cost, and value are identical. Thus if supply is scarce, construction will increase to stabilize the imbalance.

6.11 (c) the market is over-supplied.
Falling prices indicate an oversupply of commercial properties in relation to demand. In this case, construction of new supply will also slow down.

6.12 (a) have been increasing.
A rise in prices is a market signal that there is an undersupply of product in relation to demand. As the market moves toward equilibrium, builders construct more buildings to meet the unmet demand.

6.13 (c) It is often difficult to convert to cash.
Since real estate is often a large, long-term investment that has no exact duplicate, the process of a buyer's evaluating and choosing the right property is long and complex; hence, finding a buyer at a desired price can take a long time.

6.14 (b) The number of persons employed in base industries in an area
Base employment is the number of persons employed in the base industries that represent the economic foundation of an area. It is the driving component of total employment, which includes secondary and support industries, and which creates demand for all types of real estate.

6.15 (d) The total existing space of a certain type that is unoccupied at a given time
Vacancy is the amount of total real estate inventory of a certain type that is unoccupied at a given time. It is often stated as a percentage of total inventory, the vacancy rate for that property type.

6.16 (a) local government influencing the real estate market, regardless of demand.
Local governments sometimes declare a moratorium on new construction because of present or projected inadequacies of the infrastructure—water, sewer, power, roads, etc.—or because of the desire to conform to a master plan. The result may be to drive up prices, as supply cannot freely increase to meet demand.

6.17 (c) In- and out-migrations of major employers
Changes in employment numbers in a local market area, especially in major industries, have a direct impact on real estate demand in the area. Money supply, interest rates, and trade imbalances also have an impact, but they are regional or national factors rather than strictly local.

6.18 (b) Vacancy rises and prices fall.
New construction generally occurs to meet an excess of demand. By adding supply, it tends to increase vacancy and lower prices until supply-demand equilibrium is achieved.

6.19 (d) Residential
While all types of users may have these needs, they are most prominent for residential users because of concerns for family comfort and safety. Retail users are more concerned with competitive features of the trade area; office users care more about occupancy costs and suitability for the business; industrial users care more about such features as functionality, accessibility, and the labor pool.

6.20 (c) its susceptibility to swings in the local economy.
Because a real property cannot be transferred to a large, central real estate marketplace, its marketability is closely tied to local conditions. Investors and users must come to the product, unlike other types of economic product that can be moved to a place in search of greater demand.

6.21 (b) anticipation.
Anticipation is the value principle that a buyer will pay a price based on the benefits the buyer expects to derive from a property over a holding period. For example, if an investor anticipates an annual rental income from a leased property to be one million dollars, this expected sum has a direct bearing on what the investor will pay for the property.

6.22 (b) A homeowner adds a third bathroom to a house and thereby increases the appraised value by $10,000.
The principle of contribution focuses on the degree to which a particular improvement affects market value of the overall property. In essence, the contribution of the improvement is equal to the change in market value that the addition of the improvement causes. For example, adding a bathroom to a house may contribute an additional $15,000 to the appraised value. Thus the contribution of the bathroom is $15,000.

6.23 (a) assemblage.
Assemblage, or the conjoining of adjacent properties, sometimes creates a combined value that is greater than the values of the unassembled properties. The excess value created by assemblage is called plottage value.

6.24 (d) Market value is an estimate; market price is the price at which a property sold.
Market value is an estimate of the price at which a property will sell at a particular time. The market price, as opposed to market value, is what a property actually sells for. Market price should theoretically be the same as market value if all the conditions essential for market value are present. Market price, however, may not reflect the analysis of comparables and of investment value that an estimate of market value includes.

6.25 (a) Countable living area must be attached to the main house.
Generally, one cannot count an outbuilding that is not attached to the main house, i.e., a barn or shed.

6.26 (b) From the exterior walls, above grade, excluding open areas
Gross living area is measured from the outside and includes all attached and enclosed areas, minus rooms below grade and portions of area above grade.

6.27 (b) Make dollar adjustments to the sale prices of comparable properties to account for competitive differences with the subject.
The sales comparison approach consists of comparing sale prices of recently sold properties that are comparable with the subject, and making dollar adjustments to the price of each comparable to account for competitive differences with the subject. After identifying the adjusted value of each comparable, the appraiser weights the reliability of each comparable and the factors underlying how the adjustments were made. The weighting yields a final value range based on the most reliable factors in the analysis.

6.28 (d) takes into account the competitive value of specific amenities of the subject property.
The sales comparison approach is widely used because it takes into account the subject property's specific amenities in relation to competing properties. In addition, because of the currency of its data, the approach incorporates present market realities.

6.29 (a) adds value to a comparable that is inferior to the subject property.
If the comparable is inferior to the subject in some characteristic, an amount is added to the price of the comparable. If the comparable is better than the subject in some characteristic, an amount is deducted from the sale price of the comparable. This neutralizes the comparable's competitive advantage or disadvantage in an adjustment category. For example, a comparable has a swimming pool and the subject does not. To equalize the difference, the appraiser deducts an amount, say $6,000, from the sale price of the comparable.

6.30 (b) requires the fewest and smallest adjustments.
As a rule, the fewer the total number of adjustments, the smaller the adjustment amounts, and the less the total adjustment amount, the more reliable the comparable.

6.31 (c) $395,000.
Since the comparable has an extra bath, it is adjusted downward to equalize with the subject. Conversely, since it has no patio, the appraiser adds value to the comparable. Thus, $400,000 minus $7,000 plus $2,000 equals $395,000.

6.32 (d) Add the estimated land value and cost of improvements and subtract the accrued depreciation of the improvements.
The cost approach consists of estimating the value of the land "as if vacant;" estimating the cost of improvements; estimating and deducting accrued depreciation; and adding the estimated land value to the estimated depreciated cost of the improvements.

6.33 (b) is very accurate for a property with new improvements that represent the highest and best use.
The strengths of the cost approach are that it: provides an upper limit for the subject's value based on the undepreciated cost of reproducing the improvements. It is also very accurate for valuing a property with new improvements which are the highest and best use of the property.

6.34 (c) a property loses the same increment of value each year over the economic life of the property.
All property improvements have an economic life, which becomes incrementally shorter year after year as physical deterioration takes its toll. The property as a whole does not lose value, since land itself does not depreciate. Similarly, an improvement can regain value if it is repaired or updated. Finally, not all properties lose value from economic obsolescence.

6.35 (d) $575,000.
To appraise value using the cost approach, add the land value to the value of the depreciated improvement. Thus you have $150,000 + ($475,000 - 50,000), or $575,000.

6.36 (b) Divide the income a property generates by a rate of return.
An appraiser obtains an indication of value from the income capitalization method by dividing the estimated net operating income for the subject by the rate of return, or capitalization rate. The formula is: NOI / Cap rate = Value.

6.37 (c) uses a method that is also used by investors to determine how much they should pay for an investment property.
The strength of the income approach is that it is used by investors themselves to determine how much they should pay for a property. Thus, in the right circumstances, it provides a good basis for estimating market

value. The approach, however, does not project what an income property's future income will be. Moreover, it is not an applicable method for estimating value if the subject is a non-income producing property.

6.38 (a) $370,000.
First, identify net income by subtracting out vacancy and expenses. Then divide by the capitalization rate. Thus, ($60,000 –3,000 – 20,000) ÷ 10% = $370,000.

6.39 (d) 150.
The monthly gross rent multiplier for a property is equal to the price divided by the monthly rent. Thus, ($450,000 ÷ $3,000) = 150.

6.40 (c) $406,000.
Multiply the monthly gross income times 12 to derive annual income. Multiply annual income times the gross income multiplier to derive the estimate of price. Thus, $2,400 times 12 equals $28,800. This times 14.1 equals $406,080, or $406,000 rounded.

6.41 (c) the state in which the appraiser operates.
A state-certified appraiser is one who has passed the necessary examinations and competency standards as established by each state in conformance with the federal standards.

6.42 (a) The Financial Institutions Reform, Recovery and Enforcement Act (FIRREA).
Title XI of FIRREA requires that competent individuals whose professional conduct is properly supervised perform all appraisals used in federally-related transactions. As of January 1, 1993, such federally-related appraisals must be performed only by state-certified appraisers.

6.43 (a) if two similar properties are for sale, a buyer will purchase the cheaper of the two.
According to the principle of substitution, a buyer will pay no more for a property than the buyer would have to pay for an equally desirable and available substitute property. For example, if three houses for sale are essentially similar in size, quality and location, a potential buyer is unlikely to choose the one that is priced significantly higher than the other two.

6.44 (a) is physically and financially feasible, legal, and the most productive.
This valuation principle holds that there is, theoretically, a single use for a property that produces the greatest income and return. A property achieves its maximum value when it is put to this use. The use must, however, be legal.

6.45 (d) $400,000.
Market value is an opinion of the price that a willing seller and willing buyer would probably agree on for a property at a given time if: the transaction is for cash; the property is exposed on the open market for a reasonable period; buyer and seller have full information about market conditions ; there is no abnormal pressure on either party; it is an "arm's length" transaction; title is marketable; and the price does not include hidden influences such as special financing deals. The amount Lynne actually paid is the market price. The previous listing price and Ken's offer might be interesting data for the appraiser, but the appraisal must also consider other market data, such as comparable sales.

6.46 (a) there may be no recent sale price data in the market.
The sales comparison approach is limited in that every property is unique. As a result, it is difficult to find good comparables, especially for special-purpose properties. In addition, the market must be active; otherwise, sale prices lack currency and reliability.

6.47 (c) selects comparable properties, adjusts the comparables, and estimates the value.
The steps are to first identify comparable sales; then compare comparables to the subject and make adjustments to comparables; then, finally, weigh values indicated by adjusted comparables for the final value estimate of the subject.

6.48 (b) the seller offers below-market seller financing.
The principal factors for comparison and adjustment are time of sale, location, physical characteristics, and transaction characteristics. An adjustment may be made for such differences as mortgage loan terms, mortgage assumability, and owner financing.

6.49 (b) weights the comparables.
The last step in the approach is to perform a weighted analysis of the indicated values of each comparable. The appraiser, in other words, must identify which comparable values are more indicative of the subject and which are less indicative. However, all comparables are taken into account, not simply the nearest comparable.

6.50 (b) market value is not always the same as what the property cost.
The limitations of the cost approach are that: the cost to create improvements is not necessarily the same as market value; and depreciation is difficult to measure, especially for older buildings.

6.51 (b) replacement cost.
Reproduction cost is the cost of constructing, at current prices, a precise duplicate of the subject improvements. Replacement cost is the cost of constructing, at current prices and using current materials and methods, a functional equivalent of the subject improvements.

6.52 (d) functional obsolescence.
Functional obsolescence occurs when a property has outmoded physical or design features which are no longer desirable or acceptable to current users.

6.53 (b) incurable economic obsolescence.
Economic (or external) obsolescence is the loss of value due to adverse changes in the surroundings of the subject property that make the subject less desirable. Since such changes are usually beyond the control of the property owner, economic obsolescence is considered an incurable value loss.

6.54 (c) depreciation.
Depreciation is the loss of value in an improvement over time. The loss of an improvement's value can come from any cause, such as deterioration, obsolescence, or changes in the neighborhood.

6.55 (a) estimates depreciation, subtracts depreciation from cost, and adds back the land value.
The steps in the costs approach are: (1) estimate land value; (2) estimate reproduction or replacement cost of improvements; (3) estimate accrued depreciation; (4) subtract accrued depreciation from reproduction or replacement cost; and (5) add land value to depreciated reproduction or replacement cost.

6.56 (b) Uniform Standards of Professional Appraisal Practice (USPAP)
USPAP is the professional code of conduct established by the Appraisal Qualifications Board that regulates appraisal practice in the USA. Standards relate to reporting requirements, methodologies, and proper disclosures to clients and the public.

NATIONAL TEST 7: Finance

7.1 (b) A state in which a mortgagee has equitable title to a secured property.
States differ in their interpretation of who owns mortgaged property. Those that regard the mortgage as a lien held by the mortgagee (lender) against the property owned by the mortgagor (borrower) are called lien-theory states. Those that regard the mortgage document as a conveyance of ownership from the mortgagor to the mortgagee are called title-theory states.

7.2 (d) It is evidence of the borrower's debt to the lender.
A valid mortgage or trust deed financing arrangement requires a note as evidence of the debt.

7.3 (a) trust deed or mortgage.
The mortgage or trust deed is evidence of the collateral pledge of the purchased property as security for the loan.

7.4 (b) mortgagor.
The mortgagor is the borrower and the mortgagee is the lender. As a memory aid, notice that "lender" and "mortgagee" both have two "e"s. "Mortgagor" and "borrower" both have two "o"s.

7.5 (d) $1,000.
Multiply the rate times the loan amount and divide by 12 to calculate monthly interest. Thus, ($200,000 x 6%) ÷ 12 = $1,000.

7.6 (b) $1,000,000.
The equation for the loan amount is (annual interest divided by the interest rate) = loan amount. Thus, ($5,000 x 12) ÷ .06 = $1,000,000.

7.7 (a) 7.5%.
The equation for the interest rate is (annual payment / loan amount) = interest rate. Thus ($18,750 / $250,000) = 7.5%.

7.8 (b) $12,000.
A discount point is one percent of the loan amount. Thus, one point on a $600,000 loan equals ($600,000 x 2%) or ($600,000 x .02), or $12,000.

7.9 (b) Part of each periodic payment is applied to repayment of the loan balance in advance and part is applied to payment of interest in arrears.
In an amortizing loan, part of the principal is repaid periodically along with interest, so that the principal balance decreases over the life of the loan. The annual interest is never the same, since the principal balance to which the interest rate applies changes every year. Interest on a loan is always paid in arrears, not in advance.

7.10 (b) private mortgage insurance.
Mortgage insurance protects the lender against loss of a portion of the loan (typically 20-25%) in case of borrower default. Private mortgage insurance generally applies to loans that are not backed by the Federal Housing Administration (FHA) or Veterans Administration (VA) and that have a down payment of less than 20% of the property value. The FHA has its own insurance requirement for loans with a down payment of less than 20%.

7.11 (d) The fraction of the appraised value of the property offered as collateral which the lender is willing to lend.
The relationship of the loan amount to the property value, expressed as a percentage, is called the loan-to-value ratio, or LTV. If the lender's loan to value ratio is 80%, the lender will lend only $80,000 on a home appraised at $100,000. The difference between what the lender will lend and what the borrower must pay for the property is the amount the borrower must provide in cash as a down payment.

7.12 (c) buyer's down payment.
Price less loan is the down payment. This is also the buyer's initial equity.

7.13 (a) refusing a loan because the borrower does not match the lender's target market.
The Equal Credit Opportunity Act (ECOA) requires a lender to evaluate a loan applicant on the basis of that applicant's own income and credit rating, unless the applicant requests the inclusion of another's income and credit rating in the application. In addition, ECOA has prohibited a number of practices in mortgage loan underwriting, including refusing a loan based on an applicant's demographic characteristics.

7.14 (b) $1,680.
Monthly income qualification is derived by multiplying monthly income by the income ratio. Thus (72,000 / 12) x .28 = $1,680. Remember to first derive the monthly income.

7.15 (b) adjust the applicant's debt ratio calculation and lower the loan amount.
Since a lender lends only part of the purchase price of a property according to the lender's loan-to-value ratio, a lender will verify that a borrower has the cash resources to make the required down payment. If someone is lending an applicant a portion of the down payment with a provision for repayment, a lender will consider this another debt obligation and adjust the debt ratio accordingly. This can lower the amount a lender is willing to lend.

7.16 (c) All loans secured by a residence.
Regulation Z applies to all loans secured by a residence. It does not apply to commercial loans or to agricultural loans over $25,000. Its provisions cover the disclosure of costs, the right to rescind the credit

transaction, advertising credit offers, and penalties for non-compliance with the act.

7.17 (d) the borrower has a limited right to cancel the transaction within a certain period.
A borrower has a limited right to cancel the credit transaction, usually within three days of completion of the transaction. The right of rescission does not apply to "residential mortgage transactions," that is, to mortgage loans used to finance the purchase or construction of the borrower's primary residence. It does, however, apply to refinancing of mortgage loans, and to home equity loans. State law may require a rescission period and notice on first mortgage loan transactions as well.

7.18 (b) ask the buyer/borrower about his/her religion or national origin.
ECOA prohibits discrimination in extending credit based on race, color, religion, national origin, sex, marital status, age, or dependency upon public assistance. A creditor may not make any statements to discourage an applicant on the basis of such discrimination or ask any questions of an applicant concerning these discriminatory items. A real estate licensee who assists a seller in qualifying a potential buyer may fall within the reach of this prohibition.

7.19 (d) not FHA-insured or VA-guaranteed.
A conventional mortgage loan is a permanent long-term loan that is not FHA-insured or VA-guaranteed. FNMA does not "back" loans; FHA only insures FHA loans; and the VA, not GNMA guarantees loans.

7.20 (b) limited by when the loan was originated.
Rules for assumability vary according to when the FHA-insured loan was originated and whether the original loan was for an investment property or an owner-occupied principal residence. Loans originated before December 1, 1986, are generally assumable without restriction. Loans originated after December 1, 1986, require that the assumer show creditworthiness. Some mortgages executed from 1986 through 1989 contain language that is not enforced as a result of later Congressional action. Mortgages from that period are now freely assumable, despite any restrictions stated in the mortgage.

7.21 (c) how much of a loan the VA will guarantee.
A veteran must apply for a Certificate of Eligibility to find out how much the VA will guarantee in a particular situation.

7.22 (d) Zero.
If a loan is fully amortizing, its loan balance is zero at the end of the loan term.

7.23 (b) The buyer gives the seller a mortgage and note as part of the purchase price of the property.
With a purchase money mortgage, the borrower gives a mortgage and note to the seller to finance some or all of the purchase price of the property. The seller in this case is said to "take back" a note, or to "carry paper," on the property.

7.24 (c) hypothecation.
The process of securing a loan by pledging a property without giving up ownership of the property is called hypothecation.

7.25 (a) The borrower gives the lender a note and a mortgage in exchange for loan funds.
When a borrower gives a note promising to repay the borrowed money and executes a mortgage on the real estate for which the money is being borrowed as security, the financing method is called mortgage financing.

7.26 (c) The trustor conveys title to a trustee in exchange for loan funds from the beneficiary.
A deed of trust conveys title to the property in question from the borrower (trustor) to a trustee as security for the loan. The trustee is a third party fiduciary to the trust. While the loan is in place, the trustee holds the title on behalf of the lender, who is the beneficiary of the trust.

7.27 (a) title-theory state.
States that regard the mortgage document as a conveyance of ownership from the mortgagor to the mortgagee are called title-theory states.

7.28 (b) usury.
Many states have laws against usury, which is the charging of excessive interest rates on loans. Such states have a maximum rate that is either a flat rate or a variable rate tied to an index such as the prime lending rate.

7.29 (c) $7,500.
A point is one percentage point of a loan amount. Thus, 2.5 points on a $300,000 loan equal (.025 x $300,000), or $7,500.

7.30 (a) an amortized loan is paid off over the loan period.
Amortized loans retire the principal balance over the loan period. If a loan does not do this, one must make a balloon payment at the end of the loan term to complete the loan payoff.

7.31 (c) it is a negotiable instrument.
A promissory note is a negotiable instrument, which means the payee may assign it to a third party. The assignee would then have the right to receive the borrower's periodic payments.

7.32 (d) may be required to execute a release of mortgage document.
Lenders may be required to release the mortgage or trust document to the borrower when the borrower has paid off the loan and all other sums secured by the document. The release clause, also known as a defeasance clause, may specify that the mortgagee will execute a satisfaction of mortgage (also known as release of mortgage and mortgage discharge) to the mortgagor.

7.33 (a) an appraisal report.
Loan underwriting is the process of assessing the lender's risk in giving a loan. Mortgage underwriting includes: evaluating the borrower's ability to repay the loan; appraising the value of the property offered as security; and determining the terms of the loan.

7.34 (c) the ability to re-pay, the value of the collateral, and the profitability of the loan.
A lender assesses risks by examining, or qualifying, both borrower and property. In qualifying a borrower, an underwriter weighs the ability of the borrower to repay the loan. In qualifying a property, an underwriter assesses the ability of the property value to cover potential losses. In this evaluation, a lender requires that the appraised value of the property be more than adequate to cover the contemplated loan and costs. Finally, the loan must make money for the lending organization as a basic business precept.

7.35 (b) they want to ensure there is more than enough collateral to cover the loan amount.
Without an ample difference between the property value and the loan amount, a drop in property values could cause the loan balance to exceed the collateral itself. This greatly increases the risk of a loan loss should the borrower default since the balance could not be completely recovered in a foreclosure sale.

7.36 (b) consider the income of a spouse in evaluating a family's creditworthiness.
The Equal Credit Opportunity Act (ECOA) requires a lender to evaluate a loan applicant on the basis of that applicant's own income and credit rating, unless the applicant requests the inclusion of another's income and credit rating in the application. In such a case, a lender may not discount or disregard income from part-time work, a spouse, child support, alimony, or separate maintenance.

7.37 (a) insure the buyer has the earning power to make the loan payments.
Both the income and debt ratios in borrower qualification quantify how much a borrower can safely afford to pay on a mortgage loan. The income ratio focuses on the borrower's earning power.

7.38 (d) debt payments divided by gross income.
The debt ratio formula is (debt obligations) ÷ (income).

7.39 (c) the parties complete all loan origination documents and the loan is funded.
Closing of a mortgage loan normally occurs with the closing of the real estate transaction. At the real estate closing, the lender typically has deposited the funded amount with an escrow agent, along with instructions for disbursing the funds. The borrower deposits necessary funds with the escrow agent, executes final documents, and receives signed copies of all relevant documents.

7.40 (b) Truth-in-Lending laws and Regulation Z.
Regulation Z, which implements the Truth-in-Lending Act, applies to all loans secured by a residence. It does not apply to commercial loans or to agricultural loans over $25,000. It prescribes requirements to lenders regarding the disclosure of costs, the right to rescind the credit transaction, advertising credit offers, and penalties for non-compliance with the Truth-in-Lending Act.

7.41 (a) The Equal Credit Opportunity Act.
ECOA prohibits discrimination in extending credit based on race, color, religion, national origin, sex, marital status, age, or dependency upon public assistance.

7.42 (c) the Real Estate Settlement and Procedures Act.
RESPA is a federal law which aims to standardize settlement practices and ensure that buyers understand settlement costs. RESPA applies to purchases of residential real estate (one- to four-family homes) to be financed by "federally related" first mortgage loans. In addition to imposing settlement procedures, RESPA provisions prohibit lenders from paying kickbacks and unearned fees to parties who may have helped the lender obtain the borrower's business.

7.43 (b) Buying securities, changing the discount rate, and controlling banking reserves.
The Federal Reserve System regulates the money supply by means of three methods: selling or re-purchasing government securities, primarily Treasury bills, changing the reserve requirement for member banks; changing the interest rate, or discount rate, the system charges member institutions for borrowing funds from the Federal Reserve System.

7.44 (a) It cycles funds back to primary lenders so they can make more loans.
Secondary mortgage market organizations buy pools of mortgages from primary lenders and sell securities backed by these pooled mortgages to investors. By purchasing loans from primary lenders, the secondary market returns funds to the primary lenders, thereby enabling the primary lender to originate more mortgage loans.

7.45 (a) Fannie Mae, Freddie Mac, and Ginnie Mae.
As major players in the secondary market, the Federal National Mortgage Association (FNMA, "Fannie Mae"), Government National Mortgage Association (GNMA, "Ginnie Mae), and Federal Home Loan Mortgage Corporation (FHLMC, "Freddie Mac") tend to set the standards for the primary market. FHA, VA, and the Federal Reserve are not organizations in the secondary mortgage market.

7.46 (c) It purchases FHA-backed and VA-backed loans.
Fannie Mae buys conventional, FHA-backed and VA-backed loans; gives banks mortgage-backed securities in exchange for blocks of mortgages; and sells bonds and mortgage-backed securities. It does not guarantee, insure, or originate loans.

7.47 (b) It insures loans made by approved lenders.
The Federal Housing Administration (FHA) does not lend money, but insures permanent long-term loans made by others. The lender must be approved by the FHA, and the borrower must meet certain FHA qualifications.

7.48 (a) It guarantees loans made by approved lenders.
The Veterans Administration (VA) offers loan guarantees to qualified veterans. The VA partially guarantees permanent long-term loans originated by VA-approved lenders on properties that meet VA standards. The VA's guarantee enables lenders to issue loans with higher loan-to-value ratios than would otherwise be possible.

7.49 (c) the loan payments gradually increase.
Graduated payment mortgages allow for smaller initial monthly payments which gradually increase. The interest rate remains fixed as does the loan term.

7.50 (b) the borrower pays additional interest at the onset in order to obtain a lower interest rate.
A buydown loan entails a prepayment of interest on a loan. The prepayment effectively lowers the interest rate and the periodic payments for the borrower. Buydowns typically occur in a circumstance where a builder wants to market a new development to a buyer who cannot quite qualify for the necessary loan at market rates.

7.51 (c) Private mortgage insurance
If a loan's LTV ratio is too high, a lender may require that the borrower purchase private mortgage insurance, commonly called PMI. This insurance secures whatever portion of the loan amount takes the LTV ratio above the typical ratio limit – which is usually 80% of the property's value. This protects the lender from the borrower's default – which can become more likely if the borrower has very little equity in the property.

7.52 (d) Agribusinesses
The Federal Agricultural Mortgage Corporation, or Farmer Mac. Farmer Mac (FAMC) is a federal agency whose central function is to increase the availability and affordability of credit for American agriculture and American rural communities.

NATIONAL TEST 8: Investments; Taxation; Professional Practices

8.1 (b) negative leverage.
Leveraging is borrowing funds in order to make an investment that is larger than your own resource permits you to do directly. In negative leverage situations, your cost of borrowing funds to make the investment becomes greater than the income the investment returns to you.

8.2 (b) income properties.
Cost recovery, or depreciation, allows the owner of income property to deduct a portion of the property's value from gross income each year over the life of the asset. Principal residences cannot be depreciated (unless portions are treated as a home office.) Further, land cannot be depreciated.

8.3 (c) 19.5 %.
Appreciation amount is the current value of the property minus the original cost. The total appreciation rate is derived by dividing the appreciation amount by the original cost. Subtract the estimated current market value from the price originally paid (239,000 - 200,000 = 39,000) and then divide the result by the original price (39,000 / 200,000 = . 195 or 19.5%).

8.4 (d) a deduction for mortgage interest.
Deducting mortgage interest is a significant tax advantage of owning one's residence. Depreciation and cost-deductions do not apply to a non-income producing residence. Appreciation is a benefit, but not a tax benefit.

8.5 (d) $232,900.
The figure for net proceeds from sale is expressed by the formula: sale price - costs of sale = net proceeds. Thus $250,000 - (6% x 250,000) – 600 – 1,500 = $232,900.

8.6 (b) $471,000.
The beginning basis is the cost of acquiring a property. Basis is increased by capital improvements and decreased by depreciation. The basic formula for adjusted basis is Beginning basis ($450,000) + capital improvements ($9,000 + $12,000) - depreciation ($0) = adjusted basis ($471,000).

8.7 (c) $68,000.
The gain on sale (capital gain) of a primary residence is represented by the basic formula: amount realized (net sales proceeds, $420,000) - adjusted basis ($352,000) = gain on sale ($68,000). Note the purchase price of the second house is irrelevant.

8.8 (a) There is no taxable gain.
There is no taxable gain because the gain falls under the exclusion limit of $250,000. As of August 5, 1997, tax law provides an exclusion of $250,000 for an individual taxpayer and $500,000 for married taxpayers filing jointly on the gain from sale of a principal residence. The seller must have owned the property for at least two years during the five years preceding the date of sale; used the property as principal residence for a total of two years during that five-year period; and have waited two years since the last use of the exclusion for any sale.

8.9 (c) direct investment.
Individuals, corporations, or other investor entities may invest as active investors in a property by buying it directly and taking responsibility for managing and operating the property. This investment mode is called direct investment.

8.10 (a) $2,100.
Annual gross operating income ($1,500 x 12 = $18,000) - annual operating expenses ($500 x 12 = $6,000) = annual net operating income ($12,000); annual net operating income ($12,000) - cost recovery expense ($5,000) = taxable income ($7,000); taxable income ($7,000) x tax rate (30%) = tax liability ($2,100).

8.11 (b) the more the investor stands to gain, the greater the risk that the investor may lose.
The general rule in investments is that the safer the investment, the more slowly it gains in value. The more you want it to gain, and the more quickly, the more you must risk losing it. Reward in investing corresponds directly to the degree of risk.

8.12 (a) income and tax benefits.
The basic financial rewards of an investment include income, appreciation in asset value, positive borrowing leverage, and tax benefits.

8.13 (d) relatively illiquid.
Real estate is by nature more difficult to convert to cash than many other types of investment. Compare the selling of a home with the ease of drawing money out of a bank account or selling a stock.

8.14 (b) a more management-intensive investment.
Real estate tends to require a high degree of investor involvement in management of the investment. Even raw land requires some degree of maintenance to preserve its value. Improved properties often require extensive management, including repairs, maintenance, onsite leasing, tenant relations, security, and fiscal management.

8.15 (a) a general partnership.
A general partnership is a syndicate in which all members participate equally in managing the investment and in the profits or losses it generates.

8.16 (d) gross income minus expenses minus building depreciation.
Taxable income from investment real estate is the gross income received minus any expenses, deductions or exclusions that current tax law allows. Depreciation of land is not allowed.

8.17 (c) deduct interest payments from income.
Taxable income is net operating income minus all allowable deductions. The interest portion of debt service is allowed and is deducted from Net Operating Income as interest expense. Principal repayment is not an allowable deduction on investment properties. Capital gain derivation does not involve interest or principal payments.

8.18 (d) The owner may be able to avoid capital gain tax when the property is sold.
Provided the owner meets certain ownership and use tests, there is no capital gain tax on sale of the property unless the gain exceeds $250,000 for a single taxpayer or $500,000 for married taxpayers who file jointly. Since the property is not used for business, deductions for expenses against income are not allowed.

8.19 (c) may be deducted from the sale price for gains tax purposes.
Selling costs include such expenses as brokerage commissions, relevant advertising, legal fees, seller-paid points and other closing costs. These costs are deducted from the selling price to get the amount realized, which is reduced by the adjusted basis to calculate gain on sale for gains tax purposes.

8.20 (b) the difference between amount realized and adjusted basis.
The formula for gain tax is Taxable Gain on Sale x the owner's marginal tax bracket. The formula for gain on sale is: Amount Realized - Adjusted Basis = Gain on Sale. The formula for Amount Realized is: Selling Price - Selling costs = Amount Realized. Therefore, the gain tax = (Amount Realized - Adjusted Basis) x tax rate.

8.21 (c) A tax district.
Real estate property taxes are imposed by "taxing entities" or "taxing districts" at county and local levels of government. States may legally levy taxes on real property, but most delegate this power to counties, cities, townships and local taxing districts. The federal government does, however, tax income derived from real property and gains realized on the sale of real property.

8.22 (b) properties owned by a government agency.
Certain types of property are exempt from property taxes. Certain classes of property owner may also be exempted or have a reduced liability. Exemptions include government-owned properties, real properties owned by churches, and properties owned by other non-profit organizations.

8.23 (c) It adjusts assessments in a locality to make them more consistent with an average level for the state or other higher level jurisdiction.
Equalization factors level out the unevenness of valuations for groups of properties. For instance, if assessed values of properties in one county are consistently ten percent below the average for other counties, an equalization board may multiply each assessed value in that county by a factor of 110% to raise them to the average level for the state.

8.24 (c) $2,000,000,000.
The mill rate = (tax requirement / the tax base). A mill is one one-thousandth of a dollar ($.001). To solve for the tax base, reconfigure this formula to be: Base = Tax Requirement / Mill Rate. Thus the Base = $20,000,000 / .010, or $2,000,000,000.

8.25 (d) $1,323.
The library tax is ($1.00 x 441) and the fire district tax is ($2.00 x 441). Thus the tax is 441 x $3 = $1,323.

8.26 (b) $5,700.
Special assessments are based on the cost of the improvement and apportioned on a pro rata basis among benefiting properties according to the value that each parcel will receive from the improvement. Here, Mary's share is 38 / 200, or 19%. 19% x $30,000 = $5,700.

8.27 (a) A conveyance instrument for a property that is sold to enforce a tax lien.
A tax deed is a legal instrument for conveying title when a property is sold for non-payment of taxes. The application for a tax deed causes the taxing agency to institute a tax sale or tax foreclosure.

8.28 (d) a statutory right of redemption.
If the taxpayer can redeem the property after the tax sale, this right is known as a statutory right of redemption. In this case, the taxpayer must pay the amount paid by the winning bidder at the tax sale, plus any charges, additional taxes, or interest that may have accumulated.

8.29 (b) the total of all assessed values of properties minus exemptions.
The tax base of an area is the total of the appraised or assessed values of all real property within the area's boundaries, excluding partially or totally exempt properties such as those owned by the government or non-profit organizations.

8.30 (c) multiplying each district's tax rate times the taxable value of the property.
Each property owner's tax bill is determined by multiplying the tax rate for each taxing district times the taxable value of the property. Taxable value is the assessed value after all exemptions and adjustments have been taken into account.

8.31 (a) Civil Rights Act of 1866.
The original fair housing statute, the Civil Rights Act of 1866, prohibits discrimination in housing based on race. The prohibition relates to selling, renting, inheriting, and conveying real estate.

8.32 (c) race, color, religion, and national origin.
Title VIII of the Civil Rights Act of 1968, known today as the Fair Housing Act, prohibits discrimination in housing based on race, color, religion, or national origin.

8.33 (c) Advertising a property as available to individuals of a particular race.
The prohibition against discriminatory advertising states that an agent may not advertise residential

properties in such a way as to restrict their availability to any prospective buyer or tenant.

8.34 (c) An agent persuades a family to put their house on the market because ethnic minority families are beginning to move into the neighborhood.
Blockbusting, a prohibited activity, is the practice of inducing owners in an area to sell or rent to avoid an impending change in the ethnic or social makeup of the neighborhood that will cause values to go down.

8.35 (a) The Home Mortgage Disclosure Act.
The Home Mortgage Disclosure Act requires lenders involved with federally guaranteed or insured loans to exercise impartiality and non-discrimination in the geographical distribution of their loan portfolio. In other words, the act is designed to prohibit redlining, the practice of restricting loans by geographical are(a)

8.36 (c) privately owned single-family residences listed with a broker.
Among the circumstances where the Fair Housing Act might allow for an exemption is: a privately owned single-family home where no broker is used, with certain additional conditions. In other words, as soon as a broker is used in the sale, the law applies.

8.37 (a) illegal, because the agent changed the terms of the sale to discourage this particular couple.
The Fair Housing Act prohibition against discriminatory misrepresentation states that an agent may not conceal available properties, represent that they are not for sale or rent, or change the sale terms for the purpose of discriminating.

8.38 (d) The owner of a duplex who resides in one of the units refuses to rent the other unit to a non-Christian.
The Fair Housing Act would exempt the owner in this situation because it involves rental of an apartment in a 1-4 unit building where the owner is also an occupant and there is no discriminatory advertising.

8.39 (b) File a complaint with HUD and/or file suit against the offending parties in a state or federal court within the prescribed time period.
The Fair Housing Amendments Act of 1988 prohibits discrimination based on sex. If May feels she has been discriminated against in this way, she may file a complaint with the Office of Fair Housing and Equal Opportunity (OFHEO) in HUD within one year or file suit in a federal or state court within two years of the alleged violation.

8.40 (a) Inform Scott that the condition is illegal and that she cannot comply with it.
Scott is not allowed to discriminate based on race, color, religion, national origin, sex, family status, or handicap. If an agent goes along with a client's discriminatory act, the agent is equally liable for violation of fair housing laws. It is thus imperative to avoid complicity with client discrimination. Further, an agent should withdraw from any relationship where client discrimination occurs.

8.41 (c) require families without children to pay the same security deposit that families with children must pay.
Fair housing laws prohibit discriminatory advertising, discrimination on the basis of national origin, discrimination based on age in dwellings of more than four units, and discrimination against families with children. The fact that the owner is requiring the same deposit from tenants with and without children does not discriminate against families with children but actually favors them.

8.42 (d) It is a single-family house, and the owner owns only one other rental home in addition to his own residence.
Federal fair housing laws do not prohibit age and family status discrimination in residential dwellings of four units or less and in single family houses if sold or rented by owners who have no more than three houses.

8.43 (c) the Fair Housing Amendments Act of 1988.
The Fair Housing Amendments Act of 1988 prohibited discrimination based on sex and discrimination against handicapped persons and families with children. Executive Order 11063 concerned racial discrimination in housing where federal funding was involved; the Civil Rights Act of 1968 concerned discrimination based on race, color, religion, and national origin; Jones v Mayer concerned racial discrimination.

8.44 (c) steering.
Steering is the illegal practice of limiting customers' choices by encouraging or discouraging them about the suitability of an area and directing them only to areas the agent deems suitable for them.

8.45 (a) providing unequal services.
The agent may be illegally providing unequal services by altering the nature or quality of brokerage services to a party based on race, color, sex, national origin, or religion.

8.46 (a) discriminatory misrepresentation by omission.
Discriminatory misrepresentation is the concealing of available properties, representing that they are not for sale or rent, or changing the sale terms for the purpose of discriminating.

8.47 (c) Prior to the sale of an occupied 1-4 unit dwelling
The Seller's Property Condition Disclosure form must be completed by the seller prior to the closing of any resale of a 1-4-unit residential dwelling. New homes are exempted, as are commercial properties. In some jurisdictions, the property disclosure form must be completed when an offer is completed.

8.48 (d) must still be completed according to local requirements
Whether the seller lists or sells by-owner, he or she must still fulfill the obligation to complete the Property Condition form in a timely fashion. Similarly, the licensee is required to disclose all known material facts regardless of the seller's disclosures.

8.49 (c) A previous occupant died in the house
Sellers are not required to disclose fact that do not materially impact the value or condition of the property including suicides, AIDS-related illness, and other property stigmas. Licensees, however, are required to disclose known material facts.

8.50 (d) love letter.
Buyers sometimes try to enhance the attractiveness of a purchase offer by attaching a personal note to the offer. This appeal to the seller, called a "love letter," typically mentions such things as why the buyer particularly likes the home, how the buyer imagines family life in the home, and how well the buyer will care for the home.

8.51 (a) By requiring the wholesaler to have a real estate license
Some states require the wholesaler in such transactions to hold a real estate license.

NATIONAL TEST 9: Closings; Risk Management; Property Management

9.1 (c) returns funds to the buyer.
If for any reason the transaction cannot be completed, the escrow instructions usually provide a mechanism for reconveying title to the seller and funds to the buyer. In such a case, both parties return to their original status as if no sale had occurred.

9.2 (d) disclose in writing any business relationships they have with other parties involved in the transaction.
Business relationships and affiliations among real estate firms, mortgage brokers, title insurance firms and other such companies that are involved in a transaction are permitted, provided the relationships are disclosed in writing to the consumer, the consumer is free to go elsewhere for the relevant service, and the companies do not exchange fees for referrals.

9.3 (a) The item must be prorated and recorded as a debit to one party and a credit to the other party for the same amount.
An income or expense item that affects both parties is apportioned, or prorated, to each party to reflect the proper amount that each owes or should receive. A prorated item is treated as a debit to one party and a credit to the other party for the same amount.

9.4 (b) at some time after the expense is incurred.
Items paid in arrears are paid after the expense has been incurred.

9.5 (d) A debit to the seller and credit to the buyer for $580.
For income the seller received in advance, the buyer receives a credit and the seller receives a debit. In effect, the seller has received some of the buyer's income, and the seller must pay this share to the buyer. Therefore the seller is debited and the buyer is credited the $580 the buyer is entitled to earn as the new owner.

9.6 (b) A debit to the seller and credit to the buyer for $43.
For an item the buyer will pay in arrears, the buyer receives a credit and the seller receives a debit. In effect, the seller has incurred some of the expenses that the buyer will be paying for after closing. Thus the seller must pay the buyer the used portion of the expense, or $43.

9.7 (b) $546.00.
The daily tax expense, first, is ($2,190 ÷ 365) or $6.00. Since the buyer will pay the taxes after closing, the seller will owe the buyer his or her portion of the tax bill, which is the 91 days from the beginning of the year through closing. Therefore, credit the buyer and debit the seller ($6.00 x 91), or $546.00.

9.8 (d) $1,916.67.
This method assumes all months are 30 days and the year is 360 days. The daily proration is therefore $3,750 ÷ 360, or $10.42. The closing occurs on the 184th day of the year. Thus, ($10.42 x 184) = $1,916.67. Note that if the day of closing is the buyer's, there would be 183 day's worth of prorated expense.

9.9 (d) $735.34.
Assuming a 365 day year, the daily tax expense is ($1,100 ÷ 365), or $3.013. As taxes are paid in arrears, the buyer will be paying the annual bill. Thus, he will be owed a credit for the seller's share of the bill, which is $3.013 x 244 days, or $735.34.

9.10 (a) $116.03.
The buyer's share is the unused portion, or (365 days – 244 days), or 121 days. The daily expense is ($350 ÷ 365), or $.9589. ($.9589 x 121) = $116.03. The seller receives this amount as a credit and the buyer a debit.

9.11 (a) $5,075.00.
If the buyer pays $5,250 interest for 30 days, the daily expense is ($5,250 ÷ 30), or $175.00. If there are 29 days of pre-paid expense, the buyer's charge is ($175.00 x 29), or $5,075.00.

9.12 (c) $17,750.
$887,500 x .02 = $17,750. Remember, one point = 1% of the loan amount.

9.13 (d) $22,500.
$375,000 x 6% = $375,000 x .06 = $22,500.

9.14 (d) the buyer must pay the expense.
Explicit agreements in the sale contract supersede traditional expense-payment responsibilities which can vary from state to state.

9.15 (a) the excess of the buyer's debits over the buyer's credits.
To determine how much money the buyer owes at closing, the buyer's debits are totaled and compared with the total of the buyer's credits. The excess of debits over credits is the amount the buyer must bring to the closing.

9.16 (d) negligence, error or omission in carrying out professional services.
A standard E&O policy provides coverage for "damages resulting from any negligent act, error or omission arising out of Professional Services." It does not cover dishonest or illegal acts, including environmental violations and mishandling of funds.

9.17 (a) Failing to inform and disclose properly.
Agency risks commonly concern the requirement to inform and disclose. Most states require agency relationships to be in writing and to be disclosed to all parties to a transaction. In states that do not use agency, there is still the obligation to explain and disclose the nature of the relationship.

9.18 (b) failing to disclose known adverse facts.
Depending on the state, the licensee may have no further duty to disclose property condition after properly informing parties of their rights and obligations. However, the licensee may still be subject to legal action for failing to disclose adverse facts the licensee knew about or should have known about.

9.19 (d) avoid creating a false impression that the licensee is a certified appraiser.
Misuse of such terms as "appraisal" and "value" could lead to a charge of misrepresenting oneself as an appraiser.

9.20 (b) exceeding the authority of the agreement.
Licensees must stay within the bounds of the authority granted by the agency agreement and avoid doing anything requiring permission without first getting that permission in writing.

9.21 (a) use a checklist of all items, contingencies, dates and responsibilities that must be met.
One way to reduce risk in the contracting process is to use a checklist that covers all the contract items, such as inclusions and exclusions, contingency periods, documents, forms, data checking, and milestone dates.

9.22 (d) the principals may make changes as long as they sign or initial each change.
Real estate professionals who are not attorneys are usually limited to filling in blanks or making deletions on a preprinted contract form prepared by a lawyer. While a licensee may make deletions, additions to a form should be drafted by an attorney. The principals themselves can make changes as long as each change is signed or initialed by all signers.

9.23 (b) obtain education in the content and intent of the laws.
The risk of violating fair housing laws can be minimized through ongoing education that addresses both the intent of the laws and their current content.

9.24 (a) being present at a conversation where the setting of commission rates is discussed.
Antitrust laws forbid brokers to band together to set a price on their services in listing and selling property. Even being overheard discussing commission rates or being present at such a conversation can lead to charges of ***price fixing***.

9.25 (a) License discipline, fines, and possible incarceration.
Intentional misrepresentation, as a type of fraud, is a criminal act that may result in fines and incarceration, in addition to discipline from state regulators and professional organizations.

9.26 (c) stating that a client should seek legal counsel.
Unintentional misrepresentation occurs when a licensee *unknowingly* gives a consumer inaccurate information concerning a property, financing or agency service. Information that the licensee, as a professional, should have known to be false or inaccurate may be included in the definition. Telling a client that legal counsel would be advisable is not misrepresentation and, in fact, is often an important risk management technique.

9.27 (d) avoid speculative statements in all reports.
Progress reports should be accurate, timely, in writing, and free of speculation. Speculation may encourage the consumer to believe the agent has expertise that in fact is non-existent. If a consumer has a question about the meaning of something in an inspection report, the licensee should refer the consumer to the person who wrote the report rather than trying to explain it.

9.28 (b) It reduces the chance of presenting an offer from an unqualified buyer.
Using a lender to qualify the buyer protects the agent against leading a seller to believe a purchaser is fully qualified when this may not be the case. Also, lenders and loan agents are better able to look into the buyer's qualifications than a real estate licensee is. If it is necessary to show a property to a potential buyer

who has not been qualified by a lender, the licensee can gain some protection by performing an informal qualification and documenting the fact that it was based on the information provided by the buyer.

9.29 (c) the agency relationship.
Maintaining the confidentiality of any information that would harm the client's interests or bargaining position or anything else the client wishes to keep secret, unless the law requires disclosure, is one of the primary duties of agency. The duty to maintain confidentiality generally survives the termination of a listing agreement into perpetuity.

9.30 (a) performing a comparative market analysis.
In preparing a Comparative Market Analysis, licensees should guard against using the terms "appraisal" and "value," which are reserved for the use of certified appraisers. Misuse of these terms could lead to a charge of misrepresenting oneself as an appraiser.

9.31 (d) make a substantial misrepresentation.
The license laws of most states list as illegal advertising activities subject to discipline such actions as making any substantial and intentional misrepresentation, making false promises, and making misleading or untruthful statements in any advertising.

9.32 (c) fiduciary
The management agreement creates an agency relationship between the manager and the principal. This is a fiduciary relationship and, in general, the agent is charged with producing the greatest possible net return on the owner's investment while safeguarding the value of the investment for the owner/investor.

9.33 (b) financial reporting to the principal.
Financial reporting to the principal is a fundamental responsibility of the property manager. Reports may be required monthly, quarterly, and annually. Required reports typically include operating budget, cash flow, profit and loss, and budget comparison statements.

9.34 (d) revenue from all sources minus losses from uncollected rents, vacancies, and evictions.
The total of scheduled rents plus revenues from such sources as vending services, storage charges, late fees, utilities, and contracts is the potential gross income. Subtracting losses caused by uncollected rents, vacancies and evictions gives effective gross income.

9.35 (a) cost per tenant prospect generated per lease.
The efficiency of marketing activities can be judged in terms of how many prospects per completed lease they generate. The lower the cost per prospect per lease, the more effective and efficient the program.

9.36 (b) raise rental rates.
Vacancy rates are directly related to demand and competitive supply in the market. If vacancy rates in the managed property are too high, the manager may have to lower rates or identify problems in the property or its management that are contributing to vacancy level. On the other hand, if the property's vacancy rate is significantly lower than market rates, the manager may conclude that higher rental rates are called for.

9.37 (b) Routine, preventive, and corrective
The foremost maintenance objective is generally to preserve the value of the physical asset for the owner over the long term. Three general types of maintenance are required to keep a property in serviceable condition: routine (day-to-day), preventive (scheduled), and corrective (repairs and replacements).

9.38 (a) ensure that disabled employees have the same level of access to facilities that all employees have.
Employers with at least fifteen employees must follow nondiscriminatory employment and hiring practices and make reasonable accommodations to enable disabled employees to perform essential functions of their jobs. Modifications to the physical components of the building may be necessary to provide the required access to tenants and their customers. Existing barriers must be removed when the removal is "readily achievable," that is, when cost is not prohibitive.

9.39 (a) replacement value.
The amount of coverage provided by certain types of policies may be based on whether the property is insured at depreciated value or current replacement value. Depreciated value is original value minus the

loss in value over time. Current replacement value, which is more expensive, is the amount it would cost to rebuild or replace the property at current rates. Commercial policies include coinsurance clauses requiring the insured to bear a portion of the loss. Fire and hazard policies usually require the coverage to be in an amount equal to at least 80 percent of the replacement value.

9.40 (b) cash for the management firm's operating expenses.
Managers are responsible for proper handling of monies belonging to other parties (trust funds) that come into the manager's hands in the course of doing business. For property managers, such trust funds include rents collected from tenants, security deposits, and capital contributions from the property owner. Funds belonging to the management firm must not be commingled with those of the client.

9.41 (c) General
Property managers are usually considered to be general agents empowered to perform some or all of the ongoing tasks and duties of operating the property, including the authority to enter into contracts.

9.42 (b) The tenant pays a fixed rent, and the landlord pays all operating expenses.
In a gross lease, the tenant pays an established, fixed rent, and the landlord pays all property operating expenses, such as taxes, insurance, utilities, and other services. This is the arrangement commonly used in residential leases. If the tenant pays some of the operating expenses, the lease is a form of net lease.

9.43 (d) the property manager does not have to maintain it.
The lease should set forth items that are excluded or included in the leased property. For instance, a residential lease may include built-in appliances such as dishwashers but exclude freestanding ones, such as refrigerators. At issue for the landlord is the cost of maintenance. If a refrigerator is not included, it does not have to be maintained by the property manager.

9.44 (b) deliver a habitable property.
The landlord (by way of the property manager), is expected to deliver a property that is habitable. This means keeping heating, plumbing, cooling, and electrical systems in good repair as well as maintaining serviceability of floors, stairways, railings, roofs, and windows.

9.45 (c) A tenant declares a landlord in default and vacates the leased premises.
A constructive eviction occurs when a tenant vacates the leased premises and declares the lease void, claiming that the landlord's actions have made the premises unfit for the purpose described in the lease. The tenant must prove that it was the landlord's actions that were responsible and may be able to recover damages.

9.46 (a) the competitive market for the property.
In preparing a management plan, a manager must consider the owner's objectives, including financial goals; the competitive market for the property, both local and regional, depending on the property type; and the features of the particular property. The plan will also include a budget and indications of what the manager intends to do with the property to meet the owner's objectives.

NATIONAL TEST 10: Real Estate Math

10.1 (a) $.023 / SF
5/6ths of an acre = (5 x 43,560 SF) / 6, or 36,300 SF. Her commission was (.06 x $28,000) x .50, or $840. $840 / 36,300 SF = $.023 / SF.

10.2 (b) $370,170
The land costs $.50 x 43,560 SF/ac. x 1.5 ac, or $32,670. The home will cost $135 / SF x 2,500, or $337,500. The total property will cost $370,170.

10.3 (a) 12%
The lot measures 43,560 / 4, or 10,890 SF. The tennis court will take up 9,600 SF, leaving 1,290 SF. This amount is 11.8% of the total lot area.

10.4 (c) 40
The total area available for lots is 11.2 acres (16 acres x 70% for houses), or 487,872 SF (11.2 x 43,560). Dividing this area by 12,000 SF / lot = 40.66. Thus he can have a 40-lot subdivision.

10.5 (a) 6
First, the requirement = 2(13'x 9') +2 (18'x 9') =558 SF. Each roll is 2'x 50', or 100 SF. Thus she will need 6 rolls.

10.6 (d) 1,376 SF
First figure the area to be mulched. If the home is 40 x 30, the flower area adds 8' to each side of the house. Thus the outside perimeter of the flowered area is (40+8+8) by (30+8+8), or 46' by 56'. The area of the flowered area is (46' x 56') minus the house area of 1,200 SF. This is 1,376 SF.

10.7 (b) 40 acres
First, remember that a section contains 640 acres. The area in question is a forth of a half of a half of the total section. So divide 640 by (4 x 2 x 2). 4 x 2 x 2 is 16 and 640/16= 40 acres.

10.8 (c) 10 acres
The key to this question is to recall that a section has 640 acres. Theresa's property only is a ¼ of a ¼ of a ¼ of the entire section. Multiply 4 x 4 x 4 which equals 64. Savannah owns 1/64 of the section. Divide 640 by 64 and you get the answer of 10 acres.

10.9 (a) $38,955
Their fixed rent is (1,800 SF x $1.40/SF) x 12 months, or $30,240. The percentage rent is ($41,500 x .0175) x 12, or $8,715. Total rent is ($30,240 + 8,715), or $38,955.

10.10 (a) 5.04%
First, convert to decimals: 2 2/3 % = 2.67%; 5 1/5% = 5.2%; 7 1/4% = 7.25%. Thus total appreciation = (2.67% + 5.2% + 7.25%), or 15.12%. Divide by 3 to derive the average: 15.12% / 3 = 5.04%

10.11 (c) 29%.
Appreciation as a per cent can be estimated by (1) subtracting the estimated current market value from the price originally paid (239,000 - 185,000 = 54,000) and (2) dividing the result by the original price (54,000 / 185,000 = . 29 or 29%).

10.12 (c) 94%
To find the percent of listing price the offer is, divide the offer by the listing price. In this question the offer is $290,000 and the listing price is $308,000. $290,000 / $308,000 = .94 or 94%.

10.13 (a) $206,000.
Remember the formula V = I / R where V is value, I is annual income, and R is the cap rate. Variations of this are: R = I / V in solving for the cap rate, and I = V x R in solving for income. Here, first identify net income by subtracting out vacancy and expenses. Then divide by the capitalization rate. Thus, ($30,000 – 1,500 – 10,000) / 9% = $205,555, or $206,000 rounded.

10.14 (b) $375,000.
Value = Income / Cap rate. Thus, V= $30,000 / .08 = $375,000.

10.15 (b) $13,600.
First derive the annual depreciation which is the cost divided by the economic life. Then multiply annual depreciation times the number of years to identify total depreciation. Remember to subtract depreciation from the original cost if the question asks for the ending value. Thus, ($16,000 / 20 years x 3 years) = $2,400 total depreciation. The ending value is $16,000 –2,400, or $13,600.

10.16 (a) $1,077
First, Lee's depreciable basis, without the land, is $280,000 x 75%, or $210,000. The annual depreciation for the entire home is ($210,000 / 39 years), or $5,384.61. Second, his office is 20% of the house (500 sf / 2,500 sf). Therefore Lee can take annual depreciation of ($5,384.61 x 20%), or $1,076.92.

10.17 (d) $376,000.
Cost Approach formula: Land + (Cost of Improvements + Capital Additions – Depreciation) = Value. Thus you have $80,000 + ($350,000 - 54,000), or $376,000.

10.18 (c) $475,000
Use the same Cost Approach formula: Land + (Cost of Improvements + Capital Additions – Depreciation) = Value. The land is worth (100,000 x 125%), or $125,000. Remember, you cannot depreciate the land, only the cost of the improvements. Therefore, annual depreciation is ($400,000 / 40), or $10,000. Total depreciation is ($10,000 x 5 years), or $50,000. Thus the value is ($125,000 + 400,000 – 50,000), or $475,000.

10.19 (d) 125.
Use the formula: GRM = Price / Monthly Rent. Thus, $400,000 / $3,200 = 125.

10.20 (c) $582,000.
Use the formula: GIM = Price / Annual Income. To solve for price convert the formula to Price = GIM x Annual Income. Thus, ($3,300 x 12) equals $39,600 annual income. ($39,600 x 14.7 GIM) = $582,120, or $582,000 rounded.

10.21 (d) $1,500
The loan amount is $400,000 x .75, or $300,000. The first month interest equals ($300,000 x 6%) / 12 months, or $1,500.

10.22 (b) $358,000.
The equation for the loan amount is (annual interest divided by the interest rate) = loan amount. Thus, ($1,580 x 12) / .053 = $357,736 or $358,000 rounded.

10.23 (a) 4.82%.
The equation for the interest rate is (annual payment / loan amount) = interest rate. Thus ($1,000 x 12) / $249,000 = 4.82%.

10.24 (b) $1,456.95
In the first month they pay interest of ($280,000 x 6.25%) / 12, or $1,458. If their fixed payment is $1,724, they paid down the principal by $266 ($1,724 - 1,458). Now they must pay 6.25% interest on the new principal balance of $279,734. This equals (279,734 x .0625) / 12, or $1,456.95.

10.25 (b) The second option, by 150.
The first option's interest total is (6.5% x $60,000) x 5 years, or $19,500. The second option will charge (6.25% x $60,000) x 5 years, plus $600, or a total of $19,350. The 2nd option is $150 cheaper.

10.26 (b) 1.67 points
A discount point is one percent of the loan amount. Jose's loan is ($410,000 x 90%), or $369,000. If he paid $6,150, he paid 1.67% of the loan amount ($6,150 / 369,000), or 1.67 points.

10.27 (c) $4,875.
$325,000 x .015 = $4,875. Remember, one point = 1% of the loan amount.

10.28 (c) $487,500
Use the formula: Price x LTV Ratio = Loan. Then plug in the figures and calculate: Price x .80 = $130,000. Therefore, Price = $390,000 / .80 = $487,500.

10.29 (c) $379,259
First, the annual interest paid is $1,600 x 12, or $19,200. The interest rate is 6.75%. Using the formula (Loan = Interest / Rate), the loan amount is $19,200 / 6.75%, or $284,444. As this is 75% of the price, the price is ($284,444 / .75), or $379,259.

10.30 (b) $1,900.
Monthly income qualification is derived by multiplying monthly income by the income ratio. Thus (76,000 / 12) x .30 = $1,900. Remember to first derive the monthly income.

10.31 (a) $253,846

Total depreciation on this property = ($600,000 / 39 years) x 10 years, or $153,846. His adjusted basis is therefore ($680,000 original price – 153,846 depreciation taken), or $526,154. The gain is then ($780,000 – 526,154), or $253,846.

10.32 (b) $257,000.

Adjusted basis = beginning basis ($250,000) + capital improvements ($2,000 + $5,000) – depreciation (0) = adjusted basis ($257,000).

10.33 (c) $34,000.

Capital gain = amount realized (net sales proceeds, $265,000) - adjusted basis ($231,000) = ($34,000).

10.34 (d) $375,000.

The basic formula for adjusted basis is: Beginning Basis + Capital Improvements - Exclusions and Credits = Adjusted Basis. Debra's adjusted basis is therefore $360,000 + $15,000 = $375,000. The financing terms and subsequent selling price are not relevant.

10.35 (c) $15,000 overpriced.

Use the same formula V = I / R where V is the price and R is the rate of return. Then plug in the numbers to solve for V. The NOI of this property is ($60,000 - $22,000), or $38,000. The return is 11%. Therefore, the value to get this return must be $38,000 / .11, or $345,455. Since the price is $360,000, the price exceeds the amount needed for an 11% return by approximately $15,000 ($360,000 - $345,455 = $14,545).

10.36 (b) Yes, since he will yield 8.375%

Use the same formula R = I / V where V is the $2 million price, and R is the cap rate or rate of return. To identify income: (25,000 SF x $10/SF) = $250,000 gross income, minus 5% vacancy (.05 x $250,000), or $12,500, minus expenses of $70,000 = $167,500 net income. ($250,000 – 12,500 – 70,000) Now divide net income of $167,500 by $2,000,000 to derive the return of 8.375%.

10.37 (a) $1,680.

Annual gross operating income ($1,650 x 12 = $19,800) - annual operating expenses ($600 x 12 = $7,200) = annual net operating income ($12,600); annual net operating income ($12,600) - cost recovery expense ($7,000) = taxable income ($5,600); taxable income ($5,600) x tax rate (30%) = tax liability ($1,680).

10.38 (c) $10,640

The basic formula for tax liability is: Taxable Income x Tax Rate = Tax Liability. Taxable Income is Net Operating Income - Interest Expense - Cost Recovery Expense. Therefore, the annual tax is $150,000 (NOI) - $105,000 (Interest Expense) - $7,000 (Cost Recovery Expense) x 28% = $10,640. Note that the principal payment is not deductible in calculating taxable income.

10.39 (d) 31.4%

The formula for profit % is (profit / initial investment). The profit made was ($230,000 x 4) – 700,000 initial investment, or $220,000. Dividing this by the amount invested derives a profit percent of 31.4%.

10.40 (c) $1,000,000,000.

The mill rate = (tax requirement / the tax base). A mill is one one-thousandth of a dollar ($.001). To solve for the tax base, reconfigure this formula to be: Base = Tax Requirement / Mill Rate. Thus the Base = $10,000,000 / .010, or $1,000,000,000.

10.41 (a) $2,990

First, always use the assessed valuation, not the market value. Subtract out the homestead exemption to derive taxable value, or $280,000 – 50,000 = $230,000. As a shortcut to calculating the tax bill, simply add up all the mills, multiply them times .001 to convert mills to decimals, then multiply this number times the taxable value. Thus (7 + 3 + 2 + 1) x .001 x $230,000 = $2,990.

10.42 (b) 2.13%

The rate = budget / tax base. Thus, $8,000,000 / (400,000,000 – 25,000,000) = 2.13%

10.43 (d) $7,112
First calculate the total commission, then the co-brokerage splits, then the agent-broker split. Thus: $508,000 x 7% = $35,560 total commission. ($35,560 x 50%) = $17,780 total listing broker share. $17,780 x 40% = $7,112 agent's share.

10.44 (a) $6,866
Figure the total commission, then the co-brokerage splits, then the broker-agent splits. Thus, ($325,000 x 6.5%) = $21,125. ($21,125 x 50%) = $10,563. ($10,563 x .65) = $6,866.

10.45 (c) A credit to the buyer and debit to the seller for $785.34.
The daily tax expense, first, is ($3,150 / 365) or $8.63. Since the buyer will pay the taxes after closing, the seller must pay the buyer his or her portion of the tax bill at closing, which is the 91 days from the beginning of the year through closing. Therefore, credit the buyer and debit the seller ($8.63 x 91), or $785.34.

10.46 (a) $507.50.
If the buyer pays $525 interest for 30 days, the daily expense is ($525 / 30), or $17.50. If there are 29 days of pre-paid expense, the buyer's charge is ($17.50 x 29), or $507.50.

10.47 (d) Credit buyer $712.26.
For the monthly proration using the 365-day method, solve first for the daily rent amount: ($1,380 / 31), or $44.52. Since the landlord received the rent and owes the buyer portions of the rent, the buyer will be credited. The owed amount is for the 16th through the 31st, or 16 days, since the closing day belongs to the buyer. Therefore, credit the buyer and debit the seller ($44.52 x 16),or $712.26.

10.48 (d) $86,372
First calculate the transfer tax: ($322,600 / 500) = 645.2 units of $500. Round this up to 646, then multiply times $1.00 to get $646 transfer tax cost. Next figure the commission @ ($322,600 x .07), or $22,582. Next, the seller's real estate tax proration charge will be $2,000. Then, add up the expenses: ($646 transfer tax + 450 title + 550 attorney + 22,582 commission + 210,000 loan payoff + 2,000 tax proration) = $236,228. Subtracting this from the sale price = $86,372.

10.49 (d) $5,848.
Be careful here. Since the net price is $5,000, the taking price (TP) minus the commission must equal the net price. In other words, the net price is 90% of the taking price. Since TP x 90% = Net, TP = Net / 90%. So the taking price is $5,556 ($5,000 / .9). Apply the same logic to deriving the asking price: the taking price is 95% of the list price, therefore the list price = (taking price / 95%), or $5,848. Now work backwards to prove your answer: (5,848 x 95% margin x .90 net of commission) = $5,000

10.50 (d) $468,750
Use the formula: (Percent of insurable property value carried / 80% replacement cost) x claim = recovery, where the insurable property value variable excludes the land value and is valued at replacement cost. Here, the insurable portion of the property is ($740,000 - 25% land value), or $555,000. The Wildes are carrying insurance to cover 75% of the replacement cost of the entire property. Their recovery amount is therefore (75% / 80%) x $500,000, or $468,750.

10.51 (c) $280,000
Use the formula: (Percent of insurable property value carried / 80% replacement cost) x claim = recovery. Thus, (75% / 80% x $300,000) = $281,250. However, the face value of the policy is the maximum they can receive, which is $280,000.

STATE TEST 11: The Montana Regulatory Environment

11.1 (c) four
The Board is made up of five Governor-appointed members. Four must be active Montana real estate licensees and one member represents the public and may not hold a real estate license.

11.2 (d) prohibited, because the presiding officer may not be an officer or employee of a real estate association.
The presiding officer and any Department employee serving the Board may not be an officer or employee of a real estate association. The restriction protects the Board from industry capture. Board members are not otherwise barred from outside employment.

11.3 (a) the Board's administrative rules, which carry the same legal force as the statute.
The Board's rulemaking power lets it adopt administrative rules that fill in the details of the licensing statute. Those rules are found in ARM Title 24, Chapter 210, and they have the same legal force as the statute itself.

11.4 (d) writing and scoring the national portion of the licensing examination.
The Board controls the licensing examination and approves prelicense and continuing education courses, and it may reject a course that does not meet its requirements. The examination itself is developed and administered by Pearson, the state's testing service.

11.5 (b) determine guilt by majority vote following a hearing.
The Board may investigate on its own initiative or after receiving a sworn written complaint, but guilt is determined by a majority vote following a hearing. No criminal conviction or outside referral is required.

11.6 (c) grounds for suspension or revocation, because no signed listing agreement was valid on the date of the advertisement.
A licensee may not openly advertise property belonging to another without a valid signed listing agreement in effect on the date the advertisement runs. Advertising a cooperating broker's listing is permitted only with the consent of the owner and the listing agent, and the advertisement must identify that brokerage.

11.7 (a) committed unprofessional conduct by failing to disclose the family relationship.
A licensee may never recommend a service provider such as an attorney, inspector, or lender without disclosing any family, financial, or business relationship with that provider. The violation is complete when the recommendation is made, regardless of the quality of the work performed.

11.8 (b) Acting as a buyer agent without a written buyer broker agreement
ARM 24.210.641 makes it unprofessional conduct to act as a buyer agent without a written buyer broker agreement, or as a seller agent without a written listing agreement. The other three choices describe conduct the rules require rather than prohibit.

11.9 (b) the amount of harm, or risk of harm, caused to Montana consumers.
Sanctions are imposed under Section 37-1-312, MCA. The Board looks at three things: how serious the violation was, how much harm or risk of harm was caused to Montana consumers, and whether the licensee has a prior disciplinary history.

11.10 (d) the failure to respond is itself unprofessional conduct and triggers additional Board discipline.
Failing to pay the fine or file a written dispute within the response period is itself unprofessional conduct and exposes the licensee to further Board discipline. Refusing to sign the citation without disputing it is treated the same way.

11.11 (a) 5 business days
The citation process authorized by Section 37-51-324, MCA, gives the licensee 5 business days to pay the fine or file a written dispute. The citation is an administrative alternative to full disciplinary proceedings, and no hearing is required unless the licensee disputes it.

11.12 (c) has violated Montana law, because dealing with Montana real estate and soliciting Montana residents is practicing within the state.
The phrase within this state reaches beyond physical presence. Marketing or dealing with Montana real estate, or soliciting Montana residents from anywhere, is practicing in Montana. Even a single act falling within the definition of brokerage can violate Section 37-51-301, MCA.

STATE TEST 12: Montana Real Estate Licensing

12.1 (a) is not advertising, because information sent to one specific prospect on request is excluded.
The Board defines advertising as information used to promote property or services, but expressly excludes data sent to one specific prospect at that prospect's request. Had the same information been posted publicly, the internet advertising rules of ARM 24.210.430 would apply.

12.2 (d) no entity license exists, and every person in the entity who performs licensed acts must hold an individual license.
Montana does not license business entities. Every officer or partner who performs acts requiring a license must be individually licensed. If the entity does not comply, each individual acting for it is in violation.

12.3 (d) A person who, for a fee, negotiates leases of apartments owned by others
Attorneys performing legal duties, court-appointed executors, and persons prospecting or leasing land for minerals or hydrocarbons are all exempt. Negotiating leases of property owned by others for compensation is brokerage and requires a license.

12.4 (a) the examination results expire and the examination must be retaken.
An applicant must apply for a license within 12 months of passing, or the examination results expire. The state and national portions may be taken separately, and each result carries its own 12-month window.

12.5 (c) denied, because the salesperson has not been a licensed Montana salesperson for at least 2 years.
A broker applicant must have worked as a licensed Montana salesperson for at least 2 years, or hold equivalent Board-approved experience. Education does not waive the experience requirement, and the 60-hour course and 30 activity points are additional requirements rather than substitutes.

12.6 (b) obtain a supervising broker endorsement under Section 37-51-302, MCA.
A broker license by itself does not permit supervision of salespersons. A separate supervising broker endorsement is required, and obtaining it requires completing the Board-approved pre-endorsement course.

12.7 (a) at least 3 business days before the temporary supervision begins.
Temporary supervision must be in writing, signed by both the existing and the temporary supervising broker, and filed with the Board at least 3 business days in advance. A late filing draws a late fee against the existing broker. Temporary supervision is capped at 60 days per salesperson in any 12-month period.

12.8 (c) With the supervising broker, displayed at the designated address
The salesperson's license is held by the supervising broker and does not go home with the salesperson. Copies of all associated salespersons' current licenses must be displayed at the broker's designated address. What the salesperson carries is the annual pocket card.

12.9 (b) receives credit for 12 hours, and the extra 6 hours do not carry forward.
Montana requires 12 hours of continuing education every licensing year, which runs November 1 through October 31. There is no carry-over. Hours earned beyond 12 do not count toward the following year.

12.10 (d) at least 90% of the first hour and 100% of each hour after that.
The attendance rule allows a small allowance for a late start but none afterward. A licensee must complete at least 90% of the first hour and 100% of every hour following it. An hour of education means 50 minutes of instruction.

12.11 (b) the continuing education that would have been required during the inactive period, capped at 24 hours.
Continuing education requirements are frozen while a licensee is inactive, but returning to active status requires making up the hours that would have been required, up to a maximum of 24. The licensee must also submit the change form, pay the fee, and provide proof of E&O insurance.

12.12 (c) cannot renew while in cancellation status, and must first go inactive or affiliate with a new supervising broker.
Cancellation is the gap between leaving one supervising broker and joining another or going inactive. A

salesperson in cancellation status may not practice and may not renew. The status must be resolved before the renewal can be processed.

12.13 (a) the other state granting the same privileges to Montana licensees.
Reciprocity works only in both directions. The Board may waive some prelicense education or examination requirements for licensees of another state, but only where that state extends the same privileges to Montana licensees. The Montana state law portion of the examination is often still required.

12.14 (d) not permitted, because no city or county may charge a separate license fee or tax as a condition of practicing real estate in Montana.
Real estate licensing in Montana is exclusively a state function. No city or county may impose a separate license fee or tax as a condition of practicing real estate. Board fees themselves are set by rule and flow into the state special revenue fund that supports Board operations.

STATE TEST 13: Montana Brokerage and Disclosure Regulation

13.1 (a) current, because a listing must be updated or removed within 7 days of a material change.
The internet advertising rule has three requirements: accurate, identified, and current. Current means a listing must be updated or removed within 7 days of a material change such as a sale, an expiration, or an amendment.

13.2 (b) at the beginning or the end of the email message.
Identification must appear at the beginning or end of every email, news group, discussion list, and bulletin board message. Websites require identification on every viewable page or a link to it from every page.

13.3 (c) state that the material was abstracted from another source and that buyers should request further information.
MLS or listing-agent data may be reformatted or condensed, but the content may not be changed. A condensed advertisement must say that the material was abstracted from another source and direct buyers to request further information.

13.4 (d) deficient, because the brokerage must work its own name or trade name into franchise advertising.
A franchise broker must include its own name or trade name in franchise advertising or in the logo itself. The franchise logo standing alone does not identify the licensed brokerage. The rule applies in any medium, not just online.

13.5 (b) label the photographs as virtually staged.
Virtually staged photographs must be labeled as such. The same principle governs other new tools: AI-generated descriptions and images remain the licensee's responsibility, and a video tour must reflect the property's current condition.

13.6 (c) acted improperly, because the license must be returned immediately and a dispute is not grounds for delay.
The broker must immediately return the license to the Board with a termination letter. A commission dispute does not justify holding it. The broker also remains supervising broker of record until the license and release reach the Board.

13.7 (d) high-level supervision, because the salesperson closed fewer than 10 transaction sides.
High-level supervision under ARM 24.210.606 is triggered by either condition: less than 2 years of experience OR fewer than 10 transaction sides in a calendar year. Experience alone does not lower the standard when production is below the threshold.

13.8 (a) Thursday, when the supervising broker reviewed, signed, and dated it.
A listing agreement negotiated by a salesperson is not valid until the supervising broker reviews, signs, and dates it. The salesperson's signature and the seller's signature alone do not complete the agreement.

13.9 (c) before the move or within 10 days after it.
The broker must notify the Department before moving or within 10 days after, designate the new physical

address, and pay the required fee. A gap between the address of record and the actual office creates problems if a complaint or service of process is directed there.

13.10 (d) disclose to the other party that this is the salesperson's personal transaction and does not involve the broker or firm.
Section 37-51-309, MCA, lets a salesperson handle a personal sale, exchange, lease, or rental without the supervising broker. The condition is disclosure to the other party before entering the transaction. The broker and firm are then not responsible for the transaction.

13.11 (a) permitted, provided the Wyoming broker performed no services in Montana for the fee.
A Montana broker may pay a broker licensed in another state so long as that broker performed no services in Montana for the fee. The nonresident must file written consent to Montana jurisdiction and to service on the Department.

13.12 (b) decline to draft the provision or interpret the law, and recommend that the buyer consult an attorney.
Drafting complex provisions, advising on legal strategy, and interpreting statutes are the unauthorized practice of law. Failing to advise a party to seek outside professional services when appropriate is separately unprofessional conduct.

13.13 (d) exposure, because making no inquiry at all into ownership can support discipline.
A licensee must verify ownership before accepting a listing. No title search is required, but making no inquiry at all can support a discipline finding. The standard is reasonable inquiry, not a guarantee of title.

13.14 (a) not be communicated through an MLS, in any field or in the remarks.
The practice changes from the Sitzer-Burnett settlement bar any offer of buyer broker compensation from an MLS, in any field or in remarks. Sellers may still offer buyer concessions on an MLS and may still negotiate buyer broker compensation off the MLS.

13.15 (b) before the buyer tours the home, whether in person or by live virtual tour.
The agreement must be in place before the buyer tours a home, in person or by live virtual tour. Montana already required written buyer broker agreements, so the settlement adds content requirements without displacing the state rule.

13.16 (c) not acceptable, because compensation must be a specific, objectively ascertainable amount or rate.
The compensation clause must state a specific, objectively ascertainable amount or rate. Open-ended language keyed to whatever a seller happens to offer is not permitted. The clause must also bar the licensee from receiving more than the agreed amount from any source.

13.17 (a) only if a written agreement between the broker and the seller provides for it.
Any division of forfeited earnest money between broker and seller must rest on a written agreement between them. Nothing in Montana law creates an automatic split, and the broker earns a commission only when the transaction closes or terminates.

13.18 (b) must disclose the condition, because the duty to disclose adverse material facts belongs to the licensee independently of the seller.
The licensee's duty to disclose adverse material facts is independent of the seller's wishes. Flooding history is a defect affecting value. A licensee may not conceal a known defect or stay silent when asked, and a client instruction is not a defense.

13.19 (c) The results of a radon test the seller has received
Montana has no mandatory statewide property condition form. Specific hazard statutes do apply: a seller who has received radon test results must disclose them, methamphetamine contamination must be disclosed, and federal rules govern lead-based paint in pre-1978 housing.

13.20 (d) when the licensee first begins to locate property for the buyer.
With no written agreement, the licensee is a statutory broker. Under Section 37-51-314, MCA, the statutory broker gives the initial disclosure when first beginning to locate property for the buyer, not at some later point in the transaction.

13.21 (b) before or at the moment the dual agency arises, never afterward.
Dual agency consent must be signed and in writing before or at the moment the dual agency arises. Consent obtained after the fact does not cure the violation. Planning ahead by addressing dual agency in both the listing and buyer broker agreements avoids the problem.

13.22 (c) tell the buyer that the information may be maintained and by whom, and disclose any actual knowledge the licensee has about the property.
Section 37-51-105, MCA, limits the licensee's responsibility to two things: telling the buyer that registration information may be maintained and by whom, and disclosing any actual knowledge the licensee has about the property in question. There is no duty to research the registry.

13.23 (d) within 3 business days of receipt.
The deposit deadline is 3 business days from receipt unless the parties agree otherwise. Salespersons must get trust funds to the supervising broker in time for the broker to meet that deadline, and the broker remains accountable for all trust funds at all times.

13.24 (a) permitted up to $1,000, provided the broker keeps a chronological ledger of those deposits and disbursements.
A broker may keep up to $1,000 of personal funds in the trust account for maintenance and bank fees. Anything above that is commingling. Where personal funds are kept there, the broker must maintain a chronological ledger of those deposits and disbursements.

13.25 (c) within 10 business days of becoming due.
Money that becomes due to the broker must be withdrawn within 10 business days. Leaving earned funds in trust indefinitely is itself a violation, just as disbursing client funds early is.

13.26 (d) An insured checking account at a financial institution located in Montana
Trust funds must stay liquid and must sit in an insured account at a financial institution located in Montana. Sweep accounts, certificates of deposit, and repurchase agreements are all prohibited. The account must be identified by the words trust account.

13.27 (a) 8 years from the later of the date of receipt or the date the transaction was completed.
The retention period is 8 years, measured from the later of the date of receipt or the date the transaction was completed. It covers sales contracts, leases, options, agency agreements, and closing statements, and it survives a move or an office closing.

13.28 (b) committed unprofessional conduct under ARM 24.210.641.
Acting as a buyer agent without a written buyer broker agreement is unprofessional conduct, exactly as acting as a seller agent without a written listing agreement is. The buyer's satisfaction does not cure the violation.

13.29 (d) unprofessional conduct, unless the seller has consented to direct communication and that consent is documented.
Negotiating directly with a seller or buyer known to be under a written exclusive agreement with another broker is unprofessional conduct. The parties may consent to direct communication, but the consent must be documented.

13.30 (a) improper, because a listing agreement must state a specific duration.
Every listing agreement must carry a specific duration and the conditions for termination. Montana does not permit open-ended listings. Montana law sets no maximum listing term, so the defect is the absence of a definite end, not the length.

13.31 (b) permissible, because participation is free and no further commitment is required.
A drawing anyone may enter free, with no consideration and no further commitment, is permitted. What is prohibited is a prize conditioned on attending a listing presentation, signing a buyer agreement, or making an offer, and any lottery or raffle used to influence a purchaser.

13.32 (c) violates RESPA and can also support a Montana discipline finding.
RESPA prohibits giving or receiving a fee, kickback, or thing of value for referring a settlement service in

a federally related mortgage. Disclosure does not cure a payment made purely for the referral. Payment for services actually performed is a different matter, but nothing was performed here.

STATE TEST 14: Montana Agency Regulation

14.1 (a) Section 37-51-313, MCA, replaces the common law of agency, and only the five authorized statutory relationships apply.
Montana agency is defined by statute rather than common law. The five authorized relationships are seller agent, buyer agent, dual agent, statutory broker, and property manager. Nothing outside that list applies.

14.2 (b) statutory broker.
A licensee is presumed to be a statutory broker until a written agreement is signed or a different relationship is disclosed. The statutory broker is not the agent or representative of anyone in the transaction.

14.3 (c) a statutory broker, because subagency takes an explicit acceptance.
Subagency is not automatic. It requires both an offer and an acceptance. Without an explicit acceptance the cooperating broker remains a statutory broker.

14.4 (d) the agent of only the designated party, and not a dual agent.
Each designate represents only the designated party and is not a dual agent. The supervising broker does not become a dual agent by overseeing both. The arrangement still requires information barriers between the two designates.

14.5 (a) prohibited, because a licensee who is a principal in the transaction cannot be a dual agent.
A licensee buying or selling for the licensee's own account may not be a dual agent, and consent cannot cure it. Acting in the dual capacity of broker and undisclosed principal is separately unprofessional conduct under Section 37-51-321, MCA.

14.6 (b) the duty to account for money and property, and the duty of confidentiality.
Agency ends at the earliest of completed performance, the agreed expiration date, or an authorized termination. Two duties survive termination: accounting for the principal's money and property, and confidentiality.

14.7 (c) disclose the adverse material fact to the buyer.
A seller agent owes the buyer disclosure of adverse material facts about the property that the agent knows, whether or not the buyer asks. The agent is not required to inspect the property or verify the seller's statements.

14.8 (d) after written disclosure to the seller and with the seller's written consent.
The duty to act solely in the seller's best interests carries an express exception: with written disclosure and the seller's written consent, a seller agent may list competing properties without breaching any obligation. A buyer agent has a parallel exception for competing buyers.

14.9 (a) disclosing to the buyer adverse material facts about the property, disclosing to the seller adverse material facts about the buyer's ability to perform, and exercising reasonable care, skill, and diligence.
A statutory broker advocates for no one but still owes both sides honest dealing. There is no duty to inspect the property or verify anyone's statements, and no duty of loyalty or confidentiality to either party.

14.10 (b) disclose the condition, because the duty to disclose adverse material facts overrides confidentiality.
A dual agent owes each party the duties of that party's agent, with one overriding exception: the duty to disclose adverse material facts to both parties defeats confidentiality. A leaking roof materially affects value.

14.11 (c) a known structural defect in the foundation.
The four protected items are the buyer's willingness to pay more, the seller's willingness to take less, the factors motivating either party, and anything a party puts in writing as confidential. A known structural defect is an adverse material fact and must be disclosed.

14.12 (d) disclose the contractual relationship to owners and tenants, with no separate Section 37-51-314 disclosure required.
Property management is one of the five authorized relationships, governed by Sections 37-56-105 through 37-56-107, MCA. The manager discloses the contractual relationship to all customers and clients, but the Section 37-51-314 disclosure forms do not apply.

14.13 (a) does not protect the licensee, because every licensee must endeavor to ascertain all pertinent facts about a property.
The duty to ascertain pertinent facts sets a reasonable effort standard. It does not make the licensee an inspector or an attorney, but it does foreclose the defense that the licensee was deliberately incurious.

14.14 (b) That a prior occupant died by suicide in the home
Adverse material facts cover value, structural integrity, documented health risks, and a buyer's ability to perform. Montana expressly excludes the fact that an occupant has or had a communicable disease and that the property was the site of a suicide or felony. A licensee asked directly must still answer truthfully.

14.15 (c) may not use the information, because confidentiality survives termination of the agency.
Confidentiality survives the end of the agency. A former seller agent may not use the former seller's confidential information against that seller in a later transaction. Five narrow exceptions exist, and none applies to gaining an advantage for a new client.

14.16 (d) not liable, because the broker lacked actual knowledge, the subagent is not an employee, and the statement did not originate with the broker.
A broker is not liable for a subagent's misrepresentation unless the broker had actual knowledge, the subagent is an employee rather than an independent contractor, or the misrepresentation originated with the broker. None of the three applies here. Regulatory supervision duties are a separate matter from vicarious liability.

14.17 (a) at the time the listing agreement is executed.
Under Section 37-51-314, MCA, a seller agent gives the initial disclosure when the listing agreement is executed, and a buyer agent gives it when the buyer broker agreement is executed. A statutory broker gives it when first beginning to locate property for the buyer.

14.18 (b) before or at the time negotiations commence with the other side.
Negotiations means acting as an intermediary in contract discussions, completing forms for offers, counteroffers, and addendums, and presenting offers. The subsequent disclosure must precede or coincide with those activities, never follow them.

14.19 (c) reproduced in all capital letters.
The initial disclosure must carry the statutory dual agency advisory in all capital letters, describe the duties owed under Section 37-51-313, MCA, define adverse material fact, identify the relationship disclosed, and carry both signatures and the date.

14.20 (d) identification of the type of relationship, the signature of the seller or buyer, the licensee's signature, and the date.
Section 37-51-314(7), MCA, sets the required content of the subsequent disclosure. It may stand alone or be included in other transaction documents. A description of the other available relationships is permitted but not required.

14.21 (a) give the buyer a new initial disclosure reflecting the buyer agency relationship.
The relationship has changed, so a new initial disclosure is required at the time the written agreement is signed. If a disclosed relationship changes during a transaction, a disclosure documenting the change is required.

14.22 (b) permitted, because the disclosure need not be a separate document.
A relationship disclosure may be combined with the listing agreement or the buyer broker agreement. What matters is that it precede the activity it covers and contain the required content, not that it stand alone.

STATE TEST 15: Additional Montana Laws and Practices

15.1 (a) is out of compliance, because coverage must be continuous during the entire period of active licensure.
Every active Montana licensee must carry continuous errors and omissions coverage. A lapse of even a single day puts the licensee out of compliance, and the Board treats the failure as a continuing violation. Only inactive licensees are exempt.

15.2 (b) continues, because coverage under the group policy is specific to the individual licensee.
The group policy is issued to the Board with each licensee as a named insured, and the coverage is specific to the individual. It therefore follows the licensee to a new supervising broker. The other two ways to comply are an individual policy or a firm policy naming the licensee.

15.3 (c) Title 70, Chapter 33, MCA, the separate mobile home lot rental act.
Mobile home lot rentals are expressly excluded from the Residential Landlord and Tenant Act and are covered by their own parallel statute in Title 70, Chapter 33. Security deposits are addressed separately again in Title 70, Chapter 25.

15.4 (d) 30 days after the tenant terminates the tenancy and vacates.
Where no deduction is made, the entire deposit goes back within 10 days. Where deductions are proposed, the landlord has 30 days to deliver the balance with a written itemized list. Missing either deadline exposes the landlord to the withheld amount plus reasonable attorney fees.

15.5 (a) may not evict, because payment in full within the 3 days continues the tenancy.
For nonpayment of rent the landlord serves a written 3-day notice to pay or vacate. If the tenant pays in full within the 3 days, the tenancy continues. Only if the tenant does not pay may the landlord pursue eviction.

15.6 (b) A room in a hotel occupied by a transient guest
The Act reaches most residential rentals, including single-family homes, apartments, condominiums, and townhouses. Hotels, motels, and similar transient lodging are excluded, as are institutional residency, fraternal or social organization housing, and a buyer in possession before closing.

15.7 (c) must be treated as a mortgage, because a trust indenture is limited to parcels of 40 acres or less.
A trust indenture under the Small Tract Financing Act may be used only where the secured property is 40 acres or less. Above that limit the instrument is treated as a mortgage and is foreclosed judicially, which brings a 1-year right of redemption with it.

15.8 (d) may not obtain a deficiency judgment, and the unpaid balance is discharged.
Section 71-1-317, MCA, bars a deficiency judgment after a nonjudicial trust indenture foreclosure sale. The borrower is not personally liable for the shortfall. A deficiency is also unavailable in a judicial foreclosure of a trust indenture on an occupied single-family residence.

15.9 (a) on the 10th day following the sale.
Under Section 71-1-319, MCA, the purchaser at a trustee's sale takes possession on the 10th day after the sale. There is no redemption right following a nonjudicial sale. Possession after a judicial mortgage foreclosure instead waits for the 1-year redemption period to run.

15.10 (b) not acceptable, because the designated address must be a physical location.
The designated address must be a physical street address, not a post office box or a virtual office, and it must be accessible for a Board audit. A home office or a co-working space qualifies. A fully virtual brokerage with no physical location does not.

15.11 (c) continues for the full 8 years, regardless of the closing or the retirement.
The 8-year retention period runs from the later of the date of receipt or the date the transaction was completed, and it survives a move, an office closing, or a transfer of the supervisory role. A broker who sells a brokerage or retires should plan for storage and accessibility of the archive.

15.12 (d) age, creed, and marital status.
The federal classes are race, color, religion, sex, national origin, familial status, and disability. Montana adds age, creed, and marital status, so a Montana licensee treats all ten as off-limits for housing decisions.

15.13 (a) unlawful, because no exemption excuses discriminatory advertising.
The age and familial status prohibitions do not reach a dwelling for no more than two families where the owner occupies one unit. The exemption covers the rental decision, not the advertising. A discriminatory advertisement of an exempt property remains unlawful.

15.14 (b) 36 sections of one square mile each.
A township is 6 miles by 6 miles and holds 36 sections of one square mile, or 640 acres, each. Sections are numbered 1 through 36 beginning in the northeast corner, working west across the top row and then east on the next.

15.15 (c) 40 acres
A section holds 640 acres. A quarter is 160 acres and a quarter of that quarter is 40 acres. Aliquot part descriptions are read from the smallest unit backward, so the answer is one quarter-quarter.

15.16 (d) the Department of Revenue.
The Department of Revenue must approve a declaration before recording, and approval is withheld only if the name fails the similarity rule or taxes and assessments due have not been paid. The declaration must also carry local government certification on subdivision review, and floor plans are recorded at the same time.

15.17 (a) is not effective until 72 hours after the buyer received the documents, and the buyer may withdraw without penalty during that period.
When the seller constitutes a majority of the unit owners, the seller must disclose that fact before any buy-sell agreement is signed and furnish the required documents on request. The agreement is not effective until 72 hours after delivery, and the buyer may withdraw the offer without penalty in that window.

15.18 (b) a common expense of all the unit owners, including the purchaser.
A purchaser taking title through foreclosure of a first mortgage or trust indenture is not liable for common expenses that came due before the acquisition. The unpaid share becomes a common expense of all the unit owners. In a voluntary sale, by contrast, the grantee is jointly and severally liable with the grantor.

15.19 (c) cannot recover, because an agreement employing a broker to sell real estate must be in writing.
Section 28-2-903, MCA, places an agreement authorizing or employing an agent or broker to buy or sell real estate for compensation inside the statute of frauds. Montana case law on the point is long settled. This is a second, independent reason for the written agreement requirement in Section 37-51-313, MCA, and ARM 24.210.641.

15.20 (d) A residential lease for a term of one year
Section 70-20-101, MCA, requires a writing for any estate or interest in real property other than an estate at will or a term not exceeding one year. A one-year lease falls inside that exception. Listings, sale contracts, and leases running longer than one year all require a writing.

SAMPLE TEST: Montana License Examination Sample Test

S 1. (b) Trade fixtures that are personal property.
Trade fixtures are items of a tenant's personal property that the tenant has temporarily affixed to a landlord's real property in order to conduct business. Trade fixtures may be detached and removed before or upon surrender of the leased premises. Should the tenant fail to remove a trade fixture, it may become the property of the landlord through accession. Thereafter, the fixture is considered real property.

S 2. (c) Severance and affixing.
Severance is the conversion of real property to personal property by detaching it from the real estate; affixing, or attachment, is the act of converting personal property to real property by attaching it to the real estate, such as by assembling a pile of bricks into a barbecue pit, or constructing a boat dock from wood

planks.

S 3. (d) absolute fee simple estate.
The fee simple freehold estate is the highest form of ownership interest one can acquire in real estate. It includes the complete bundle of rights, and the tenancy is unlimited, with certain exceptions. The fee simple absolute estate is a perpetual estate that is not conditioned by stipulated or restricted uses.

S 4. (c) the estate may revert to a grantor or heirs if the prescribed use changes.
The defeasible fee estate is perpetual, provided the usage conforms to stated conditions. Essential characteristics are: the property must be used for a certain purpose or under certain conditions; and, if the use changes or if prohibited conditions are present, the estate reverts to the previous grantor of the estate.

S 5. (a) conventional life estate.
A conventional life estate is a freehold estate that is limited in duration to the life of the owner or other named person. Upon the death of the owner or other named individual, the estate passes to the original owner or another named party. A legal life estate is created by law as opposed to a property owner's choice.

S 6. (a) a condominium owner owns a unit of air space whereas the co-op owner owns a proprietary lease.
The owner of a condominium has a fee-simple ownership interest in his/her unit and its air space. Whereas, a co-op owner has a leasehold, not fee-simple, interest with the property's corporation. Since the corporation owns an undivided interest in the cooperative property, debts and financial obligations apply to the property as a whole, not to individual units as in a condominium.

S 7. (d) Trustor, trustee and beneficiary.
In an estate in trust, a fee owner-- the grantor or trustor-- transfers legal title to a fiduciary-- the trustee-- who holds and manages the estate for the benefit of another party, the beneficiary.

S 8. (c) fee simple ownership of the airspace in a unit and an undivided share of the entire property's common areas.
A condominium is a hybrid form of ownership of multi-unit residential or commercial properties. It combines ownership of a fee simple interest in the airspace within a unit with ownership of an undivided share, as a tenant in common, of the entire property's common elements, such as lobbies, swimming pools, and hallways.

S 9. (a) the date of recordation.
Among junior liens, date of recording determines priority. The rule is: the earlier the recording date of the lien, the higher its priority. For example, if a judgment lien is recorded against a property on Friday, and a mortgage lien is recorded on the following Tuesday, the judgment lien has priority and must be satisfied in a foreclosure ahead of the mortgage lien.

S 10. (b) A state in which a mortgagor retains title to the property when a mortgage lien is created.
In lien-theory states, laws give a lender on a mortgaged property equitable title rather than legal title. The mortgagor in a lien theory state retains legal title.

S 11. (b) transfers with the property.
The term appurtenant means "attaching to." An easement appurtenant attaches to the estate and transfers with it unless specifically stated otherwise in the transaction documents.

S 12. (c) Giving constructive notice of one's rights and interests in the property.
Recorded instruments may include deeds, mortgages, liens, easements, sale contracts, and marriage, probate and tax records. The primary purpose of recording and maintaining records of these instruments is to provide constructive notice of the conditions of a property's title-- who owns it, who maintains claims against it.

S 13. (c) A chronology of successive owners of record of a parcel of real estate.
Chain of title refers to the succession of owners of record dating back to the original grant of title from the state to a private party. It is thus more than a mere list; it is a chronological list as reflected in title records.

S 14. (c) Title insurance.
A title insurance policy indemnifies the policy holder against losses arising from defects in the title and is thus generally accepted as the best evidence of marketability after a Torrens certificate, which is not available in every jurisdiction. A signed deed is no evidence of marketability, only of an intent to convey title. An attorney's opinion and a title certificate, while forms of evidence of marketability, do not guarantee clear title or offer any protection against a defective title.

S 15. (c) percentage lease A percentage lease allows the landlord to share in the income generated from the use of the property. A tenant pays percentage rent, or an amount of rent equal to a percentage of the tenant's periodic gross sales.

S 16. (d) net lease.
A net lease requires a tenant to pay for utilities, internal repairs, and a proportionate share of taxes, insurance, and operating expenses in addition to rent.

S 17. (b) The leased property is foreclosed.
A foreclosure extinguishes all prior interests in a property, including a leasehold.

S 18. (c) the construction conforms with applicable building codes.
Building inspectors inspect a new development or improvement for code compliance. If the work complies, the municipality or county issues a certificate of occupancy which officially clears the property for occupation and use.

S 19. (b) takes title subject to the same restriction.
Deed restrictions attach to the title of the property. Therefore, the restriction passes to the new buyer.

S 20. (a) She has the right to re-possess the property because the grantee has violated the condition.
A deed condition may restrict certain uses of a property, much like a deed restriction. However, violation of a deed condition gives the grantor the right to re-take possession of the property and file suit for legal title.

S 21. (a) To create a consistent, unchanging standard for identifying a property's unique location.
A legal description of real property is one which accurately locates and identifies the boundaries of the subject parcel to a degree acceptable by courts of law in the state where the property is located. The general criterion for a legal description is that it alone provides sufficient data for a surveyor to locate the parcel. A legal description identifies the property as unique and distinct from all other properties.

S 22. (b) They identify an enclosed area, beginning and ending at the same point.
The metes and bounds description always identifies an enclosed area by starting at an origination point, called point of beginning, or POB, and returning to the POB at the end of the description.

S 23. (a) is void.
By changing any of the terms of an offer, the offeree creates a counteroffer, and the original offer is void. At this point, the offeree becomes the offeror, and the new offeree gains the right of acceptance. If accepted, the counteroffer becomes a valid contract provided all other requirements are met.

S 24. (a) may be assigned.
A real estate contract that is not a personal contract for services can be assigned to another party unless the terms of the agreement specifically prohibit assignment. Listing agreements, for example, are not assignable, since they are personal service agreements between agent and principal. Sales contracts, however, are assignable, because they involve the purchase of real property rather than a personal service.

S 25. (c) A two-year lease.
A contract may be in writing or it may be an oral, or parol, contract. Certain oral contracts are valid and enforceable, others are not enforceable, even if valid. For example, most states require listing agreements, sales contracts, and leases exceeding one year to be in writing to be enforceable.

S 26. (b) a dual agent.
Dual agency occurs whenever a single broker represents both principal parties to a transaction. Here, since Bob and Sue work for Bill, Bill is the dual agent.

S 27. (a) upon first substantive communication.
The agent must provide written notice to all parties or their agents as soon as substantive communication occurs, which can include initial face-to-face contact.

S 28. (d) neither seller nor buyer.
In recent years, the brokerage industry has striven to clear up the question of who works for whom, and who owes fiduciary duties to whom. One solution allows a broker to represent no one in a transaction. That is, the broker acts as a transaction broker, or facilitator, and has no allegiance to buyer or seller.

S 29. (b) the principal has proposed an illegal act, which should not be obeyed.
An agent must comply with the client's directions and instructions, provided they are legal. If the directive is illegal, the agent must also immediately withdraw.

S 30. (b) negotiated with clients.
The amount of a broker's commission is whatever amount the client and broker have agreed to.

S 31. (b) the client may be liable for a commission and marketing expenses.
With an exclusive right-to-sell listing, if the property sells during the term of the revoked listing, the client is liable for the commission. If the property does not sell, the client is liable for the broker's actual costs.

S 32. (b) the agent has a claim to a commission if the owner sells or leases to a party within a certain time following the listing's expiration.
Many listings include a protection clause stating that, for a certain period after expiration, the owner is liable for the commission if the property sells to a party that the broker procured, unless the seller has since listed the property with another broker.

S 33. (c) the advertising must not be deceptive.
Advertising may not be misleading or deceptive in promoting the brokerage or listed properties. Blind ads are also prohibited without exception. Sales agents, moreover, must identify their employer.

S 34. (a) collusion.
Collusion is the illegal practice of two or more businesses joining forces or making joint decisions which have the effect of putting another business at a competitive disadvantage.

S 35. (b) The brokers have illegally fixed prices.
Price fixing is the practice of two or more brokers agreeing to charge certain commission rates or fees for their services, regardless of market conditions or competitors.

S 36. (a) The seller may cancel the contract, since it can be ruled invalid.
A contingency that is too broad, vague, or excessive in duration may invalidate the entire contract on the grounds of insufficiency of mutual agreement. To avoid problems, the statement of a contingency should be explicit and clear, have an expiration date, and expressly require diligence in the effort to fulfill the requirement.

S 37. (d) claim the deposit as compensated damages for the buyer's failure to perform.
If a buyer fails to perform under the terms of a sale contract, the breach entitles the seller to legal recourse for damages. The usual remedy is forfeiture of the buyer's deposit as liquidated damages, provided the deposit is not grossly in excess of the seller's actual damages.

S 38. (b) The optionor must perform if the optionee takes the option, but the optionee is under no obligation to do so.
An option-to-buy places the optionee under no obligation to purchase the property. However, the seller must perform under the terms of the contract if the buyer exercises the option. An option is thus a unilateral agreement. Exercise of the option creates a bilateral sale contract where both parties are bound to perform.

S 39. (b) a decline in demand for all types of real estate in the real estate market.
Businesses that support the departing company will lay off or fire new employees, causing some to leave town in search of work. Some of these businesses may also have to cease operations. Hence the demand for

residential real estate, as well as for commercial and industrial, will decline, and new construction will probably also halt until some other factor increases demand again.

S 40. (b). rental prices in that market will rise
An undersupply of commercial properties in relation to demand will most likely increase prices, as renters have fewer choices and less bargaining power.

S 41. (b) absorption.
Absorption is the amount of available property that becomes occupied over a period of time, usually measured in square feet.

S 42. (b) $17,000.
First derive the annual depreciation, which is the cost divided by the economic life. Then multiply annual depreciation times the number of years to identify total depreciation. Remember to subtract depreciation from the original cost if the question asks for the ending value. Thus, ($20,000 ÷ 20 years x 3 years) = $3,000 total depreciation. The ending value is $20,000 – 3,000, or $17,000.

S 43. (b) Apartment buildings.
The income capitalization approach, or income approach, is used for income properties and sometimes for other properties in a rental market where the appraiser can find rental data. The approach is based on the principle of anticipation: the expected future income stream of a property underlies what an investor will pay for the property.

S 44. (c) estimates net income and applies a capitalization rate to it.
The steps are: estimate potential gross income; estimate effective gross income (potential minus vacancy and credit losses); estimate net operating income (effective minus total operating expenses); select a capitalization rate; and apply the capitalization rate. Use the formula: income ÷ cap rate = value.

S 45. (c) potential gross income minus vacancy and credit loss minus expenses.
Net operating income, or NOI, is always income after vacancy, credit loss and expenses. It does not, however, include debt service.

S 46. (b) $400,000.
Value = Income ÷ Cap rate. Thus, V= $40,000 ÷ .10 = $400,000.

S 47. (a) the interest rate may vary.
Adjustable rate mortgages (ARMs) allow the lender to change the interest rate at specified intervals and by a specified amount. Federal regulations place limits on incremental interest rate increases and on the total amount by which the rate may be increased over the loan term.

S 48. (b) A wraparound lender can profit when the interest rate of the wraparound exceeds that of the underlying mortgage.
In a wraparound loan arrangement, the seller receives a junior mortgage from the buyer, and uses the buyer's payments to make the payments on the original first mortgage. This potentially enables the seller to profit from any difference between a lower interest rate on the senior loan and a higher rate on the wraparound loan.

S 49. (b) a blanket mortgage loan.
A blanket mortgage is secured by more than one property, such as multiple parcels of real estate in a development.

S 50. (b) Payments are not sufficient to retire the loan.
Negative amortization causes the loan balance to increase over the term. This occurs if the borrower's periodic payment is insufficient to cover the interest owed for the period. The lender adds the amount of unpaid interest to the borrower's loan balance.

S 51. (b) the loan amount needs to be less than the property's value.
Lenders must have a margin of borrower equity to protect against falling real estate values which increase the risk of the loan. Without this margin, a lender can incur a loan loss in a foreclosure sale since the proceeds may be less than the loan amount.

S 52. (b) Truth-in-Lending laws
Truth-in-Lending Laws, implemented by the Federal Reserve's Regulation Z, regulate the disclosure of costs, the right to rescind the credit transaction, advertising credit offers, and penalties for non-compliance with the act.

S 53. (d) Participants sell mortgage-backed securities in order to buy pools of loans.
Secondary mortgage market organizations buy pools of mortgages from primary lenders and sell securities backed by these pooled mortgages to investors. By selling securities, the secondary market brings investor money into the mortgage market. By purchasing loans from primary lenders, the secondary market returns funds to the primary lenders, thereby enabling the primary lender to originate more mortgage loans.

S 54. (a) cost recovery expense.
Cash flow is the difference between the amount of actual cash flowing into the investment as revenue and out of the investment for expenses, debt service, and all other items. Cash flow concerns cash items only, and therefore excludes depreciation (cost recovery), which is not a cash expense.

S 55. (c) dividing net income by the price paid for the property.
The investment return measure known as return on investment (ROI) is calculated by dividing net income by the value of the investment. This yields a rate of return on investment.

S 56. (a) Installing a higher capacity air conditioning and purifying system.
Basis is increased by the cost of capital improvements made to the property. Examples of capital improvements are: putting on an addition, paving a driveway, replacing a roof, adding central air conditioning, and rewiring the home. Repairs, maintenance, and redecorating are not generally considered capital improvements.

S 57. (c) There are no federal ad valorem taxes on real property.
There are no federal taxes on real property. The Constitution of the United States specifically prohibits such taxes. The federal government does, however, tax income derived from real property and gains realized on the sale of real property.

S 58. (b) the assessed value of property.
General property taxes are levied on an ad valorem basis, meaning that they are based on the assessed value of the property. Assessed value is determined according to state law, usually by a county or township assessor or appraiser.

S 59. (d) The prohibition may be legal if performed correctly.
The condominium association may be exempt from fair housing prohibitions against age discrimination if it is established as a retirement community in which 80 % of the dwellings have one person who is 55 years of age or older and it has amenities for elderly residents.

S 60. (c) The agent and the owner.
The owner has illegally discriminated, and the agent, by going along with the owner, is equally guilty of violating fair housing laws.

S 61. (b) Inspection fees.
Prorated items are expenses that both parties must share. Non-prorated items are one-time individual charges such as sale commissions, recording fees, and title insurance.

S 62. (d) A lender paying a fee to a broker for referring a borrower to the lender.
RESPA prohibits the payment of fees as part of a real estate settlement when no services are actually rendered. This prohibition includes referral fees for such services as title searches, title insurance, mortgage loans, appraisals, credit reports, inspections, surveys, and legal services.

S 63. (b) Copies of required communications to principals.
Some communications with transaction parties are good and necessary for business. Others are required by law, and records of them must be maintained for a statutory period. Required records typically include listing agreements, offers, contracts, closing statements, agency agreements, disclosure documents, correspondence and other communication records, notes and any other relevant information.

S 64. (a) refuse to use terms that refer to or describe any of the classes of persons protected by the laws.
Before entering into a listing agreement, a licensee should explain that it is necessary to comply with fair housing laws and obtain the potential client's acknowledgment and agreement. The agent should make it clear that the agent will reject the use of terms indicating race, religion, creed, color, national origin, sex, handicap, age or familial status to describe prospective buyers. Such terms should be avoided in conversation as well as in advertising.

S 65. (a) Alterations to a rental space made to fit a particular tenant
Alterations made specifically for certain tenants are called build-outs or tenant improvements. The work may involve merely painting and re-carpeting a rental space, or erecting new walls and installing special electrical or other systems.

S 66. (c) maintain a special trust account in a qualified financial depository.
State laws and real estate commission rules specify how a property manager is to manage trust funds. In general, the agent is to maintain a separate bank account for these funds, with special accounting, in a qualified depository institution. The rules for how long an agent may hold trust funds before depositing them, and how the funds are to be disbursed, are spelled out. The fundamental requirements are that the owners of all funds must be identified, and there must be no commingling or conversion of client funds and agent funds.

S 67. (c) 3
The total area of the living room is (8' x 14' + 8' x 18' + 8' x 16' + 8' x 18') = 528 SF. They will therefore need 528 / 200 SF, or 3 whole gallons.

S 68. (d) 218'
Since the investor paid $100,000 total, and that equals $250 per frontage foot, there are 400 frontage feet (100,000 / 250). If the property is two acres, it totals 87,120 SF. Dividing this by 400 produces a lot depth of 217.8'.

S 69. (c) Yes with $360 left over.
The loan she can get amounts to ($240,000 x 80%), or $192,000. The points charge is ($192,000 x .02), or $3,840. Total closing costs are then $3,840 + 800, or $4640. Thus she has $360 to spare.

S 70. (c) $90,000
First, the sale price is 115% of the appraised value, so the appraised value is $230,000 / 115%, or $200,000. The lender will lend $140,000 (70% of appraised value), so the investor will have to come up with $90,000 ($230,000 – 140,000).

S 71. (c) $96,000.
Since the comparable has an extra half-bath, it is adjusted downward to equalize with the subject. Conversely, since it has no patio, the appraiser adds value to the comparable. Thus, $100,000 minus $5,000 plus $1,000 equals $96,000.

S 72. (c) $508
The total assessed value is ($84,550 + 235,000), or $319,550. The annual tax is based on ($319,550 / 100) = 3195.5 100's. Round up to 3196. To derive the annual tax, multiply 3,196 x 1.91, or $6,104.36. Divide this by 12 for the monthly escrow: ($6,104 / 12) = $508.

S 73. (d) $92,000
The formula for equity is (current value – indebtedness). The current value is ($180,000 + 25% x 180,000), or ($180,000 x 125%), or $225,000. The current debt is ($180,000 x 80%) - $11,000, or $133,000. Their equity is therefore $92,000.

S 74. (b) $166,150
Use the formula: Gain = (Net selling price – adjusted basis) where adjusted basis = (beginning cost – depreciation). The selling price is $240,000 x 5% annual appreciation x 10 years, or ($240,000 + 50% x 240,000), or $360,000. Since land cannot be depreciated, the depreciable basis is ($240,000 total cost – 60,000 land value), or $180,000 (land = 25% total value). Annual depreciation = ($180,000 / 39 years), or

$4,615. Thus total depreciation is ($4,615 x 10 years), or $46,150. The adjusted basis is therefore ($240,000 – 46,150), or $193,850. The total gain is therefore ($360,000 – 193,850), or $166,150.

S 75. (c) $80,000
Applying the formula (percent of insurable property value carried / 80% replacement cost) x claim = recovery), divide the amount of coverage carried ($160,000) by 80% of the insurable property value ($250,000) to get the percent of the claim the company will pay (80%). Multiply this percentage by the claim amount to get $80,000, what the company will pay.

S 76. (a) may not hold a Montana real estate license.
The Board has five Governor-appointed members. Four must be active Montana real estate licensees and one represents the public and cannot hold a license. All five require Senate confirmation and must be Montana residents.

S 77. (d) too many violations in one audit, repeat violations across audits, or a single severe violation.
Most trust account violations are handled through the citation process as an administrative alternative to full disciplinary proceedings. Escalation is reserved for significant violations, defined by volume within one audit, repetition across audits, or severity.

S 78. (c) the supervising broker and the designated address.
The pocket card is issued annually by the Department and certifies that the holder is a licensed Montana broker or salesperson. A salesperson's card names the supervising broker and the designated address, and it must be updated when the broker changes.

S 79. (a) 30 activity points earned within the prior 36 months.
A broker applicant must show 2 years of licensed Montana salesperson experience, complete the 60-hour broker prelicense course, and demonstrate 30 activity points earned in the prior 36 months from transactions, education, supervision, and instruction.

S 80. (d) must be displayed in the banner, or the banner must link to a page that displays it.
ARM 24.210.430 requires a banner advertisement either to display licensee identification or to link to a page that does. Multimedia advertising must display identification as part of the message.

S 81. (a) also receives the complaint and must respond to it.
A complaint filed against a salesperson goes to the supervising broker as well, and the broker must respond. A supervising broker is exposed to discipline for the conduct of every supervised salesperson.

S 82. (b) the corresponding deposit has been verified.
No disbursement may be made until the corresponding deposit has been verified. Trust funds otherwise remain in the account until the transaction closes or terminates, unless they are disbursed to the closing agent on the written agreement of the parties.

S 83. (d) 8 years
All compensation arrangements must be documented and retained for 8 years, the same period that applies to trust account records and other real estate documents. The period runs from the later of the date of receipt or the date the transaction was completed.

S 84. (c) before engaging or recommending the title company.
Any family relationship, financial relationship, or financial interest must be disclosed before the licensee engages or recommends an attorney, title company, appraiser, escrow agent, insurance agent, or maintenance service.

S 85. (a) when the property is offered for sale or lease.
Disclosure under Title 75, Chapter 10, Part 13, MCA, is required when the property is offered for sale or lease. It is one of the specific hazard disclosures that apply even though Montana has no mandatory statewide property condition form.

S 86. (d) only if a written agreement identifies it as compensation for services performed.
Interest may be payable to the broker only where a written agreement identifies it as compensation for services performed. A broker who receives interest from a trust account must also disclose the arrangement

to the principal.

S 87. (b) how any shortfall in the expected compensation will be handled.
Since an offer of buyer broker compensation can no longer be published through an MLS, the agreement must address who is expected to pay and what happens if the amount collected falls short of the agreed rate or amount.

S 88. (a) A separate chronological ledger for each transaction, with a running balance
The broker keeps a chronological record of all receipts and disbursements plus a separate ledger for each transaction, each carrying a running balance. Reconciliation is monthly and may be done by the broker, and records may be kept electronically so long as they can be audited.

S 89. (c) Contract preparation review and pre-closing document review
Reasonable supervision under ARM 24.210.605 covers written office policy, file audits, regular contact, training, and advertising review. High-level supervision under ARM 24.210.606 adds office procedure training, contract preparation review, transaction monitoring, and pre-closing document review.

S 90. (d) unprofessional conduct, because the prize is conditioned on a commitment.
A drawing anyone may enter free, with no strings attached, is permitted. A prize that requires attending a listing presentation, signing a buyer agreement, or making an offer is not. The dividing line is free participation with no further commitment.

S 91. (a) remain with the broker, who must immediately notify all principals.
Listings and pending transactions belong to the broker, not the salesperson. On a departure the broker must immediately notify all principals. The departing salesperson may request a certified statement of the transactions worked in the prior 3 years.

S 92. (b) after written disclosure to each buyer and with each buyer's written consent.
The duty to act solely in the buyer's best interests carries an express exception. With written disclosure and written consent, a buyer agent may represent multiple buyers interested in the same or similar property. A seller agent has the parallel exception for competing listings.

S 93. (d) the seller or the seller's agent.
The subsequent disclosure goes to the other side of the transaction when negotiations commence. For a statutory broker working with a buyer, that means the seller or the seller's agent. The initial disclosure went to the buyer when the broker began locating property.

S 94. (a) maintain information barriers so one principal's protected information does not reach the other.
Each designate represents only the designated party and is not a dual agent, and the supervising broker does not become one by overseeing both. The arrangement works only if information barriers keep each principal's protected information from the other side.

S 95. (c) ends, though the duties of accounting and confidentiality survive.
Agency ends at the earliest of completed performance, the agreed expiration date, or an authorized termination. Two duties survive: accounting for the principal's money and property, and confidentiality.

S 96. (d) a contract between the property manager and the owner.
The property management relationship runs from a contract between the manager and the owner, governed by Sections 37-56-105 through 37-56-107, MCA. The manager discloses that contractual relationship to owners and tenants, with no separate Section 37-51-314 disclosure required.

S 97. (a) the name and address of the person authorized to manage the property.
The landlord must disclose who manages the property and who is authorized to accept service of process and receive demands and notices, and must keep that information current. A written list of existing damages must also be given before the tenant pays a security deposit.

S 98. (c) 1 year from the date of the sale.
A judicially foreclosed mortgage carries a 1-year right of redemption running 365 days from the sale, and a borrower whose property is a residence may remain in possession during that period. A nonjudicial trust

indenture sale carries no redemption right at all.

S 99. (d) passes with the unit even if the deed does not mention it.
The undivided interest cannot be separated from the unit and is conveyed or encumbered with it whether or not the instrument says so. Common elements remain undivided and partition is prohibited. The percentage may be altered only by unanimous agreement of the affected owners plus a recorded amendment.

S 100. (b) 180 days of the discriminatory act.
The Montana Human Rights Bureau deadline is 180 days. A complaint may instead, or also, be filed with HUD within 1 year, and many complaints are dual-filed. A substantiated complaint also triggers Board discipline under Section 37-51-321, MCA.

Appendix: Performance Programs Company's Test-Taking Tips

Introduction

Effective test-taking is more of an art and a practiced skill than a guarantee of success. Students preparing for the state license exam should take exam preparation very seriously. Since there are no guarantees to passing, it behooves students to optimize their chances of a successful outcome. Simply put, this is accomplished by purposeful, intensive study and question-taking practice. The harder you study and prepare, the better your odds become of passing.

There are a few beneficial pointers that can be made to improve your overall test-preparation effort. These are contained in the following compilation of tips assimilated by professional educators and test-prep experts. Please take the time to peruse these observations as they will serve to better your overall chances of passing. And in any case, we wish you the best of success!!

Make and use flashcards

Understanding tested real estate terminology is a large part of passing your exam. As you prepare for the license examination, study. Don't just memorize specific definitions. Memorize contexts of content as well. Understand, for example, that a question about a deed is a question about conveying property in some way, shape or form; a question about eminent domain falls into the "terminology environment" of rights in property. A question about the cost approach relates to the challenges of identifying value. The more you know about "the environment" of each word, in addition to the term's specific definition, the more likely you will be able to use that information to lead you to the correct exam response.

Take notes

As you read and study, take notes. Often, just the act of writing information down helps cement it in your mind. Visualizing how your notes about a particular topic appeared on the page is helpful for students who appreciate visual cues.

Immerse yourself

Form or join a study group, review topics with friends and colleagues, chat with real estate experts, and read real estate blogs. In other words, immerse yourself in the world of real estate. To obtain a deeper understanding of a term or concept, Google it (using whatever search engine you employ with your computer or phone). This will shed light on varying perspectives or iterations of a term's meaning.

Prepare a "date and key quantity" sheet

As a memory device, students are well-advised to create a "date and key quantity sheet" to be able to efficiently refer back to in future study sessions. This particular summary sheet includes facts and data that are very commonly tested, including deadlines, dates, and quantities.

Some examples:

- 1978 – cutoff date for lead paint disclosure
- Base times height divided by two: area of a triangle
- CE requirement in hours
- Deadline (in a given state) for conveying a trust deposit to the broker
- Protected classes (in a given state)
- # acres in a section
- LTV calculation
- loan payment given a rate and loan amount
- criteria for a valid contract
- criteria for distinguishing real vs. personal property
- Recovery Fund – maximum fine per licensee per incident
- adverse possession prescription period (in your state)

Plan study time

Set a goal for yourself. Avoid the trap of just "studying until you're ready." Instead, determine the date you want to apply to take your exam and set aside enough time to finish your test preparations by that date. Try to limit how long each of your study / cram sessions will be. Study periods should not be too much in excess of one hour – after which time students begin to lose concentration and attention span.

Finally, select your study environment so as to avoid distractions and interruptions!

Reading is not studying

It may seem odd, but *reading* is not *studying*. Studying is an active process. Creating and reviewing your flashcards is studying. Develop study guides. Teach someone about difficult or complex topics. Relate what you are learning to your own experiences or the real estate topics you hear about in conversations or on the news. Create your own memory devices such as mnemonics, rhyming, acronyms, or images. These can be invaluable ways to remember cut and dry facts and figures.

Dissect exam questions

Take and review as many practice exams as you can find. Take and re-take quizzes in your textbook and any exam prep resource that you can find. Write down the topics you tend to miss questions on, then re-study those topics. When reviewing a missed question, be sure to understand the correct response and why the incorrect answers were not right.

Review the exam provider's handbook

A wealth of knowledge exists in the exam provider's test preparation resources. Review these materials thoroughly! You will learn the general topic areas covered and the relative weighting of a given subject. For example, appraisal methods will be tested more vigorously than an intricate metes and bounds description.

Exam prep materials generally present the key content of a topic and how many questions will appear on your exam, particularly if the resource is state-specific. The testing service candidate handbook will further describe how your exam is scored. This knowledge will help you to understand how to answer questions you may not be sure about. In other words, you should know whether or not you are penalized for wrong answers.

It's almost time! Your exam is tomorrow. What do you do?

Candidate handbooks will provide full instructions about the exam day itself—what you can and can't take with you, how long you have to complete the exam, and how long you have to wait before you get your results, and so forth.

Immediately prior to the exam, you should limit how much to cram. At some point, nothing new should be introduced into your mind. In short, you either know it or you don't. Make a quick final pass-through, then leave it alone.

Okay, it's exam time. How do I avoid being a nervous wreck?

To alleviate stress, you can do a couple of things:

- Drive by the testing center so you know where it is and how long it will take to get there. On test day, allow extra time for traffic snarls, etc.
- Be sure you have an acceptable calculator (information will appear in the exam provider's handbook). Note that some providers don't allow you to bring a calculator in. Instead, you'll use one they provide or one embedded on the computer you'll use to take the exam.
- Assemble everything you need to take with you. Include test registration documents, required identification, a calculator, and a sweater or light jacket. Put everything in a bag or your car.
- Eat a well-rounded meal the evening before your exam and get a good night's sleep.
- Most exam providers give you a few minutes before you begin the exam to acquaint yourself with how the system works. You can answer a few practice questions, use the calculator, etc. Use this time not only to familiarize yourself with the environment but also to take a few deep breaths and get comfortable. You can do this!
- Budget your time. Know how many questions you must answer (more information from the provider's handbook).
- Read every question carefully. Be sure you understand what it's asking, in particular if the question is in the negative ("which of the following is NOT....," or "which of the following is NOT TRUE....". Then read EVERY possible response before you respond. Exam providers generally want you to select the BEST answer, not the only possible answer.

Answering questions

In most circumstances, you should answer every question. You will certainly receive a score deduction if you don't answer a question, but if you guess, you could guess right. So you come out ahead by answering every question.

This issue raises the question: "how much time should I spend on a question?" This becomes easy math. Know how much time you have for a given section and how many questions you must answer in that section. Then divide the number of questions into your time allocation to get your per-question time allowance. Do not stray too much from that estimate as you complete the section!

If you aren't sure of the answer to a question, keep these tips in mind:

- Are there responses that you know are incorrect? Eliminate them. If you eliminate two responses, you've increased your odds of correctly answering the question to 50/50!
- Dissect the remaining possible responses. Are there key words that indicate a correct or incorrect answer?
    - Terms like "always," "never," and "only" MAY indicate an incorrect response because seldom are things as definitive as these terms suggest.
    - Terms such as "usually," "generally," "typically," "most," and "some" are more likely to appear in the correct response.
- If you see a response that includes something you've never heard of, don't choose it! If you didn't see that information in your preparations, it's unlikely to be the correct response.
- Be particularly cautious about organization names. "The Department of Housing and Urban Development" sounds suspiciously like "The Division of Housing and Development."

After the exam

Depending on the exam provider and state, you may know right away if you passed. You may also receive a report from the testing center that details topic area scores.

If you're not successful on your first attempt, don't panic...and understand that you're not alone. Real exams can be notoriously difficult. As soon as you leave the testing center, write some notes to yourself about questions you recall struggling with or topics that you may need to review.

Then, dig in again. Use the textbook, your notes, and the information you remember from the exam and keep studying. Your career is far more important than not passing the test!

Appendix: Useful Websites

Montana Real Estate Candidate Handbook
This contains crucial information regarding the Pearson Montana Real Estate Examination, including the state and national content outlines, examination fees, identification requirements, and scoring.
https://www.pearsonvue.com/content/dam/VUE/vue/en/documents/publications/092700.pdf

Montana Board of Realty Regulation
301 S. Park Avenue, 4th Floor
Helena, MT 59601
(406) 444-6880
dlibsdhelp@mt.gov
https://boards.bsd.dli.mt.gov/realty-regulation/
Statutes and administrative rules:
https://boards.bsd.dli.mt.gov/realty-regulation/regulations

Pearson VUE (Pearson Professional Assessments)
Montana Real Estate
Attn: Regulatory Program
5601 Green Valley Drive
Bloomington, MN 55437
(888) 366-9520
pearsonvuecustomerservice@pearson.com
https://www.pearsonvue.com/us/en/mt/realestate.html

Montana Association of REALTORS
1 South Montana Avenue, Suite M-1
Helena, MT 59601
(406) 443-4032
info@montanarealtors.org
https://www.montanarealtors.org

Montana Local REALTOR Associations
A directory of the local boards serving Billings, Bozeman, Butte, Great Falls, Helena, Kalispell, Missoula, and the other Montana markets.
https://www.montanarealtors.org/about/local-associations/

Montana Human Rights Bureau
P.O. Box 1728
Helena, MT 59624-1728
(406) 444-2884 or (800) 542-0807
https://erd.dli.mt.gov/human-rights/

If you liked Montana Real Estate License Exam Prep, check out the other titles of Performance Programs Company!

Cramming for the Montana real estate exam? You need Montana Real Estate License Exam Prep!

Where can you buy Montana Real Estate License Exam Prep?
Montana Real Estate License Exam Prep (MT-RELEP) is available as a printed book or e-book through nearly all online retailers.

Looking for a real estate principles textbook? Get what all the students love -- Principles of Real Estate Practice in Montana!

Principles of Real Estate Practice in Montana is invaluable reference material for Montana real estate professionals. Its 602 pages contain the essentials of real estate law, principles, and practices taught in real estate schools and colleges across Montana.

Where can you buy Principles of Real Estate Practice in Montana?
Principles Real Estate Practice in Montana is available as a printed book or e-book through nearly all online retailers

Struggling with real estate math? The solution to that equation is Real Estate Math Express!

Real Estate Math Express is a concise, easy-to-study test preparation guide to help real estate students improve their real estate math scores to pass the state licensing test. The primary feature of Real Estate Math Express is that it contains all necessary formulas and practice questions in 100+ pages.

Where can you buy Real Estate Math Express?
Real Estate Math Express is available as a printed book or e-book through nearly all online retailers.

Publisher Contact

Ryan Mettling
Performance Programs Company
6810 190th Street East, Bradenton, FL 34211
ryan@performanceprogramscompany.com
www.performanceprogramscompany.com

www.ingramcontent.com/pod-product-compliance
Lightning Source LLC
Chambersburg PA
CBHW061203240926
51846CB00006B/1095
9781965482698